Picturing the beast

One only gets to the centre of
the problem by taking a detour.

Stephen Bann,
The Inventions of History

Picturing the beast

Animals, identity
and representation

STEVE BAKER

MANCHESTER UNIVERSITY PRESS

MANCHESTER AND NEW YORK

*distributed exclusively in the USA
and Canada by St. Martin's Press*

Copyright © Steve Baker 1993

Published by Manchester University Press
Oxford Road, Manchester M13 9PL, UK
and Room 400, 175 Fifth Avenue, NY 10010, USA

Distributed exclusively in the USA and Canada
by St. Martin's Press, Inc., 175 Fifth Avenue, New York, NY 10010, USA

British Library Cataloguing-in-Publication Data
A catalogue record for this book is available from the British Library

Library of Congress Cataloging-in-Publication Data
Baker, Steve, 1953–
    Picturing the beast: animals, identity, and representation/Steve Baker.
        p.   cm.
    ISBN 0-7190-3377-2 (hardback),-- ISBN 0-7190-3378-0 (paperback)
    1. Animals--Symbolic aspects. 2. Human–animal relationships. 3. Animals and
civilization. 4. Animal rights. I. Title.
    GR705.B35   1993
    398'.369--dc20   92-31521
                                                                          CIP

ISBN 0 7190 3377 2 *hardback*
     0 7190 3378 0 *paperback*

Conversion and pagination in Monophoto Photina
by August Filmsetting, Haydock, St Helens

Printed in Great Britain
by Bell & Bain Limited, Glasgow

Contents

List of figures

Acknowledgements

For their invaluable advice, criticisms and comments on drafts of various chapters, my particular thanks go to Grahame Ashcroft, John Banks, Martin Barker, Anne Brownlow, Gérard Mermoz, Katharine Reeve, Linden Reilly, Dave Russell, Kim Stallwood, and most of all to Aly Baker. Their support and encouragement helped to sustain my own belief that there was a topic here – however elusive it may sometimes have seemed – about which it was worth writing.

While little of the material here relates in any direct way to the subject of my doctoral thesis, completed a few years ago at the University of Kent at Canterbury, the stimulating advice which I received there from my supervisor, Stephen Bann, continues to shape my understanding of the imaginative detours which may usefully be taken in order to get to the centre of a problem.

In addition to the individuals mentioned above, I am grateful to colleagues in the Department of Historical and Critical Studies at the University of Central Lancashire for a period of study leave in the autumn of 1991 which enabled me to complete the text, and to both Sue Rathmell and Norman Cowell for their generous assistance with the illustrations. I would also like to thank all those at Manchester University Press who have been involved in the editing, design and production of this book for their helpfulness and their interest in the project.

Picture credits

Illustrations reproduced by kind permission of: Aitken & Stone Ltd (figs 23 & 25); Animal Liberation Front (fig. 37); Animal Photography Ltd (fig. 33); Animal Rights Advocates of the Hudson Valley (fig. 40); Associated Press (fig. 8); Steve Bell (fig. 28); © Casterman/References de l'ouvrage (fig. 32); © The Daily Telegraph plc 1983 & 1989 (figs 14 & 18); Express Newspapers plc (figs 13, 17, 21 & 22); Stanley Franklin/ The Sun (fig. 16); The Guardian (fig. 31); Merrily Harper (cover illustration); Imperial War Museum (fig. 19); London News Service Ltd (fig. 9); Methuen Children's Books (fig. 26); Alex Pacheco/People for the Ethical Treatment of Animals (fig. 38); Press Association (fig. 12); Royal Society for the Prevention of Cruelty to Animals (fig. 35); Today Newspaper (figs 29 & 36); World Society for the Protection of Animals (fig. 39).

FOR MY FATHER
JAMES GEOFFREY BAKER
1917–1989

Preface

The signifying animal

In 1974 Roy Willis introduced the subject of his book *Man and Beast* as follows: 'I am interested in what animals signify to man. I am also an anthropologist of a "structuralist" persuasion, meaning that I find pleasure in discovering the way symbolic ideas are interrelated within human society and culture ...'. He went on to explain his conviction that the way humans related to animals 'could, when subjected to the detailed examination of a structuralist analysis, be used as a key to "read off" certain otherwise inaccessible information about the way human beings conceived of themselves'. Almost two decades later, notwithstanding the recent collection edited by Willis entitled *Signifying Animals*, there is still much work to be done in pursuit of a broadly post-structuralist reading of 'what animals signify'. In particular, for those of us working outside anthropology, there is an ever more urgent need for interdisciplinary study in this area because the anthropologists have continued to choose, almost without exception, to explore the topic only in relation to societies and cultures other than their own.

What happens when the question of what animals signify is asked in relation to our own experience? It is clear that Western society continues to draw heavily on symbolic ideas involving animals and that the immediate subject of those ideas is frequently not the animal itself, but rather a human subject drawing on animal imagery to make a statement about human identity. In what follows I shall be considering some of those representations and some of those symbolic ideas in order to assess their operation and their influence in contemporary culture. No attempt is made to be comprehensive; the choice of examples, indeed, is sometimes unashamedly idiosyncratic.

The book sets out to tackle three main questions. First, why should it be that the animal, frequently conceived as the archetypal cultural 'other', plays such a potent and vital role in the symbolic construction of human identity in such a variety of contemporary instances? Of course, if representations of the animal can be used to make almost *any* kind of statement about humans and human identity, it might reasonably be asked to what extent the animal constitutes a meaningful connecting theme at all. Part of the book's purpose, however, is precisely to question and to demythologize the idea of animal imagery as a 'natural' resource for saying-things-about-humans.

Secondly, what is the relation of these kinds of cultural representations to the circumstances of actual living animals in that same culture, and what can the animal rights movement learn from this evidence in its attempt to develop and promote a less contemptuous and condescending attitude to animals throughout the culture? Thirdly, is the creation of a more 'positive' image for animals necessarily the most effective way forward here, or do other more oblique tactics for bringing about change in public attitudes need to be explored?

The greater part of the book is necessarily concerned with that first immense question of how animals figure in our thinking about human identity, but it has been the other two questions which have provided much of the motivation for trying to answer it. There is no very obvious reason why the destabilizing of entrenched stereotypes of human identity resulting from the post-structuralist strategy of 'decentring the subject' might not be made to work, indirectly at least, to the animals' advantage. In the end it should not simply be a matter of our studying what animals already signify in the culture but rather, through a benevolent manipulation, of exploring what animals might yet be *made to signify*.

Part I

History and power

I

From massacred cats to lucky cows: history and *mentalités*

We are lucky cows,
We chew the cud and browse,
'Cos we're eating up our greens
It makes our butter taste supreme.
  – jingle from a TV commercial for 'Anchor Butter', late 1980s

An invitation to the reader: try to envisage the whole of the culture, the contemporary culture of which we are part, and then call to mind all the ways in which animals figure in its everyday operation. This may not be particularly easy, but a moment's reflection will show that the task has little to do with thinking about real, living animals; any list arrived at in this way will be largely about representations of one kind or another. Many of them, like the verse above, are disconcertingly banal. This is no reason to dismiss them. The intention here will be to consider what such representations might reveal about attitudes both to animals and to other humans: in other words to inquire into the consequences of their apparent inconsequentiality. As a means of getting under way, let me list the kind of examples that came readily to mind as I began work on this project in 1990 – some of them will already seem quaintly nostalgic, but they probably remain as representative as any.

It was summer, and outside in the street an ice-cream van had again been playing its distorted tape-loop of 'The Teddybears' Picnic', a tune I'd known since childhood and to which I could probably still recite most of the words if I thought about them. My colleague at work was near to completing her troublesome PhD thesis, which she referred to without fail as 'the Beast'. The news at the time was dominated by the start of the 1990 Gulf crisis, and as the West was left wondering whether Iraq's Saddam Hussein could be persuaded not to invade Saudi Arabia after his annexation of Kuwait, I heard that the *Daily*

Mail, with characteristic reserve, had expressed the opinion that 'you cannot sweet-talk a rabid dog'. In contrast, I recall, my best friends often affectionately addressed their two-year-old daughter as 'Bear'; they did it so unselfconsciously that at the time it somehow seemed almost impertinent to ask them why. The local paper, meanwhile, delighted in punningly reporting the manager of the town's Woolworth store to be 'shell-shocked' by the demand for any merchandise linked to the newly-popular Teenage Mutant Ninja Turtles, though it made no mention of the fact that the craze had led in turn to a significant increase in the demand for living turtles as pets. And that strange advert was still on television all the time, the one for Anchor Butter, the one with the girl-group singing 'We are lucky cows'.

The juxtaposition of public and private and of the innocent and the exploitative across these various identifications and enthusiasms, these rhetorics of loathing or of condescension, is itself important; ours is a culture in which animal references can be employed in any context, and in which animals can apparently be used to mean anything and everything. This of course is part of the difficulty – it may be far from clear what one could meaningfully say about the role of the animal in relation to such diverse examples as a rhetorical device for characterizing political opponents, an affectionate family nickname for a child, and the cynical international marketing of a television cartoon. We are however dealing here with the products of a shared culture, with commonplaces, with stereotypes (which is not to say that the public necessarily consents to all these stereotypes, but certainly that it recognizes and understands them). The question then is what is to be made of this understanding.

The inquiry begins from the stubborn insistence that this apparently banal material is *not* without significance. It will be the contention of this book that much of our understanding of human identity and our thinking about the living animal reflects – and may even be the rather direct result of – the diverse uses to which the concept of the animal is put in popular culture, regardless of how bizarre or banal some of those uses may seem. Any understanding of the animal, and of what the animal means to us, will be informed by and inseparable from our knowledge of its cultural representation. Culture shapes our reading of animals just as much as animals shape our reading of culture.

These matters are raised at the outset in order to make quite clear the kind of book that this is meant to be. It has been written at a time when the range of books on animal-related issues within the humanities disciplines is beginning to burgeon. Most of this recent literature, one way or another, is concerned to construct an historical understanding of the ways in which animals themselves have been treated (or more often mistreated) by humans. The present book, though very much in sympathy with that larger project, tries to do something rather different. It is in fact almost the opposite of those histories of how right-thinking folk have struggled against the odds to improve the lot of animals. Its main subject, in all but the final chapter, is how the animal currently figures in the thinking of people who for the most part don't care, or don't care much, or don't consciously think much about animals. It is about the forms and structures of the symbolic availability of animals – an availability which is of course in no way restricted to those who have a particular view on animal rights. It addresses neither the 'moral' nor the 'immoral' but rather the amoral use of animals in popular culture and the popular imagination, *and it does so in the conviction that any effective cultural strategies on behalf of animals must be based on an understanding of contemporary cultural practice.*

It is partly because of this central concern with the popular and the commonplace that common usage is to be followed throughout the book in relation to certain contentious terms. Regardless of delicate sensibilities, non-human animals will be referred to simply as *animals*, and human animals simply as *humans*. Similarly, the text will not act on the proposal that 'referring to a non-human animal as an "it" strips *him* or *her* of dignity and perpetuates the view that other animals are objects, inferior things or property'.[1] This is not to dispute the fact that perceptions are shaped by language, but it seems doubtful that the rallying-call for the liberation of language in this particular way will prove a sturdy enough proposal to achieve acceptance in a popular context; and without the prospect of its acceptance the call would do little more than allow both writer and readers to feel unjustifiably self-righteous. In any case, in the present context, the continued use of 'it' can serve instead as the typographic reminder of a point to be elaborated as the book progresses: that the animal is necessarily a construction, a representation, and not an accessible essence or reality.

The book's emphasis on representation and the fairly extensive use of illustrations should not, of course, lead the reader to expect a conventional contribution to the art-historical tradition of writings on animal symbolism. It does concern the symbolic use of animals, but from a perspective which can better be described in terms of what has come in recent years to be called the 'new cultural history'.

Animals are good to think:
a contemporary mentalité

The woods are full of eager interpreters.
Clifford Geertz[2]

The methods to be used here draw particularly on the idea of historical *mentalités*. Although this term has been employed by French historians (notably those of the Annales school) since at least the 1960s, it has been popularized over the last few years by the new cultural history, within which the study of *mentalités* might be broadly defined as 'the cultural analysis of popular behaviour and attitudes'.[3]

In the Introduction to his exemplary *The Great Cat Massacre and Other Episodes in French Cultural History*, Robert Darnton usefully describes the history of *mentalités* as treating 'our own civilization in the same way that anthropologists study alien cultures. It is history in the ethnographic grain'. Its concern is 'the way ordinary people made sense of the world'. The historian must therefore read the evidence, like a text, 'for meaning – the meaning inscribed by contemporaries in whatever survives of their vision of the world'.[4] The procedure has been characterized elsewhere as one of 'symptomatic reading'.

The project of *Picturing the Beast* will proceed by similar means. The main questions with which the book will be concerned are these: What place does the animal hold in our imagination, and how are we to understand the uses to which our imaginative conception of the animal is put? Above all, why is it that our ideas of the animal – perhaps more than any other set of ideas – are the ones which enable us to frame and express ideas about *human* identity? This inquiry into the symbolic and rhetorical uses of the animal, and into the implications those uses may have for our attitudes to animals themselves, might reasonably be thought of as the study of a *mentalité*. The book is an attempt to describe the evidence of this collective state of mind, to demonstrate it, to lay it out for the reader's inspection.

In both its subject-matter and its approach the book is admittedly quite different from some of the earlier studies of *mentalités* by cultural historians and by the anthropologists whose methods they have sometimes followed. Robert Darnton took as his starting point a single contemporary text recounting the ritualized massacre of local alley cats by the apprentices in one Parisian printing shop in the 1730s:

> The hunt is soon organized. ... This man arms himself with the bar of a press, that one with a stick from the drying-room, others with broom handles. They hang sacks at the windows of the attic and the storerooms to catch the cats who attempt to escape by leaping outdoors. The beaters are named, everything is organized. Léveillé and his comrade Jerome preside over the fête, each of them armed with an iron bar from the shop. The first thing they go for is *la grise*, Madame's pussy. Léveillé stuns it with a quick blow on the kidneys, and Jerome finishes it off. ... The men produce terror on the rooftops. Seized by panic, the cats throw themselves into the sacks. Some are killed on the spot. Others are condemned to be hanged for the amusement of the entire printing shop.
> Printers know how to laugh; it is their sole occupation.

From this extraordinary graphic account, written by one of the delighted participants, Darnton endeavoured to construct a framework for understanding the culture of the typical eighteenth-century urban artisan: a culture in which – quite incidentally, as it were – there was thought to be 'nothing unusual about the ritual killing of cats'. Similarly, some years earlier, the anthropologist Clifford Geertz had based his interpretation of Balinese village culture in the late 1950s on the institution of the cockfight, a popular but illegal sport which he took not merely as the starting point for his analysis but as a microcosm of the whole culture.[5] The present book, though much influenced by such strategies, is less concerned with the idea of a single explanatory or even revelatory case study, and instead explores a variety of more modest examples.

The most obvious difference from the cases mentioned above, however, is that the time of this book's proposed *mentalité* is the present. The attitudes and prejudices under review are therefore our own, and not those of an historically or geographically distant group of 'others'.[6] Their proximity and familiarity, however, is no guarantee that their significance will be self-evident. This prompts two further questions. First, in what sense is this present *mentalité* inaccessible to us, and thus in need of description or demonstration? Secondly, if it can be shown to be inaccessible, how is it to be approached?

To understand how something that is part of everyday life and thought can be so taken for granted that it becomes invisible, it's useful to recall Roland Barthes's account of the process of naturalization, given in *Mythologies*. Calling the workings of everyday culture 'myth', he writes: 'Myth hides nothing and flaunts nothing: it distorts; myth is neither a lie nor a confession: it is an inflexion'.[7] What it distorts and inflects is the historical and the cultural, so that they appear entirely natural. But what is most useful here is the idea that *nothing is actually hidden*: it's just that the culture typically deflects our attention from these things, and makes them seem unworthy of analysis. It is rather like the means by which the luscious imagery of a modern cigarette advertisement unfailingly works to divert the viewer's attention from the health warning below. The unwritten priorities of the culture enable even that which is in full view to be rendered effectively invisible – or if still visible to be drained, by common consent, of any significance. The dominant cultural view that the subject of animals is essentially trivial, or is associated principally with memories of childhood, is a clear case in point.

This leads directly to the question of how the subject *is* to be approached if it is to be rendered serious and worthy of attention. A degree of stealth may be called for. The case studies by Geertz and Darnton which were mentioned a moment ago both happen to focus on the place of animals in a culture, but there the animal subject-matter is introduced partly as a pretext for discussing something else, something more general within the culture. For them the animal theme is a kind of chink in the culture's armour, a way in, or a means of getting around the culture's naturalization of itself. This strategy has a parallel in the *mentalité* to be described here, where the chink, the way in, is to be the *visual* image of the animal. The visibility of the subject is to be re-established, in other words, by attending to the visual evidence.

It is perhaps too easy for readers with, say, an art-historical or media studies background to forget that their own dexterity with the visual is far from typical. The feelings of the general public as well as those of many academics may be more accurately caught in the admission by one historian that 'we are particularly uneasy when faced with the visual'.[8] The very difficulties and ambiguities which are often associated with the visual image may nevertheless, if we proceed with care, serve as the means of circumventing some of the mental pitfalls on the subject of the animal into which our verbally-oriented culture might otherwise lead us.

In summary, this is what is being proposed: if we want to understand how the animal operates as a flexible symbolic device within the everyday life of the culture, and why Lévi-Strauss's classic assertion that animals are 'good to think' still seems to hold true,[9] there is much to be learnt from the varied and often surprising evidence of how that culture deals specifically with *picturing* the beast.

At this point any readers whose principal interest is in the analysis of the contemporary evidence could, if they preferred, move straight to the start of Chapter 2, where I begin to put together a picture of the interweaving of human and animal identity in this proposed *mentalité*, and where the argument starts to draw more heavily on the accompanying illustrations. The remainder of the present chapter takes a more theoretical turn. Its purpose is *to shape a way of thinking about animals*. Its contention is that the existing histories of attitudes to the animal lead us to think about the subject in certain ways and not in others. The implicit claim of these historical narratives is a simple 'this is how things were'. It is never easy to challenge the unique explanatory force that history is able to claim for itself – the culturally-entrenched belief that 'true' meaning is invariably located in the accurate record of 'real' events. Any challenge will appear marginal and partisan; any veering from established historical priorities can be stigmatized as ahistorical. Nevertheless, to explain how this book's proposed analysis of the present is to make sense in relation to the existing histories, there is no option but to call into question certain of those historical priorities.

Representing animals, representing history

The specific advantages of an emphasis on the visual in the mapping out of this contemporary *mentalité* may emerge only slowly, but it is easy enough to explain why this apparently eccentric approach has been chosen in preference, say, to simply asking people what and how they think about animals. The problem with 'simply asking', it will

readily be acknowledged, is that members of any society will not typically see through the ways the topic in question has been thoroughly
naturalized by their own culture. Describing her research into the
significance of the animal symbolism used in the Lele society of what is
now Zaire, the anthropologist Mary Douglas has written: 'I was frustrated in my direct inquiries seeking reasons for their food avoidances.
They would never say, "We avoid anomalous animals because in defy-
ing the categories of our universe they arouse deep feelings of dis-
quiet".'[10] It's clear enough that the researcher in any modern Western
society would be equally unlikely to elicit answers of this order. A less
direct approach looks altogether more promising.

It has already been noted that questions about contemporary attitudes to animals will be concerned largely with cultural representations of the animal. Culture does not allow unmediated access to
animals themselves. Our attitudes, our prejudices and indeed our sympathies are all filtered through or clogged up in this thick but transparent mesh (or mess) of history, culture, public opinion, received ideas.

Animals themselves, living animals, 'real' animals: where are they
in all this? The difficult idea of the real animal is one which will need
repeatedly to be addressed as this book progresses. For now it's enough
to acknowledge that cultural history and cultural anthropology, like
many other areas of contemporary theory, are loath to draw a sharp
distinction between representation and reality, or between the symbolic and the real. Such distinctions are usually at a cost to the former
term in each pair. Geertz expresses it nicely, complaining of the widespread prejudice 'that "symbolic" opposes to "real" as fanciful to sober,
figurative to literal, obscure to plain, aesthetic to practical, mystical to
mundane, and decorative to substantial'.[11] Instead, the representational, symbolic and rhetorical uses of the animal must be understood
to carry as much conceptual weight as any idea we may have of the
'real' animal, and must be taken just as seriously.

These matters will now be considered in relation to two of the most
persuasive contributions to what might be called, albeit a little clum-
sily, a history of the thinkability of animals. The first is John Berger's
'Why look at animals?'; the second is Keith Tester's more recent
Animals and Society. There is a particular reason for concentrating here
on these, rather than on more conventional historical accounts –
works such as Keith Thomas's *Man and the Natural World* or Harriet
Ritvo's *The Animal Estate*, for instance. Berger and Tester, I would sug-

gest, are more directly concerned to show how historical knowledge shapes the understanding of the present. Both writers focus principally on the modern urban experience of the animal. I intend eventually to dispute the 'thinkability' which their accounts enable, but to do so it will be necessary to examine in some detail the way they have constructed their versions of history.

Animals in the city: Berger on looking and loss

John Berger's 'Why look at animals?', the opening piece from his 1980 collection *About Looking*, is one of the very few texts to pay much attention to the interconnection of real and symbolic issues in human dealings with animals. It has the additional advantage of being perhaps the one text on animal issues with which a majority of readers of the present book will already be familiar. It is worth reviewing this common ground. As it appears in *About Looking*, the essay runs as a piece of continuous prose uninterrupted by subheadings, but the work was first published in the magazine *New Society* in 1977 as three distinct pieces with the titles 'Animals as metaphor', 'Vanishing animals', and 'Why zoos disappoint'.[12] Berger summed up the aim of the whole piece as follows: 'What we are trying to define, because the experience is almost lost, is the universal use of animal-signs for charting the experience of the world' (p.6). As the definitive title indicates, the essay puts much emphasis on the evidence of sight.

Two interrelated questions will be pursued in relation to this essay. The first asks what Berger has to say about the changing status of animals. The second asks, as Berger himself does, what knowledge is to be gained from a specifically visual encounter with the animal. The questions overlap, of course, because the status of animals, just as much as the image of animals, is inevitably a matter of representation.

The history Berger was proposing was a history of a loss – a loss founded on the recognition (or rather, on his contention) that modern culture has placed animals 'in a *receding* past' (p.10). But even prior to what emerges as a specifically urban or metropolitan loss, the relation of animals and humans is characterized by Berger as one of an absence of contact, which is epitomized by the pathos of an unrecognizing looking, an imperfectly-met gaze:

> The eyes of an animal when they consider a man are attentive and wary.
> ... Other animals are held by the look. Man becomes aware of himself

> returning the look. The animal scrutinizes him across a narrow abyss of
> non-comprehension. .... The man too is looking across a similar, but not
> identical, abyss of non-comprehension. And this is so wherever he looks.
> He is always looking across ignorance and fear. (pp.2–3)

This early passage is an important one because in it Berger alludes to
what he sees as humanity's sympathy for the animal, and to its symbolic investment in the animal. The animal has power, secrets, *difference*: 'a power is ascribed to the animal, comparable with human
power but never coinciding with it' (p.3). In this seemingly timeless –
which is to say pre-industrial, pre-modern – but 'now irredeemable'
relation (p.26), human dealings with animals, Berger seems to be saying, were more direct and honest. Animals 'were subjected *and* wor-
shipped, bred *and* sacrificed' (p.5). To those familiar with Berger's
idealization of the rural it will come as no surprise that the passage
continues:

> Today the vestiges of this dualism remain among those who live inti-
> mately with, and depend upon, animals. A peasant becomes fond of his
> pig and is glad to salt away its pork. What is significant, and is so difficult
> for the urban stranger to understand, is that the two statements in that
> sentence are connected by an *and* and not by a *but*. (p.5)

This, for Berger, is evidently an authentic relation to the animal: an
authentic relation, what is more, to the *real* animal. The culture of
capitalism has in his view consistently eroded and corrupted that relation. The essay provides an outline of how this has happened.

'In the last two centuries', Berger asserts, 'animals have gradually
disappeared. Today we live without them' (p.9). The theoretical break
into this new and impoverished world had come earlier, first with
Descartes's conception of the animal as a soulless machine, and then
with the eighteenth-century French naturalist Buffon's classificatory
project which effectively drained the animal of its 'experience and secrets' – the sources of its previous power in the eyes of humanity.
Nineteenth-century industrialization confirmed and completed this
theoretical break. In the early stages of industrialization 'animals were
used as machines', and later they were regarded as raw material:
'Animals required for food are processed like manufactured commo-
dities'. Not surprisingly, animal experimentation is given as the clin-
ching example of 'this reduction of the animal' (p.11).

At this point in the essay, however, Berger begins to use the animal as something of a rhetorical blunt instrument with which to hammer home his view of the inauthenticity of contemporary urban culture. To this end the 'disappearance' argument is deftly turned on its head: 'Is there not one way in which animals, instead of disappearing, continue to multiply?' What he has in mind is the institution of the pet, which he introduces as the living epitome of the animal reduced, the animal drained: mere 'mementoes from the outside world' (p.12).

It is important here to bear in mind a point Berger had made earlier. Thinking, perhaps, of something like Hegel's view that a self-consciousness can gain recognition and satisfaction only in another self-consciousness, Berger had resignedly proposed that 'No animal confirms man, either positively or negatively' (p.3). It is a key sentence in the essay. It defines the animal in the fullness of its difference, and is perhaps the clearest statement of Berger's genuine commitment to the idea of animals' independence, dignity, power and worth. In contrast, the pet-owner's relation to the pet is described as inherently corrupt: 'The pet *completes* him, offering responses to aspects of his character which would otherwise remain unconfirmed' (p.12). The implication of these contrasting statements is clear enough: the modern urban pet *is not a real animal.*

The essay thus sets up an idiosyncratic contrast which is certainly not quite that of contemporary animal rights orthodoxy. The 'outside' world, the authentic reality of the good meat-eating peasant, is set against capitalism's claustrophobic interior where the overt exploitation of animals goes hand in hand with the narcissistic fictions of the pet-owning animal-lover – the powerful symbolism of that older and outer world contrasting with the hollow echoes of what we might call the modern urban–symbolic.

In this urban–symbolic the reduced animal is typically 'co-opted' into relations of family or of spectacle (p.13). Pets, Beatrix Potter books and Disney films exemplify the family relation; zoos, game reserves and wildlife photography attest to the spectacular relation. The old symbolic is perceived as inadequate and must be replaced by a new urgent realism, whether in the form of the sudden 'demand for verisimilitude in animal toys' in the nineteenth century (p.21), or in that of the sharp-focus 'technical clairvoyance' of current nature photography (p.14). For Berger, it seems, the varied instances of this spurious realism can largely be explained in terms of a bourgeois insistence on meaning, on contact, and on the elimination of the distance between 'us' and the animal. This is the significance of his observation, for instance, that 'the manufacture of realistic animal toys coincides, more or less, with the establishment of public zoos' (p.21). Both developments betray that crucial loss of the animal's symbolic power, mystery and authenticity, only to replace it with a rather literal and unsatisfying form of visual knowing: 'The zoo to which people go to meet animals, to observe them, to see them, is, in fact, a monument to the impossibility of such encounters' (p.19).

There is much with which to disagree in Berger's 'Why look at animals?' – notably the idea of the inauthenticity of urban experience, and the worrying implication that the urban pet is somehow inherently less worthy than the wild animal or the field animal. It is also true that Berger's basic history of the marginalization of animals in industrial society is a fairly familiar one, and one which has been traced in far greater detail, for instance, in Harriet Ritvo's more recent book *The Animal Estate*. But Ritvo, like most other writers on animals' history, is quite explicitly concerned with what she calls the 'real animal'. She describes the approach of her various chapters thus:

> They present interpretations based primarily on texts produced by people who dealt with real animals – the records of organizations concerned with breeding, veterinary medicine, agriculture, natural history, and the like ... Canonical art and literature have provided only occasional corroborative examples; the large literature of animal fable and fantasy, which has little connection to real creatures, none at all.[13]

Much of the lasting value of Berger's essay stems from his reluctance to draw that kind of distinction. He has a conception of the real animal, certainly, but it is one he employs rhetorically.[14] His outline of a politico-cultural history of the animal makes no claim to speak of anything more real than human imaginings. 'Animals first entered the imagination as messengers and promises'; by the nineteenth century they inhabit that imagination largely 'as meat or leather or horn' (p.2).

For Berger, this 'reduction' of the animal is everywhere linked to an impoverishment of the imagination and to the loss of a meaningful symbolic relation to the animal, and this is frequently most apparent in our dealings with representations rather than with living animals. The traditional and essentially symbolic hobby horse is replaced for the middle-class Victorian child with the literalism of the rocking horse: 'an elaborate "reproduction" of a horse, painted realistically, with real reins of leather, a real mane of hair, and designed movement to resemble that of a horse galloping' (p.20). The imaginative decline continues into the corporate-capitalist present. Berger gives the example of Grandville's famous engravings from the 1840s, where the clothed animals 'are not being "borrowed" to explain people, nothing is being unmasked; on the contrary. These animals have become prisoners of a human/social situation into which they have been press-ganged'. This ambivalent imagery, this 'disturbing, prophetic dream', is presented as the noble beginning of a graphic tradition which is soon enough to end in 'the banality of Disney' (p.17). And 'with the advent of vast display and selling systems like Disney's', of course, the poverty of the middle-class imagination becomes the heritage 'of all childhoods' (p.20).

Living animals offer further evidence of this decline, and again that evidence comes from *looking*: 'in the zoo the view is always wrong. Like an image out of focus' (p.21). But whose view is this? In the urban gaze which is typically mediated by either the photographic lens or the bars of the cage, 'animals are always the observed. The fact that they can observe us has lost all significance. They are the objects of our ever-extending knowledge. What we know about them is an index of our power, and thus an index of what separates us from them' (p.14). Berger doesn't actually say so, but what he is describing here is the white male gaze, the empowered gaze: his account of it is remarkably similar to the terms in which, in his earlier and more famous book *Ways of Seeing*, he had described the male artist's objectification of the female model through looking. In our dealings with animals, Berger shows, the relation of knowledge and image can be a difficult one – the practice of looking is at the heart of both our sympathy for and our oppression of the animal. But the final answer to his question 'Why look at animals?' must surely be this: only by understanding who has power over the image can we begin to elaborate a worthwhile cultural history of the animal.

This brief review of Berger's position suggests an agenda for the rest of this chapter. What it needs most urgently to account for is the way in which our own historical experience of the animal is particularized. What are we allowed to see, and what are we able to say about what we see? And who exactly is this 'we'?

Animals in the city: Tester on the modern episteme

In trying to clarify the characteristics of our contemporary *mentalité*, much can be learned from a recent book of considerable importance, Keith Tester's *Animals and Society: The Humanity of Animal Rights*.[15] Tester's subject is the historical development of the claims made by the contemporary animal rights movement, so he is only incidentally concerned with the attitudes of the bulk of the public – the animal-complacent majority – in any given period. Nevertheless, he offers a valuable way forward on the question of the particularization of historical experience. 'Animals', he rightly insists, 'are a historical object' (p.70).

Tester's approach is marked by an absence of overt expressions of sympathy for animals. His deliberate detachment may not always be convincing, but it does allow him to adopt an admirably forthright style. He refers, for instance, to Darnton's example of the eighteenth-century Parisian print-workers' gleeful slaughter of local cats (including *la grise*, the favourite of the bourgeois printing-shop master's wife), and he summarizes the implications of Darnton's argument thus:

> Darnton makes the point that the important feature in the cat massacre was not the death of the cats but the entertainment it gave the workers. The printers thought their actions absolutely hilarious. A lack of embarrassment which we now find abominable? No. A set of cultural meanings around cats that we cannot understand because our culture differs from that of pre-industrial Europe? Yes. (p.69)

Darnton, of course, uses this lack of understanding as the starting-point for his exploration of an eighteenth-century *mentalité*. Tester's intention is to place our incomprehension in a rather different historical model, as will be seen in a moment. But since the present chapter is adopting Darnton's and the new cultural history's model of *mentalités*, why return here to the example of the cat-massacre at third-hand, via Tester? The answer is that Tester's main concern is to fix that example within a history of *attitudes to animals*, and not, like Darnton, just to focus on it as a revealing case study within a broader history of popular attitudes. It is therefore vital to consider how useful Tester's model might be for our own purposes.

Tester puts much emphasis on the idea of the unthinkable: for us the cat massacre is unthinkable 'because we do not know the taxonomies that make it thinkable, not just because it is abhorrently violent' (p.69). His search for taxonomies that would return it to the thinkable leads him straight to Michel Foucault, whose historical priority was the writing of a history of the present. As Foucault himself pointed out, 'to diagnose the present is to say what the present is, to say how the present differs from all that it is not, that is from our past'.[16] He further acknowledged that the writing of this history of the present is essentially a matter of constructing a usable fiction. This, of course, is exactly what John Berger's essay appeared also to be doing.

It is to Foucault's classic *The Order of Things* that Tester turns for his historical model. The choice is an appropriate one in relation to animals' histories: the 'archaeology' of knowledge proposed in that book, drawing as it does on competing historical models of classification, takes some of its evidence from the orderings of medieval bestiaries, from those of Enlightenment natural history, and even from bizarre instances of animal classification in Borges's fiction. This is also the book which elaborates Foucault's grand notion of the 'Western *episteme*' and its important historical divisions: the Renaissance, Classical and modern *epistemes*. Foucault describes these divisions as 'those great caesuras, furrows, and dividing-lines which traced man's outline in the Western *episteme* and made him a possible area of knowledge'.[17]

One commentator offers a usefully concise definition of the term *episteme* while simultaneously emphasizing its distinctly urban focus. She notes that in contrast to Foucault's earlier book *Madness and Civilization*, where the town walls served to symbolize the boundary 'between the community and the spaces of exclusion', *The Order of Things* approaches that boundary

> from within the town, through the different ways in which the community positively constituted its space of inclusion. Foucault calls the principles governing a space of inclusion an *episteme*. Epistemic principles determine what objects can be identified by the community, how they can be marked, and in what ways they can be ordered; they make certain perceptions, certain statements, certain forms of knowledge possible, others impossible.[18]

Foucault locates the break between the Renaissance and the Classical *epistemes* in the mid seventeenth century, and that between the Classical and modern *epistemes* around the year 1800. In reviewing the development of expressions of sympathy towards animals across these breaks, Keith Tester's key question is this: 'What was the status of animals in these different eras of knowledge?' (p.79). Understandably, his main concern is to explore the distinction between the Classical and the modern: the Classical period encompassing both Enlightenment natural history and the 'unthinkable' cat massacre; the modern period allowing the emergence of today's animal rights theory, which he persuasively contends would itself have been unthinkable in an earlier time.＊ Would it?

In constructing his own history/fiction of the present, his own version of that present, Tester cleverly plays off Foucault's theoretical model against more conventional histories, notably Keith Thomas's *Man and the Natural World*.[19] He (Tester, that is) writes that 'Foucault identifies changes in the structure of knowledge at the end of the eighteenth century, and we already know from Keith Thomas ... that this period also experienced fundamental transformations in the social treatment of animals' (p.79). The system of knowledge which for Foucault is exemplified by the Renaissance bestiary's all-inclusive listing of fact and fable 'is broadly the world of symbolic meaning which Keith Thomas says was undermined by urbanization and objective observation' (p.80). Foucault gives less weight than Thomas to 'the theological dimension' of anthropocentrism; 'Foucault's Renaissance *episteme* is much the same as Thomas's anthropocentrism', but Thomas has no real equivalent to Foucault's intermediate and distinct Classical *episteme*: instead he 'rather simply juxtaposes anthropocentrism with non-anthropocentrism' (p.80). For Tester, however, Thomas scores over Foucault in his explanation of epistemological change: in place of Foucault's vague references to the erosion of an *episteme* from outside, Thomas 'is right to stress the radical importance of urbanization in changing social perceptions of the natural world' (p.81).＊

The relevant passages in Thomas, in Foucault and in Tester should really be read in the original; these brief comments cannot do them justice, and in any case the purpose of these comments is only to trace the emergence of a few common themes in this tentative history of the thinkability of the animal. Although Tester makes no reference to John Berger's essay, their accounts overlap in certain important respects. The shift to a broadly 'modern' attitude to animals is presented by both as occurring around the start of the nineteenth century; both writers attribute this shift largely to the effects of urbanization; and both regard it as marking the demise of a symbolic relation between humans and animals. Neither writer expresses it quite so crudely, but their version of this history is one in which the city and the symbolic are presented as opposing terms.

This is not a question of the accuracy or reliability of Berger's or Tester's historical research. It is rather a matter of acknowledging that this is their operative fiction. As questions of history, animals and representation converge, this is the shape and sense that is being made of them. This is the story of the modern, the received idea of the modern, at what is still virtually the moment of its writing, as far as the thinkability of the animal is concerned.

The opposition of the city and the symbolic certainly looks rather persuasive as a theoretical motif in terms of its adaptability. As Tester suggests, it is quite likely to have operated in some quarters even prior to the shift into the modern *episteme*. Commenting on the urban base for the development of science, for example, he speculates that 'no doubt Linnaeus and his fellow cataloguers mocked the "yokels" who continued to believe that animals possessed symbolic meanings' (p.83). This opposition of 'real' and symbolic knowledge is a complex one, though. Noting that in England 'it was the intellectuals and the urban middle class who first suggested that animals were morally relevant', Tester writes:

As they sat by the fireside, examining fossils and stroking the dog, they could see that anthropocentrism was a myth; their science laid the foundations for a new, objectively true classification of the universe. Meanwhile, the rural population carried on its old ways; it still had a direct, personal relationship with animals, it retained a stake in the anthropocentric attitudes without which the definitions of human and animals in the rural world would collapse. (p.54)

The symbolic concerns of the rural 'yokel' are thus contrasted with the scientific pretensions of the modern urban intellectual. But cutting across this too-clean distinction is a contradiction. It is specifically the *pet-keeping* middle classes who Tester (following Thomas) explains to be the early supporters of both a humanitarian concern for animals and a scientific interest in them, and yet this is the group he describes as having 'the least strong direct relationship with animals' (p.53) and 'the least first-hand knowledge of animals' (p.54). The rural population, meanwhile, 'still had a direct, personal relationship with animals'. The authenticity of rural experience of the animal is thus contrasted with something very close to Berger's notion of a self-deluding modern experience, which I characterized earlier as that strange lesser category of the urban-symbolic. It is hard to avoid the bizarre conclusion that in Tester's just as much as in Berger's version of animals' history, *cats are simply less real than cows.*

To explain why the internal inconsistencies of these histories matter, and why, in the end, Tester's use of Foucault's model will not suit our particular purposes, it is necessary to focus more closely on the fate of the symbolic in the shift from the Classical to the modern episteme. Foucault's *The Order of Things* charts the shifting relation of three grand historical themes, which he names as Labour, Life and Language. He describes a 'general redistribution' of the Western *episteme* whereby the Classical concerns with the analysis of wealth, with natural history, and with a general grammar give way, respectively, to the distinctly modern 'empiricities' of economics, biology and linguistics.[20] It is the 'Life' theme – the shift from natural history's visual cataloguing to biology's spirit of scientific inquiry – which is most directly of concern in the context of the present discussion.

In the Classical era, Foucault contends, knowledge of things was generally ordered by means of a tabular classification which sought to display the outward visual relation of one thing to another. In contrast, the scientific drive of the modern *episteme* led to a belief in the greater reliability of a system of classification which dealt with underlying, hidden, structural, organic connections between things. These were regarded as more substantial and more real than the deceptive superficiality of surface appearances. To be modern, it might be said, is to doubt or to deny the visual.

Foucault describes the shift from Classical natural history to modern biology very much in terms of a diminished visibility. In the eighteenth century, prior to the constitution of biology as a recognized field of inquiry, living beings including animals 'were viewed through a grid of knowledge constituted by *natural history*', and 'natural history is nothing more than the nomination of the visible'. Under the modern *episteme*, however, 'abandoning the space of representation, living beings took up their places in the specific depths of life'. The rhetoric of modern science located the essence of the living being in 'those elements most hidden from view'.[21]

Keith Tester accepts the general drift of Foucault's analysis of these issues, and this has an important consequence for Tester's own argument. By concentrating on the theme of Life – 'the modern period is the era of *life*' (p.86) – Tester is necessarily more concerned with attitudes to the animal as a living being than he is with the wider cultural symbolism of the animal. This is evident in his emphasis on the approaches and beliefs of various nineteenth-century elites: he shows how the reality or rights of the animal were fought for both in the writings of the intellectuals and in the new bourgeois welfare organizations' policing of working-class pastimes, but it is clear that neither the intellectuals nor the bourgeoisie expressed much interest in *what made animals meaningful to the masses*. Tester himself is thus led largely to ignore those popular urban cultural practices in which the symbolic still played (and still plays) a part. The priorities of the modern *episteme*, it seems, result in the overlooking and undervaluing not only of the visual but also of the symbolic and the popular.

It is my contention that the pronouncedly visual 'space of representation' described by Foucault is not just the space of an outdated Classical learning but is also, vitally, the space of contemporary popular understanding of the animal. It is not that Tester somehow fails to recognize this; his principal concerns are simply with other matters. But on the basis of what has now been said about his use of Foucault, it is possible to explain why this model for the historical understanding of the animal will be inappropriate for my own purposes.

First, as stated above, it is insufficiently concerned with the contemporary 'symbolic', and thus with the forms of popular understanding. As a result of Foucault's characterization of the modern, such a position almost necessarily entails a refusal to treat the evidence of the visual with any degree of seriousness. For many a social historian or historical sociologist, the evidence of the visual will tend to be regarded as really too trivial, too transparent, to be of much political or historical import. One of the central aims of the present book is to undermine such a view.

Secondly, with regard to our thinking on animals, both Tester and Berger describe what amounts to a two-hundred-year period of the modern. They are both alert to the significant historical shifts and to the varied (and usually class-specific) attitudes to animals which are evident *within* that modern, of course, but my intention is to try to focus on something much more specific. The contemporary *mentalité* of animal representation has in some respects taken shape over less than the last twenty years, let alone the last two hundred.

Thirdly, there is the question of a 'committed' history, for want of a better word. In principle, at least, there is no reason why any contemporary cultural or social history of the animal should be founded upon a sympathy for animals or a support for the broad cause of animal rights – though without such things the motive for writing that history may be less than altogether clear. In Tester's case the attempt to maintain a certain objectivity or detachment from the issues has an important consequence in terms of the way he characterizes the modern *episteme*. Foucault allows for the idea of a certain freedom of movement within that *episteme* – the possibility, however limited, that the individual or group can effectively exert pressure for change and can thus reshape the confines of the *episteme*. Tester does not develop this idea, for he has no need of it: it is not the purpose of his history to explore what freedom there is intentionally to change things with regard to or on behalf of animals.[22]

episteme – knowledge.

The space of representation

Many British readers will hardly need reminding of the advertisement. By means of some careful editing of the tape, the jerky repetitive 'dance' movements of the cows made them appear periodically to be kicking and heading between each other the yellow dot or ball which for the rest of the time bounced across the subtitled lyrics, guiding the viewers' listening as the female singers doing the voice-over for the cows sang in unison:

> We are lucky cows,
> We chew the cud and browse,
> 'Cos we're eating up our greens
> It makes our butter taste supreme.

Once in a while a slightly longer version of the advertisement was shown, with an extra couplet which added little to the sense of the thing:

> We girls all do state
> That year-round grass makes butter great.

In either version, the girls sang as the sound faded out: 'Anchor (the green green grass) Butter (the green green grass) ...'. From 1989 to

22

1991 it never seemed to be off the television screen. It was perplexingly popular. People laughed at it, thought it was hilarious, and even sang it themselves. The infuriating memorability of the jingle was enhanced, if anything, by the verse's lack of sense.[23] Its wilful meaninglessness was reminiscent of an old Cicely Courtneidge musical comedy song, the chorus of which went something like:

> Why has the cow got four legs?
> I must find out somehow.
> You don't know, and I don't know,
> And neither does the cow! (Ha ha ha . . .)

It is hardly a sufficient explanation, but both these little nonsense rhymes seem to call on a common view that almost anything to do with animals is somehow funny, or at least is likely to be funny. This funniness in animal representation – a release from the usual constraints of meaning – may range from the endearingly amusing to the surrealistic and bizarre, and it need have nothing whatsoever to do with the idea of an inherently warm-hearted response to the animal. The hilarity provoked by massacred cats in the 1730s is clearly not on the same point of a hypothetical sliding scale of humour as the enjoyment taken in watching Anchor Butter's lucky cows, but it may be useful to think of both experiences as being located somewhere on the same scale. This goes directly against Darnton's and Tester's notion of the unthinkable, but with good reason. To categorize the cat massacre as unthinkable – to say that it is simply *off* any contemporary scale – is to say that it is neither our problem nor our responsibility. That may be so, but it actually hinders our thinking about contemporary cultural attitudes, since it deprives us of one means of comprehending what it was that people found funny about the grotesque televisual dance that the 'lucky cows' were locked into.

Here it will be well to acknowledge that the readers and writer of the previous paragraph do not and could not constitute a unified 'we'. The cat massacre – its violence graphically reported by Darnton – will be regarded by some as an event which still has the power deeply to shock, and by others merely as a fascinating historical curiosity. Some will be struck by the idea that this distant historical example finds a distressing counterpart in the revived enthusiasm for dog-fighting in contemporary Britain and America; others will consider the comparison far too superficial. Some will see the butter advertisement as exploi-

23

tative, at least at a symbolic or representational level, in its perpetuation of the cultural stereotype of the animal as an object of mindless amusement.]Others will be inclined to mock such sensitive souls for taking 'a bit of harmless fun' so seriously. It is unlikely that these or other similar reactions can now be slotted into neat class-specific categories.[24] On the one hand, as Berger observes, many of what in the nineteenth century were distinctly middle-class values with regard to animals have now (by means of the mass media and suchlike) been largely universalized. On the other hand, this contemporary middle-class hegemony is itself able to encompass diverse and conflicting sensibilities.

The clearest way to illustrate this may be by means of a personal anecdote which provides a glimpse of the *mentalité* in action. In the course of researching this book I have continued to collect a wide variety of literature in order to clarify for myself the ways in which animals and animal issues figure in the mysterious workings of the contemporary popular imagination. The material has ranged from cheap but obscure comics to serious academic texts. Often what I wanted was not available locally. In one instance, tipped off by a friend in America about the publication in Britain of Carol Adams's *The Sexual Politics of Meat*, I went to look for it in the only nearby bookshop big enough and 'serious' enough to be likely to have it in stock. The sexual politics of meat? The assistant guffawed, and immediately went across to tell a colleague, who seemed to find the prospect of such a book equally preposterous. Doing my best to imagine myself as the detached viewer of a piece of curious but instructive anthropological behaviour rather than get angry, I ordered the book anyway. By the time I went back to collect it some two weeks later, it seemed as though every employee of the shop had been shown this extraordinary item, this prize joke – though none, as far as I could gather, had actually turned beyond the cover.

Some months later I was looking for another new book, Susan Herbert's *The Cats Gallery of Art*. As the title suggests, it comprises copies of famous paintings in which the human figures have been replaced by cats adopting the same poses. To be honest, I went in search of this book with a certain embarrassment – it isn't the kind of art book that I would ordinarily buy. But was I laughed at, or sneered at, or given the kind of supercilious stare I'd half-expected? Not at all. The assistant was politeness itself, and could only apologize that this popular book was temporarily out of stock. They were expecting more in on the next Wednesday. I went back, of course, but too late: by the time I got there the new stock had already sold out.

Readers must make what they will of the anecdote. I present it here because it was the thing that most clearly enabled me to see that the contemporary hegemony of which Berger speaks is made hazardous by its own 'abysses of non-comprehension'; those (like Adams) who try to construct a theoretical discourse aimed at the re-representation of the animal will be derided by many of those who take it for granted that everyone likes cute pictures of cats, and vice versa.

Both groups may of course be derided by some within the animal rights movement for concerning themselves at all with issues of representation rather than with immediate 'realities'. It is therefore worth restating that one of the central purposes of this book is to consider the possibility that attitudes to living animals are in large part the result of the symbolic uses to which the concept of the animal is put in popular culture. This is not to set the representational or the popular–symbolic 'over' the real. It is simply to say that any understanding of the animal is inseparable from knowledge of its cultural representation. Regrettable as it may seem, it is not easy to escape what has memorably been called 'our Walt Disney consciousness'.[25]

'We', and 'our culture'

Within the new cultural history and related literatures, there is evidence of a growing concern over what might constitute the legitimate use of terms such as *we* and *our culture*. One writer complains, for instance, of 'an entirely too comfortable sense of solidarity signed by the heavy-handed pronouns of the method'.[26] The complaint is not a call for their complete avoidance in favour of a pretended objectivity or transparency of communication, but certainly for their more cautious use. In the present context the issue is of importance because, as indicated above, readers may have conflicting views over what constitutes 'their' culture and their relation to or endorsement of that culture's dealings with animals. It is a matter, in other words, of the place and status of animals in relation to questions of identity.

There is no easy answer to what would be an appropriate use of the terms here. It may in any case be better to leave 'we' as a deliberately and radically unstable sign. Any attempt to pin it down would betray an anxious effort to put ourselves at the centre of things, at the source of meaning – an anthropocentrism which is in keeping neither with the purposes of this book nor with the state of contemporary theory. As Foucault has influentially argued,

> the researches of psychoanalysis, of linguistics, of anthropology have 'decentred' the subject in relation to the laws of its desire, the forms of its language, the rules of its actions, or the play of its mythical and imaginative discourse.[27]

This notion of the decentring of the human subject is of paramount importance. Once any textual 'we' is recognized of necessity to be a decentred subject, it is beside the point to agonize over its identity, its meaning and its 'truth'. This has consequences for thinking about animals and representation. As in other fields, it entails the recognition that the individual is not a free agent in the cultural space of representation, and is not able to change its meanings at will. But beyond this, and in a sense despite this, the decentring of the human subject opens up a valuable conceptual space for shifting the animal out from the cultural margins. It does so precisely by destabilizing that familiar clutch of entrenched stereotypes which works to maintain the illusion of human identity, centrality and superiority.

Animals, stereotypes and mentalités

> Once a friend came to visit and said, looking out on the soothing view: 'And it *would* have to be a *white* horse; the very image of freedom'. And I thought, yes, the animals are forced to become for us merely 'images' of what they once so beautifully expressed.
>
> Alice Walker, 'Am I Blue?'[28]

How is the *mentalité* of contemporary animal representation to be characterized? How do the complex and inconsistent accretions of meaning around the image of the animal actually work within the culture? The fact that they have been constituted historically will mean nothing to most of those who use them. It has been persuasively argued that any cultural system of values 'is obviously the product of history, but it functions in the present, synchronically, in ignorance of history (or, more accurately, by virtue of a particular myth of history)'.[29] It is clear that the past can offer no reliable guide to what any animal sign will mean in the present state of things: large chunks of that past have in any case been presented as 'irredeemable' (Berger) or 'unthinkable' (Darnton, Tester) by the particular myth of history that applies here. The history seems effectively and perhaps appropriately to have shorn itself of its own explanatory power.

What is left is a multiplicity of animal signs circulating in an only randomly-historical 'space of representation' – typically the space of the modern city. This is not an abstraction. These signs can carry considerable force. Of the very few studies to touch on this matter, an essay by the American anthropologist Elizabeth Lawrence called 'Mounted police: A symbolic study of urban horses' is especially useful. Through extensive interviews with police and public she shows how crass distinctions between the real and the symbolic are subsumed in the representational complexity of the living animal.

Lawrence takes as her starting point the presence and visibility of the horse in the city. She notes that 'high *visibility*' is 'the most important and frequently cited advantage of the mounted force', and that for the public the horse/rider unit constitutes 'an image whose mere presence has a strong impact'. Symbolism is in no sense secondary here; she argues that the mounted police are an effective force '*because* of the profound meanings the horse has in the human consciousness'. She also gathers evidence that the police themselves 'utilize people's perceptions of the complex and contradictory nature of the horse – the wild versus the tame – to increase the effectiveness with which they carry out their work'. This calculating manipulation of the image of the horse is often balanced, for the mounted officer, by what Lawrence calls 'a merging of self with the animal, the investing of one's identity as well as energy in the animal'. In this sense 'an officer's mount is regarded ... not as a creature of an alien order but rather as one who partakes of the human social realm on city streets'.[30]

Little would be gained by exploring the scattered historical origins of the meanings which Lawrence describes. For all the rich complexity of some of these representations, it is the immediacy and obviousness of their present-day meaning which is far more important to those involved in using them. One of the officers she interviewed clearly spoke for many when he explained that white horses were 'not at all suitable for the police' because they were 'silly-looking'. There is no gainsaying such an argument; it is no more wrong than the view of Alice Walker's fictional character that in a quite different context the white horse is 'the very image of freedom'. Like the definitions in

Flaubert's caustic *Dictionary of Received Ideas* (such as STALLION: Always 'fiery'), their truth is inseparable from their stupidity.

These meanings are the common currency of our animal *mentalité*. They are, quite simply, stereotypes. For precisely that reason they are able to operate as a surprisingly coherent body of knowledge. This kind of knowledge has been uncompromisingly described (though not specifically with regard to animal representations) as follows:

> It is the knowledge of common-sense consciousness, what the consensus of received opinion in a given society assumes and offers as Reality. It is what Aristotle called *endoxon* ('current opinion'), and, following Aristotle, we may perhaps call the discourse which repeats and reinforces consensus knowledge the endoxal discourse, the language of common-sense, the language of the stereotype, whose function it is to cover a world historically produced with the mantle of the universal and the permanent and of which the classic forms are the maxim, the proverb, the platitude, the *idée reçue*.[31]

The cute cat, the lucky cow, the white horse as the 'very image of freedom' ... The viewer is not invited to consider their historical production, nor to call into question the certainty of their vacuous meanings as they circulate in the space of representation. They are there, they are in use; it is their complex systematicity which needs to be understood rather than engaging in a search for the origins of their individual or collective meanings. Within the vicious circularity of the present animal *mentalité*, only that which is already known will be readily recognized as having meaning. Such meanings as there are will operate largely independently of the living animal even if they once derived from it or even now apply to it. The intelligibility of these stereotypes is entirely dependent on their conformity, and that conformity is not (and never was) to some 'truth' of the animal.

The emotive word *stereotype* is employed here to describe the individual instances of this common-sense consciousness, this Walt-Disney-consciousness, though it is used only partly in a combative sense. Most of the instances described in the following chapters will involve visual encounters of one kind or another, whether it be with a static pictorial image, or the more involved continuity of a cinematic or comic-book narrative, or the problematic visibility of a living animal. The notion of the stereotype has certain specific advantages in relation to examples such as these. It avoids the studied neutrality of the word *sign*, and it does less to encourage the idea that these standardized clusters of image and thought will necessarily have a fixed iconographic form. As one workaday definition has it, a stereotype is:

> An over-simplified *mental image* of (usually) some category of person, institution, or event which is shared, in essential features, by large numbers of people. ... Stereotypes are commonly, but not necessarily, accompanied by prejudice, i.e. by a favourable or unfavourable predisposition towards any member of the category in question.[32]

The connection with prejudice makes the stereotype a particularly useful concept in the study of how animals figure in the construction of competing identities. Additionally, the operation of the stereotype is consistent in certain important ways with that of the semiological sign. Summarizing in retrospect the earlier and more openly political phase of his semiological project, Roland Barthes has stated:

> It was a question, in short, of understanding (or of describing) how a society produces stereotypes, i.e., triumphs of artifice, which it then consumes as innate meanings, i.e., triumphs of Nature.[33]

– of understanding, that is, the process which in *Mythologies* Barthes had termed *naturalization*. It is made clear elsewhere in his writings that stereotyping is not restricted to the way in which any individual characterizes and dismisses the threat of others, but is also typical of the way in which personal identity is constructed. The 'I', Barthes realized, 'is not an innocent subject'. It is a complex interweaving of influences drawn from shared cultural knowledge which is then naturalized as personal history, so that even the individual's subjectivity 'has ultimately the generality of stereotypes'.[34] In the present context it is therefore not a matter of 'us', as superior outsiders, berating an ill-defined 'them' for enjoying stupid representations of lucky cows or cute cats. Everyone is implicated in the workings of this *mentalité* because everyone's attitudes to the animal have been constituted within its narrow boundaries. Change, whether by the construction of an appropriate historical perspective or by other means, can only be achieved from within this space of the popular.

Notes

1 The brief manifesto 'Liberate your language' was first printed in the American magazine *Animals' Agenda*, 6, no.8 (1986), p.18, and is reproduced in Carol J.

Adams's *The Sexual Politics of Meat: A Feminist-Vegetarian Critical Theory* (Oxford: Polity, 1990), p.65. In the same year a very similar point had been made in Jane Rich's letter 'The meaning of the word' in the British Union for the Abolition of Vivisection (BUAV) magazine *Liberator*, April/May 1986, p.18.

2 Clifford Geertz, *Local Knowledge: Further Essays in Interpretive Anthropology* (New York: Basic Books, 1983), p.21.

3 See Lynn Hunt (ed.), *The New Cultural History* (Berkeley: University of California Press, 1989), passim. For a detailed and exceptionally useful account of where the new cultural history is located within the broader context of contemporary theory, see Alan Liu, 'Local transcendence: Cultural criticism, postmodernism, and the romanticism of detail', *Representations*, no.32 (1990), pp.75–113.

4 Robert Darnton, *The Great Cat Massacre and Other Episodes in French Cultural History* (London: Penguin, 1985), pp.11 and 13.

5 See Robert Darnton, 'Workers revolt: The great cat massacre of the rue Saint-Séverin', in *The Great Cat Massacre*; and Clifford Geertz, 'Deep play: Notes on the Balinese cockfight', in *The Interpretation of Cultures* (London: Hutchinson, 1975).

6 The assertion that this is a *mentalité* of the present should not be taken to limit its historical scope too strictly. While in certain specific details it may be particular to, say, the late 1980s and the 1990s, some of the cultural clichés and symbolic meanings on which it draws may have been in place in much the same form for many decades. The emphasis, however, will be on taking a synchronic slice across the culture in order to study how contemporary meanings operate, rather than taking a diachronic perspective to show how those meanings came about historically. In this sense a *mentalité* is consistent with and rather similar to the semiological notion of a language-state, which Saussure defined thus: 'In practice a language-state is not a point but rather a certain span of time during which the sum of the modifications that have supervened is minimal. The span may cover ten years, a generation, a century, or even more.' Darnton himself has noted that 'precision may be inappropriate as well as impossible in the history of *mentalités*', and he makes this point in relation to an example extending across three centuries! See Robert Darnton, *The Great Cat Massacre*, p.30; and Ferdinand de Saussure, *Course in General Linguistics*, translated by Wade Baskin (London: Fontana, 1974), p.101.

7 Roland Barthes, *Mythologies*, translated by Annette Lavers (London: Jonathan Cape, 1972), p.129.

8 Raphael Samuel, 'The figures of national myth', in *Patriotism: The Making and Unmaking of British National Identity*, Vol.III: *National Fictions*, edited by Raphael Samuel (London: Routledge, 1989), p.xxviii. Samuel assumes here that he is speaking for a majority of historians.

9 Claude Lévi-Strauss, *Totemism*, translated by Rodney Needham (Harmondsworth: Penguin, 1973), pp.161–2 ('in totemism ... natural species are chosen not because they are "good to eat" but because they are "good to think"'). See also S.J. Tambiah, 'Animals are good to think and good to prohibit', *Ethnology*, 8 (1969), pp.423–59.

10 Mary Douglas, *Purity and Danger: An Analysis of Concepts of Pollution and Taboo* (London: Routledge & Kegan Paul, 1969), p.173.

11 Clifford Geertz, quoted in Lynn Hunt (ed.), *The New Cultural History*, p.78.

12 See John Berger, 'Why look at animals?' in *About Looking* (London: Writers & Readers, 1980), pp.1–26. The shorter pieces in *New Society* appeared in the 1977 issues of 10 March, pp.504–5, 31 March, pp.664–5, and 21 April, pp.122–3. Page numbers henceforth given in the main text are to the version in *About Looking*.

13 Harriet Ritvo, *The Animal Estate: The English and Other Creatures in the Victorian Age* (Cambridge, Mass.: Harvard University Press, 1987), p.4.

14 This remark should not be taken as an attempt to compare Ritvo unfavourably to Berger. Her approach is certainly not lacking in subtlety, and shortly after announcing her primary concern with the living animal, she distinguishes 'material animals' and 'rhetorical animals', explaining that their respective positions 'in the physical world and in the universe of discourse were mutually reinforcing' in the imaginative life of the nineteenth century (p.5).

15 Keith Tester, *Animals and Society: The Humanity of Animal Rights* (London: Routledge, 1991). As with the previous section on Berger, page references to Tester's book will be incorporated in the main text.

16 Michel Foucault, writing in 1969, quoted (in her own translation) in Eve Tavor Bannet, *Structuralism and the Logic of Dissent: Barthes, Derrida, Foucault, Lacan* (London: Macmillan, 1989), pp.103–4.

17 See Michel Foucault, *The Order of Things: An Archaeology of the Human Sciences* (London: Tavistock/Routledge, 1989), p.378. The French original, entitled *Les Mots et les choses*, was first published in 1966.

18 Eve Tavor Bannet, *Structuralism and the Logic of Dissent*, p.144. Elsewhere she evocatively describes the modern *episteme* as 'a structure which gives reality its thick and consistent historicity' (p.161).

19 See Keith Thomas, *Man and the Natural World: Changing Attitudes in England 1500–1800* (London: Allen Lane, 1983).

20 See Michel Foucault, *The Order of Things*, pp.x, 250 and 345.

21 *The Order of Things*, pp.128, 132, 345 and 268.

22 On the degree of freedom available within the *episteme*, see the closing chapter of *The Order of Things*, and also Eve Tavor Bannet, *Structuralism and the Logic of Dissent*, pp.162–3. With regard to Tester, the motives for his 'uncommitted' history are not entirely clear. He certainly wants to demonstrate the extent to which contemporary animal rights thinking wilfully refuses to acknowledge its own historical and social specificity, but there is little indication that in so doing he wishes to *strengthen* the conceptual base for animal rights.

23 Vance Packard long ago commented on this phenomenon in relation to American children's enjoyment of television commercials. See his *The Hidden Persuaders* (Harmondsworth: Penguin, 1960), pp.133–4.

24 Animals can still figure significantly in the maintenance of class boundaries, of course. The high brow press in Britain, for instance, understandably outraged by the growing popularity of dog-fighting in recent years, has often presented the phenomenon as though it were the epitome of all that continues to be incomprehensible about working-class culture as a whole.

25 Jack Zipes, *Breaking the Magic Spell: Radical Theories of Folk and Fairy Tales* (London: Heinemann, 1979), p.8.

26 Alan Liu, 'Local transcendence', p.94. At this point Liu is referring to the philosopher Richard Rorty's *Contingency, Irony, and Solidarity* (Cambridge: CUP, 1989), especially to his idea of a community of 'we liberals'. The problematic use both of *we* and of *culture* is also explored in the introduction to James Clifford's *The Predicament of Culture: Twentieth-Century Ethnography, Literature and Art* (Cambridge, Mass.: Harvard University Press, 1988).

27 Michel Foucault, quoted and translated in Jonathan Culler's *The Pursuit of Signs: Semiotics, Literature, Deconstruction* (London: Routledge & Kegan Paul, 1981), p.33. The quotation is from Foucault's 1969 *L'Archéologie du savoir*. Regardless of Foucault's strenuous denial that he was ever himself a 'structuralist', his explora-

tion of the decentring of the subject has been of great significance in the development of post-structuralist theory.

28 Alice Walker, 'Am I Blue?', in *Through Other Eyes: Animal Stories by Women*, edited by Irene Zahava (Freedom, California: Crossing Press, 1988), pp.5–6.

29 Derek Attridge, 'Language as history / history as language: Saussure and the romance of etymology', in *Post-structuralism and the Question of History*, edited by Derek Attridge, Geoff Bennington and Robert Young (Cambridge: CUP, 1987), p.191.

30 Elizabeth Atwood Lawrence, 'Mounted police: A symbolic study of urban horses', chapter 4 of *Hoofbeats and Society: Studies of Human–Horse Interactions* (Bloomington: Indiana University Press, 1985).

31 Christopher Prendergast, 'Flaubert: Writing and negativity', *Novel*, 8, no.3 (1975), p.207.

32 *The Fontana Dictionary of Modern Thought*, edited by Alan Bullock and Oliver Stallybrass (London: Fontana, 1977), p.601.

33 Roland Barthes, *A Barthes Reader*, edited by Susan Sontag (London: Jonathan Cape, 1982), p.471. The contentiousness of the term *stereotype* seems to have increased in recent years. Martin Barker's weighing of the evidence has even led him to assert that 'the concept of a "stereotype" is useless as a tool for investigation of media texts' – see his *Comics: Ideology, Power and the Critics* (Manchester: MUP, 1989), p.210. His objections do not however seem to invalidate Barthes's use of the term, which is the sense in which it is employed here.

34 Roland Barthes, *S/Z*, translated by Richard Miller (London: Jonathan Cape, 1975), p.10.

2

Eagles, lions and bulldogs: an iconography of power

Power is in its fraudulent as in its legitimate forms always based on distance from the body.

Elaine Scarry[1]

This chapter will begin to explore in more detail the status of *the animal as image*, and to question precisely how the visual image of the animal prompts the kind of meanings and connotations that it does. In doing so, rather than seeing pictorial material as a form of transparent evidence – evidence of an underlying historical reality, for instance – the intention will be to concentrate on the workings of the pictorial material itself, or on what Barthes has famously called 'the rhetoric of the image'. At the start, at least, this will not involve following any particular method; it is more a matter of trying to keep alert to what is going on at a visual level in each example, and then of risking some generalizations on the basis of these specific instances.

Animals and nation

National animal symbols have been chosen as the central subject of this chapter; they are images which wield a certain power, and which may therefore be taken to matter both to those who have invested in that power and to those against whom it is wielded. There are other more detailed reasons for the choice at this early stage of our investigations. First, these images are typical examples of 'animal symbolism' as it is traditionally conceived, by art historian and general public alike. The symbols commonly have a pictorial form, but their imagery is taken to be an illustration of concepts grounded in the broader culture: they are seen as an 'expression' of national characteristics or whatever. This leads on to the second point, which is that they are clear

33

examples of animals being used (intentionally, and not through inadvertent anthropomorphism) to symbolize human identity and human values. This relation of animal image and human concept is at the core not only of this chapter but of the book as a whole. These first two considerations continue to exploit the rather crude and uncritical distinction between the real and the symbolic, which the previous chapter has already called into question. For the moment, however, given its widespread use and intelligibility, there are certain advantages to leaving it in place.

The third reason for focusing on these symbols is that their meanings are generally taken to be fairly straightforward: this animal standing for this country, that one for that. This, however, is a mistaken impression, and it will be important to show that there is in fact no consistent and reliable relation between the animal depicted and the meanings conveyed or even intended. The apparent power of these images rests on a most fragile foundation.

The present state of play

The opening example, a newspaper photograph, reflects what was a growing enthusiasm for the 'photo-opportunity' as a tactic in British political campaigning in the 1980s. Although the image is now some years old, it is still as clear a statement as any of current attitudes to the animal as symbol, and is a particularly useful indicator of the complexity of those attitudes. Taken during the 1987 General Election campaign, it shows Norman Tebbit, at that time chairman of the ruling Conservative Party, posing with a bulldog named 'Duke' which features in the Conservative election poster seen behind them in the photograph (fig. 1). This photo-opportunity, by no means the most ludicrous one of the campaign, was used in the weekend television news but was committed to print only in the unwaveringly Conservative *Sunday Telegraph*.

Although any reading of the election poster will certainly be modified by the characters in the foreground of the photograph, it is the poster itself on which I want to concentrate for the moment. Designed by Saatchi & Saatchi, the advertising agency which the Conservatives had used since the late 1970s, it favourably compares Britain's economic growth to that of other European nations through the depiction of three dogs of different sizes. The smallest is a French poodle wearing a

"You can tell an election is on when the Tory
chairman starts patting dogs" said Mr Tebbit
yesterday as he made friends with Duke, an
18-month-old bulldog. Mr Tebbit was in
Hammersmith for the "unveiling" of a Conservative
election poster in which Duke is featured.

1 A complex circularity: the Conservative Party chairman poses with
the real bulldog which, in the election poster behind them, stands
symbolically for Britain or, more precisely, for the Conservatives themselves. From the front page of the *Sunday Telegraph*, 17 May 1987.

beret and a string of onions; next in size is a German shepherd dog
dressed in a feathered Tyrolean hat and with a stein of beer at its feet;
and largest of the three is the bulldog, long established as one of Britain's national symbols, which is unadorned except for a small Union
Jack tag hanging from its collar.

The poster's crude humour is obvious enough, at least to a British
audience, but whether or not one disapproves of its stereotypes it is an
instructive marker of contemporary attitudes to the roles animals can
play in the depiction of identity and nationhood. There is, quite clearly,
some life left yet in the notion of animal symbolism in a political context. The poster's jokiness may be very much of its time, depending as it
does on the dubious belief that in the image-cluttered present one can
employ potentially offensive visual stereotypes without intending any
real offence. Its basic strategies, however, still have much in common
with the pictorial propaganda techniques of the two World Wars,
where animal imagery and symbolism were very widely used to distinguish the good from the bad, us from them. In the present example,
Britain's superiority is asserted not simply on the basis that 'biggest is
best', but because the photographically-smaller rivals are made to look
rather ridiculous, and certainly to lack the dignity required of national
animal symbols. This is not only because of their human headgear and
their gastronomic attributes, but above all, of course, because unlike
the bulldog these dogs are *not* the chosen national animal symbols of
France and Germany.

Within the intended humorous context, then, a simple and traditional opposition is at work. The national self is depicted on its own
terms; the rival others are simply made to conform to that nation's
most entrenched and least flattering image of them. This may partly
have seemed a matter of necessity as far as the originators of the poster
were concerned. Could they have relied on the significance of, say, a
cockerel and an eagle being as unambiguously recognized as that of
the convenient stereotypes they in fact chose to use? The Union Jack
tag on the bulldog's collar seems to betray just a little concern that
even in its own country that animal's symbolic meaning might not be
quite as familiar as it once had been, and might thus need some discreet
pictorial reinforcement.

If the poster's reluctant acknowledgement of the fading intelligibility
of traditional national animal symbolism is a further mark of its con-
temporaneity, the physical details of the animals' contrasting appear-

ances accord to longer-standing principles. Again disregarding for the present the effect of the real bulldog 'Duke' in the newspaper photograph, the look of that bulldog in the poster is largely anonymous, as it should be. That anonymity is achieved through its conformity to our intuitive expectations of such symbols: it is 'dignified', still, self-contained, solid, and its gaze is direct and certain. Because it has no obvious qualities which obtrusively distract us from such expectations, we pay little attention to it. As a physical animal it is effectively invisible: a mere vehicle for the transparent transmission of a symbolic meaning. The opposite is true of the other two dogs, where everything attests to their absurd physicality, their obtrusive visibility. Acutely aware of his presence, as he is not of theirs, they gaze across and up to him – enviously eyeing his lack of a bowler hat and cigar, perhaps. For the effect of the human and 'national' attributes they have been forced to carry is simply to make their bodies look comical. We are *meant* to look at them, to inspect all this comic detail and to revel in their curious otherness, while knowing that we don't need to study the familiar bulldog in this way.

It is obviously somewhat rash to generalize from a single example, but this particular image already suggests several promising themes which might be pursued. The first is the proposal that, in a political context at least, pictorial animal symbolism has traditionally worked by means of an opposition centred on the contrasting depictions of the rival animals' bodies. Secondly, there is the question of the stability of this symbolism, this 'rhetoric', which arises from doubts about how effectively its meanings are now transmitted in popular culture. Finally, the example prompts more general questions about the 'seriousness' of animals as a vehicle for the transmission of symbolic meanings. The chapter will tackle these issues in turn, but their interconnection will be evident throughout.

The animal body in the First World War

The contrasting of one nation's animal symbol with its less favourable animal depictions of its neighbours, rivals or enemies is not always or only sustained by showing those others in a comic light. It very frequently seems to be the case, however, that they will be distinguished from the nation's own symbol by the attention which is drawn, one way or another, to their depicted bodies. This is especially clear in some

JOIN THE
ARMY AIR SERVICE
BE AN AMERICAN EAGLE !
CONSULT YOUR LOCAL DRAFT BOARD. READ THE ILLUSTRATED
BOOKLET AT ANY RECRUITING OFFICE, OR WRITE TO THE CHIEF
SIGNAL OFFICER OF THE ARMY, WASHINGTON, D.C.

2 *Be an American eagle!*, a First World War recruiting poster by Charles Livingston Bull. Bull specialized in animal imagery and was active in conservation, but here (like other artists of the time) he turns his naturalistic skills to symbolic effect.

of the posters from the First World War, where the general impression is of a popular rhetoric of rival national animals battling it out.

Consider Charles Livingston Bull's recruiting poster, *Be an American eagle!* (fig. 2). Some of its pictorial strategies are typical of a wide variety of visual propaganda. Like the bulldog of the previous example, for instance, the American eagle is shown on the right of the image; echoing the common inter-cultural stigmatization of the left, this has more to do with the sense of being 'in the right' than specifically of being on the political right (though for the Conservative bulldog that too is an apt and doubtless deliberate connotation). Unlike that bulldog, the American eagle is not shown larger than its rival, but it is shown above it in the image and thus in what would still commonly be taken to be the morally superior position.[2]

Those particular considerations do not relate directly to the poster's *animal* symbolism, but they do in fact reinforce some of the connotations triggered by the form of the animals' bodies. As with the dogs of the previous poster, the contrast here is not between entirely different species, and although the American bald eagle is immediately distinguishable from the German eagle, the artist's intended meanings still need to be marked out on their bodies. In one sense the poster is a most unusual example of its kind. When an enemy was depicted in animal form in the posters of the First World War, it might be shown as a snake, or as a dragon, or most commonly of all – at least in the Allies' posters – as an ape or ape-like creature. What seldom happened, for reasons already indicated in relation to the Conservative poster, was that the enemy was shown in the form of its own chosen national symbol. Beyond this, *Be an American eagle!* is almost alone in juxtaposing two rival countries' national animal symbols in a single image. None the less, the German eagle is clearly not depicted in a way the German authorities might have chosen, and not only because it appears to be losing the fight. It has been drained of its power and authority by subtler pictorial means.

Much depends on a comparison of the birds' feathers and thus of their silhouettes. The outline of the bald eagle is predominantly smooth, its feathers are all down, and even the open beak and the single talon that break out into the surrounding space are described in sleek and gradual curves. What the viewer seems to be faced with here is the visual expression of the body, the national self's body, as a perfect container. This is an idea whose cultural resonances can be felt even in

39

quite remote examples. In his essay on Flaubert's intolerance of stupidity (*la bêtise*), Christopher Prendergast has written of the novelist's contempt for the bourgeois urge 'to draw over the void a veil fabricated from a bland and nauseous tissue of reassuring, instantly consumable meanings, to create a world with a totally smooth surface, without leaks and gaps'. In *Mythologies* Roland Barthes notes the absorption of this general principle into the domestic details of bourgeois life, as he comments on the glazed surfaces of the recipes typically featured in *Elle*: 'a cookery which is based on coatings and alibis, and is for ever trying to extenuate and even to disguise the primary nature of food-stuffs, the brutality of meat or the abruptness of sea-food'.³ The smooth outline of Bull's American eagle seems intended similarly to disguise its 'primary nature', presenting instead the 'instantly consumable' meaning of a secure and clearly defined nationhood.

In contrast, the German eagle, which must certainly be registered by the viewer as symbolizing Germany, must then without delay be shorn of this safe symbolic distance and presented instead in its full and immediate physical reality. The detailed individuation of its tattered feathers not only gives it a greater three-dimensional 'reality,' but also presents an outline which is far from smooth, perfect, safe and 'human' in its associations. At one level this spiky outline, supported by the flailing tongue and the emphatic hook of the sharp beak, suggests not only that the bird is aggressive but – far more importantly from a propagandistic standpoint – that it is conceptually cast in the role of the aggressor. These same details can also be read, however, as signalling both its otherness and its vulnerability. It is not only that the bird lacks the visual self-containment and restraint of the American eagle, the eagle as symbol. The breaking up of the German eagle's outline can also suggest the breaking, opening and wounding of its body by its rival; the tattered state of its feathers would certainly support such a reading.

These pictorial details are important because it is they that establish the bird's physical immediacy in contrast to the bald eagle's symbolic distance or unembodiedness. Elaine Scarry has argued that the image of the opened body is the ultimate image of reality: 'It is as though the human mind, confronted by the open body itself (whether human or animal) does not have the option of failing to perceive its reality'. For the viewer it is a reality 'that rushes unstoppably across his eyes and into his mind'.⁴ Scarry's comments are made in the context of her discussion of how, in extreme situations such as war, the physical body in human or animal sacrifice has been used to substantiate or to confer a reality upon abstract ideas. In the case of Bull's poster, the openness of the German eagle's body (its inside attested to by the prominent tongue as well as the broken outline) seems principally to emphasize its lack of a sustainable symbolic status.

The kind of rhetorical opposition described here is widespread in First World War pictorial propaganda, despite the fact that much of the imagery was not produced by professional artists, and that very little of it was produced by people whose pre-war work gave them any experience in the subtle manipulation of national symbols. There is some evidence that it conforms, however, to wider cultural assumptions about perceptions of identity. The idea that the image of the opened body is most definitely not the image of the self's body seems consistent, for instance, with the widespread proscription (not only in the First World War) of the graphic or photographic representation of a country's own war wounded and war dead.[5]

From the point of view of its being *animals'* bodies that are depicted in the posters, however, there is a further matter to be considered. Here it will help to introduce another image into the discussion, a cartoon by H.T. Webster with the caption 'The thrill that comes once in a lifetime', which was reproduced in the Chicago-based monthly magazine *The Poster* in 1918 (fig. 3). The cartoon shows a row of posters, accurately drawn versions of the real poster *Teufel Hunden* by an artist identified only by the initials B.H., which would certainly have been familiar to the cartoon's contemporary readers. The poster shows the U.S. Marines in the form of the 'devil dog' seeing off the ludicrous and ungainly German dachshund, and in the cartoon the local boys are seen doing their own bit towards this part of the war effort.

A general point can now be made about the three images so far reproduced in this chapter: the British press photograph of Norman Tebbit and the Tory poster, the Charles Livingston Bull poster, and the cartoon depicting the *Teufel Hunden* poster. In each of these images one of the depicted animals represents *us*, or at least the intended viewer's 'us'. This is how animal symbolism works, of course, but in each of these three, additionally, there is evidence of a direct and particularly enthusiastic identification with the animal. The Tory poster shows not just a national symbol, but that symbol appropriated by a single party, as the legend 'Conservative' is printed directly below the bulldog; it's

3 Kicking the dog with impunity: putting the patriotic boot into the German dachshund, which the American cartoonist H.T. Webster characterizes here as 'The thrill that comes once in a lifetime'. From *The Poster*, September 1918, p.14.

hard to see this in the photograph as it's blocked from view by the party chairman's head, though that in itself reinforces this identification. Rather similarly, Bull's poster invited its viewers not simply to recognize their national symbol but positively to *be* an American eagle! And according to the Webster cartoon, in kicking the dog (and of course in only kicking the German dog) the boys manage patriotically to elevate a mischievous pastime into 'the thrill that comes once in a lifetime'.

What is clear from all three examples is that this kind of identification is unproblematic; it is exploited by the image-producer without apparent contrivance, in the confident (and very largely justified) expectation that the viewer will grasp it at once, without needing consciously to think through its conventions. It appears to be something which is simply *available*, out there in the culture. If this seems surprising, it is because of the particular choices that have been made in the making-visual of 'our' identity. Mary Douglas has observed from an anthropological perspective that 'the human body is always treated as an image of society',[6] but the three present examples use a form of symbolism in which the self's collective body is depicted as *animal*, not human. Some of the wider questions raised by this kind of totemic practice will be dealt with later, but a word must be said here to summarize how this common form of animal symbolism seeks to maintain its *pictorial* intelligibility.

In the culture at large, the practice is widespread and apparently unproblematic ('Will the Lions catch the Kangaroos on the hop?' asks a typical recent sports-page headline, for example); it is in its pictorial form that the internal tensions are perhaps more evident. The British bulldog; the American eagle; as animal symbols of the national self they are already known, and they are there simply to be recognized. Their particular visual form in any given poster will matter hardly at all to viewers, as long as it does not contradict the expected connotations such as dignity and strength. As already remarked, because of the immediacy with which the symbol is recognized it is already effectively invisible. But what is betrayed in the effort (and skill) with which the propagandists concentrate our attention on the physical bodies of the depicted rival animals is the extent of their need to distract us from the very *animality* of the self's symbol. In other words, what is evident from these pictorial examples is that we are able to identify with 'our' animal symbol because we have been led to overlook its animality. In relation to the Saatchi & Saatchi poster in figure 1, the irony is that the

43

presence of the real 'Duke' in front of the poster flatly contradicts and confounds the denial of the symbolic bulldog's animality. How is it, then, that a technique which worked so well in the First World War poster should have been so plainly misunderstood in this 1987 photo-opportunity?

The historical instability of the animal body

There are several issues to be dealt with here. First, how secure was the animal symbolism used in the posters of the First World War itself (and in any case why has that period been chosen as a particular point of reference)? Secondly, why does this kind of symbolism seem to have become more problematic in recent years, and what explains its persistence in the face of any such difficulties? These rather specific questions will be used as a way into the broader cultural evidence of the ambiguities of meaning in the display of the animal body, and in the use of the animal as sign.

An unexpected consensus

The posters of the First World War, whether or not they depicted animals, can claim an especially important place in the history of pictorial communication. That war marked the first significant use of the poster to communicate or consolidate ideas about *identity* (as opposed to its widespread use in the nineteenth century for purposes such as advertising), and it was also the point at which, in Philip Meggs's words, 'the poster reached the zenith of its importance as a medium of communication'.[7] Its impact at this time was a matter both of the scale of production and of the size of the audience. The mass audience was, realistically speaking, a new phenomenon. It was quite clear to contemporary writers that the scale of operations was unprecedented. In 1915 an article in the British *Windsor Magazine* (which mixed topical features with poetry and fiction) noted that it was 'well-nigh impossible to avoid seeing' the two and a half million copies of Parliamentary Recruiting Committee posters which had been distributed by that time.[8] The scale of the American campaigns also caused much comment. During the war the Poster Advertising Association's magazine, *The Poster*, carried articles with titles like 'Poster art and the multitude',

44

'Aiming the poster at the multitude', 'Ten million posters for new loan', and so on. One such article referred specifically to the new mass intelligibility of the medium, claiming that the war 'has magnified "poster advertising attention" many times and has given it an intimate recognition by the masses'.[9]

Pictorial printed propaganda had sometimes been aimed at a mass audience prior to the First World War, but, as a number of writers have acknowledged, it was generally far harder to reach such an audience. R.W. Scribner has discussed early sixteenth-century German Reformation prints which were aimed at 'the entire German people', but he notes that owing to the limited literacy of the society, the captions of these propaganda prints had laboriously to be explained to the mass by the educated few. There was also the question of the speed of communication. Scribner describes these prints as often making skilful use of complex 'layers of signification'; E.H. Gombrich has suggested that the typical purchaser of a symbolic propaganda engraving in the later sixteenth century 'would regard it as food for thought, contemplation and conversation during the long winter evenings for weeks to come, and for these the detailed references added richness to the fare'; and Roy Porter has made a similar point about later satirical prints and caricatures, noting that 'the prints themselves presented challenging hieroglyphs to be deciphered, whose full messages can have been intelligible only to those familiar with the features and foibles of the great and steeped in the learning of both Bible and Classics'. In contrast, and with specific reference to the First World War poster, an American commentator stated in 1918 that 'the poster that needs explanation or close examination has failed in its purpose'.[10] Just as importantly, in the course of the war the public learned not only how to decipher the rhetoric of the poster but also how to construct and manipulate it: in many countries the phenomenon of the poster competition met with popular success as part of the drive to produce patriotic propaganda on a massive scale.

Contemporary writing about the First World War poster, of which there was a great deal, contained almost no critical discussion of its subject-matter or its use of symbolism.[11] It therefore seems fair to surmise that in their use of animal symbolism, as in other aspects of their content, these posters were drawing on ideas and images with which the new mass audience was already familiar. This evidence of the security or fixity of their symbolism is important, and perhaps unex-

45

pected. Of pictorial media *other* than poster design, it has been possible to argue with the benefit of hindsight that artists responded to changing circumstances as the war progressed, albeit in varied ways. Writing of three of the official British war artists, for instance, Sue Malvern has suggested that in the period 1916–17 'the shift from the safe and derivative work of Bone to the difficult and independent paintings of Nash and Nevinson reflects changes in the nation's need for differing visualizations of its experience of war'.[12] The response of cartoonists was rather more conservative, but it also seems to have shifted to some extent. According to Frank Huggett:

> Although the old-style allegorical cartoon with its circus animals and labelled parts continued to be produced in abundance by such artists as Frank Holland who worked regularly for *John Bull*, there were far more cartoons in a new naturalistic style showing soldiers as real live men and not merely as symbols. The soldiers were still caricatured as generalized types, but they were recognizable human beings with thoughts, fears, and hopes of their own … [13]

In contrast, the symbolism of the First World War poster generally scorns these humanistic refinements. It is historically monolithic and does not deal with responses to events, other than the abstract and overarching 'the war'. Both sides for example, as is well known, issued posters depicting themselves as Saint George vanquishing the enemy dragon. The security of the symbolism rested precisely on the fact that the dragon, like many of the heraldic beasts and national animals populating these posters, was an emblem with a useful place in the visualization of identity and opposition – a place which did not 'date' or change because the imagery had no specific link to the events of the war. It was a necessary condition of this ahistorical rhetoric that 'our' side was always winning, and that 'our' animal was always the good and noble one.

Symbols in and out of history

Here it is possible to make a highly speculative remark about the operation of symbolism in an historical context. In a recent essay called 'Finding symbols in history', which discusses the ways in which significance is read into some of the earliest forms of mark-making such as prehistoric rock drawings, Whitney Davis uses the term *seeing-as* to describe this process of reading for significance. Although it is not quite what Davis has in mind, more recent forms of pictorial symbolism clearly also involve conventions of *seeing-as*. The First World War poster artist intended that viewers would see (and contemporary viewers seem to have had no difficulty in seeing) the lion or the eagle *as* a convenient and evocative means of signifying a particular nation pictorially. This much, I take it, is obvious and uncontroversial. The useful point about Davis's analysis, however, is his emphasis on the point that seeing-as is something that viewers – contemporary or otherwise – do unpredictably and regardless of the mark-maker's intentions. He therefore writes that 'it is, as it were, "outside" history ... Although it took place in history, seeing-as often has no history'.[14]

I now want to put Davis's argument to ends quite different to those for which it was intended. I am going to suggest that the success of the First World War poster's rhetoric, the apparent consensus (among artists and viewers) on the meanings of its animal symbols and images, depended in large part *on the fact that it was an ahistorical rhetoric*, a rhetoric independent of the ongoing events of the war. The next two (more recent) examples should help to test this hypothesis by describing, among other things, what happens to the animal symbol when it is more firmly fixed in its historical context.

The consensus broken

By the Second World War something seemed to have gone badly wrong. Animal symbolism could no longer be relied on. The reasons for this may not be immediately clear, and the source of the evidence for it is an undeniably obscure and slight publication, but the evidence itself is unambiguous. In 1942, on America's entry into the war, the advertising agency Young & Rubicam issued a booklet entitled *How to Make Posters That Will Help Win the War*. It was based on a survey taken in March 1942 of war posters already in use in Canada, and the posters it reproduces are accompanied by comments from the survey's respondents. In the general advice it gave, the categories of the real and the symbolic are pitted against each other in a particularly dramatic way. The introduction, for instance, gave the following instruction:

> The poster should be a picture ... And by a picture is meant a true and literal representation, in photographic detail ... of people and objects as

they are, and as they look to the millions of average people who make up the bulk of the population of the United States.[15]

Here the concern is again explicitly with the effectiveness of mass communication, and for these purposes reality – things 'as they are' – is defined as being as it looks to the masses, to 'the bulk of the population', to 'average people'. This turn of phrase implies the existence of certain excluded minorities who were allowed no part in that society's formulation of reality, but that is perhaps of less immediate relevance here than the evident belief that designers could no longer afford to aim their messages at an elite which was steeped, say, in Classical learning. It was, in a way, the American equivalent of Hitler's view that the most successful propaganda would be that which was aimed at the lowest mental common denominator.

For the Young & Rubicam writers, the crucial advice was that 'abstract design and symbolism are to be avoided, as they are likely to be misunderstood or not understood at all'. They hammer the point home relentlessly with regard to the symbolic posters they illustrate: viewers 'had no idea what meaning this poster was intended to convey, or else misunderstood it completely'; they 'did not understand the message it conveys, or else misinterpreted it entirely'; they 'missed the point, or got a totally different meaning out of it than was intended'. What is important here is that the clearest cases the authors can find of such misreadings relate to *animal* symbolism. One page of the booklet is headed 'Another case where symbolism went wrong'. It shows a Canadian poster captioned 'To Victory' which depicts the British lion and the Canadian beaver marching along together (fig. 4). Both these national symbols carry swords, the lion wears a crown and smokes a Churchillian cigar, and the beaver wears an army helmet and a sash labelled 'Canada'. Despite the reinforcements to the poster's intended meaning provided by these various attributes, there was still room for misinterpretation among its Canadian viewers. The extraordinary responses recorded below the image include the following: 'Does it mean all men are equal?'; 'It represents the Russian bear and the Japs'; 'Germany and England, the ape and the bulldog, each out against the other'; 'Britain has courage and Canada does all the work'. These responses are not exceptional. Another of the 'unsuccessful' symbolic posters, which showed a white elephant and the caption 'If you don't need it, don't buy it', was thought by one respondent to represent

48

4 'Germany and England, the ape and the bulldog, each out against the other' according to one inattentive viewer. The Canadian poster *To Victory*, from 1942, is therefore described in Young & Rubicam's *How to Make Posters That Will Help Win the War* as 'Another case where symbolism went wrong'.

5 Courage and determination or inanity and thuggery? An image of national pride or an invitation to 'Brit-bashing'? Opinion was sharply divided on Bulldog Bobby, the Football Association's logo for the England team in the 1982 World Cup finals.

India, and was interpreted by another as meaning 'Do not buy liquor, or you will see pink elephants'![16]

Doubts as to the authenticity of these comments are immaterial. What is undoubtedly true is that the writers of the booklet saw the serious misinterpretation of pictorial animal symbolism as a real possibility by this time, especially if second-rate designers with fancy ideas were to be given free rein. In order to understand why, this example will be juxtaposed with a more recent piece of equally mediocre symbolic design, but one which has the distinct advantage that the authenticity of its misreadings is better documented.

Late in 1981, in the run-up to the soccer World Cup finals which were to be staged in Spain in June 1982, a small British firm called Alf Cooke Ltd designed a logo for the use of the England football team during the World Cup competition. The logo depicted a character named 'Bulldog Bobby' (fig. 5). The case of this rather bizarre creature is worth describing and discussing at some length, because although commercial identity design still abounds with animal symbolism, it is hardly ever the subject of sustained public discussion. Here, however, much to its originators' surprise, it was. In bringing us back to the question of the bulldog as a national symbol, this example will also help to fill out our reading of the newspaper photograph which the chapter began by considering.

Although Bulldog Bobby served to identify the England team itself in the 1982 World Cup, the principal intended purpose of the logo was to raise revenue for the Football Association Youth Trust, a registered charity, through its use on a variety of merchandise. Even its origin was commercial: it was commissioned not by the Football Association but by Admiral Sportswear, the company which marketed the England football team strip.[17] These commercial considerations were rather lost sight of in the controversy over its use as a national symbol, but they are not without significance if we are to understand how the logo's problems came about.

The extent of the controversy should not be exaggerated; it was restricted to a couple of news broadcasts and around nine reports in the national press, mostly on the sports pages, and all within the month of December 1981.[18] The media attention focused on the question of the logo's suitability as an image to be associated with the England team, which had been disputed by some commentators. The basic issue was this: what was it that the bulldog meant, or rather what was it that it would be taken to mean?

There can be no substantial doubt that Bulldog Bobby was always meant to work as a symbolic logo: the image makes no sense in this context if viewed as a simple non-symbolic depiction of a (clothed) dog. Bert Millichip, the chairman of the FA, acknowledged this symbolic aspect of the logo by saying in its defence that 'we are the bulldog breed'. It is important to establish at the outset this rather obvious point about the symbolic connotations generated by the logo because most of the arguments for and against the image concerned such connotations.

The British public's conception of the bulldog's character and of the symbol's meaning has a long history (throughout which, incidentally, the problem of whether it is properly a symbol of England or of Britain never seems to have been satisfactorily resolved). The bulldog was described by John Caius in 1570 as 'vaste, huge, stubborne, ougly, and eager, of a hevy and burthenous body ... terrible, and frightfull to beholde, and more fearce then any *Arcadian* curre'. Samuel Johnson's *Dictionary* of 1755 claimed that the breed was 'particular to Britain' and that the dog was 'remarkable for his courage'. Earlier that century Hume had also mentioned the breed's courage, and Addison had written that 'they are tame no longer than they are not offended'. By the early nineteenth century the bulldog was being widely used as a symbol of Britain in prints and cartoons, as it subsequently was during both world wars. In 1857 Charles Kingsley referred to the 'British bull-dog breed', an idea popularized by Sapper's 'Bulldog Drummond' stories of the 1920s and 1930s, and widely associated with Churchill during the Second World War. Kingsley was probably also the first writer to apply the word *bulldog* metaphorically to mean a person of obstinate courage, and like Addison he warned that 'once stroked against the hair' the bulldog 'shows his teeth at you for ever afterwards'.[19]

Applied to the England football team, in terms of this popular tradition, the bulldog is likely to convey the idea that the team is a united, courageous, determined and formidable opponent. The idea of opposition is important here, because this kind of identification brings in its tow implications of moral superiority. We, the England team, are strong and fearless; that must mean that you, the opposition teams, are weak, cowardly and (perhaps worst of all) un-English. Bulldog Bobby is thus a commercial example of animal symbolism working in very much the same way, albeit far less forcefully, that it has done in more overt propaganda such as war posters.

The controversy over the suitability of this logo pivoted on two interrelated issues. One was whether the pictorial style of the logo was appropriate to its symbolic connotations; the other was whether its actual appearance overshadowed its symbolic intentions. Paradoxically, those criticizing the logo had to stress the importance of its symbolic connotations while actually concentrating on the dog's appearance, whereas those defending it had to emphasize the qualities it symbolized rather than its appearance and at the same time to *play down* the seriousness of those symbolic connotations. The quotations below will help to clarify the positions taken by either side in this rather confusing state of affairs.

Neil MacFarlane, the Minister for Sport at that time, was the most widely quoted critic of the logo. Presumably referring to its cartoon style, he claimed that it reduced the significance of England's achievement in qualifying for the World Cup to 'an inane level' and that its aggressive appearance gave 'the hooligans something with which to identify'. He also implied that it could even encourage 'Brit-bashing in Spain'. Other critics concentrated on the dog's bared teeth or 'fangs', its closed eyes and its 'beer belly', equating these features to the appearance of a typical football hooligan. Strong words were used. The logo was described as 'utterly crass' and 'manifestly offensive', and the FA's decision to use it was 'astonishingly insensitive'.

Behind all these criticisms lies the implication, never openly stated, that even for a football competition the choice of a national symbol is a matter of some importance; that it should be dignified and instil pride in its supporters; and that although Bulldog Bobby gives a poor impression of England, this impression will be taken seriously *because symbolism is a powerful means of expression*. Nevertheless, despite their apparent belief in the effectiveness of symbolism, these critics' impressions of the logo seem closer to John Caius's description of the bulldog's appearance than to subsequent uses of the dog as a symbol, to which the design was intended to allude. Only one reporter, Brian Glanville, pointed out that one of the logo's symbolic connotations was just as unfortunate as its appearance, since the Young National Front, which had an interest in recruiting football supporters, also used a bulldog as its logo.

As the connotations of brutality and national dignity are regarded as incompatible by the general public (except perhaps by extremists such as the National Front), those defending the England team logo had to take a different approach. Despite the fact that the name Bulldog Bobby had been selected by the FA and was recognized by Bert Milli-chip to have a symbolic purpose, both he and the FA Secretary, Ted Croker, seemed embarrassed by the possibility that the bulldog's estab-lished symbolic meanings should be read into their logo. Croker claimed that 'Bulldog Bobby is meant as a fun character', and in re-sponse to Neil MacFarlane's suggestion that the dog should be replaced by a lion he asked 'are lions more genteel than a bulldog?'. Millichip also said that bulldogs 'are very gentle animals'. In the *Daily Telegraph* Donald Saunders suggested that the dog in the logo 'is a close relative of the amiable canine character who appears regularly in Tom and Jerry cartoons, and is regarded . . . as a lovable old dog'. In other words the symbol of the bulldog breed was defended as a symbol by depriving it of precisely those qualities which allowed it to qualify as a symbol.

If Bulldog Bobby is finally judged, as I think it must be, to be yet 'another case where symbolism went wrong', it is easy enough to see why. It would not be unreasonable to sympathize with the plight of the poor designer at Alf Cooke Ltd who was faced with the job of combining the conflicting demands of national symbolism, publicity for a football shirt and a sense of fun in one logo, however unsatisfactory the result. Equally, it is quite understandable that the England team's logo for the 1990 World Cup in Italy – a graphically weak image of a footballer's leg superimposed on a map of Italy – was justified by commentators as a means of avoiding a repetition of the kind of controversy caused by Bulldog Bobby.[20] Animal symbolism had come to seem an unprofitable liability.

As they seem to have fallen into a similar state of symbolic confu-sion, it's worth considering what Bulldog Bobby and the poster *To Victory* have in common. Alongside their symbolic purpose, both images clearly have an intentionally comic element to them.[21] The comic effect is achieved principally through the fact that the figures are anthropomorphized: they walk on two legs, smoke, wear hats or other clothes, stand nonchalantly with one foot on a football, and so on. This has much to do with their problems. It is not only that such features contrast starkly with the pictorial seriousness of the eagles in Charles Livingston Bull's poster (fig. 2); they also resemble the means by which the French poodle and German shepherd were deprived of their pictorial credibility in the Saatchi & Saatchi election poster (fig. 1).

54

A further connection between Bulldog Bobby and *To Victory* lies in the topicality of their references, whether deliberate or not. The lion in *To Victory* does not just symbolize Britain as a whole, Britain as it always has been; its cigar is a quite specific and contemporary reference to Churchill. Similarly, Bulldog Bobby failed to universalize the image of England and Englishness; critical commentators saw, instead, a reflection of their own mental image of a 1980s football hooligan, or else an even more embarrassing link with the thuggish image of the then-prominent National Front. The *intended* process of seeing-as – seeing-as a timeless national symbol – is undermined by the (unsurprising) failure of these two images to transcend their historical specificity.

The problem, in both cases, lies in the connotations and references which are prompted by the pictorial image of the animal body, and which have perhaps always threatened the security of its meanings. The popular mental image of a national animal symbol, timeless and heraldic, is seldom achieved pictorially. In Bull's poster the American eagle retains much of its heraldic image despite its naturalistic rendering, but the body of its German rival is of course inscribed with a quite different range of connotations. Even in this period which I have tendentiously proposed as one of symbolic consensus, then, appearance can override symbolism, and can be used to manipulate or subvert its meanings. Bull's skill as a propagandist lies in his ability to handle both currencies simultaneously. In the later examples, with the consensus broken, what seems to have happened is that the potentially subversive pictorial connotations have come inadvertently but irreversibly to swamp the heraldry and the symbolism.

A subverted symbolism

The difficulties described above raise the question of why animal symbolism persists at all in its visual forms. To answer this we might begin by pointing to the relative poverty of inanimate symbols of identity, at least from the contemporary image-maker's perspective. The classic heraldic forms of the swastika or the hammer and sickle may be among the most stunning and evocative of symbols, ones which are branded on the public imagination, but they cannot easily be used to convey subtler meanings. In their response to the demolition of the Berlin Wall and the fragmentation of Eastern European politics at the end of the

1980s, for instance, Western cartoonists very quickly exhausted the ways in which the image of the hammer and sickle could be manipulated and distorted to convey something of the new circumstances.

In contrast, the richness of pictorial animal symbolism (as well as its vulnerability and precariousness) lies to a considerable extent in the potential for giving character and expression to the image of the animal body. Here an example from recent art-historical writing provides a useful way forward. In his book *Vision and Painting* Norman Bryson develops his discussion of meaning in Renaissance paintings by calling for a distinction between the iconographic codes (which enable a particular configuration of images to be identified as a Nativity, a *Pietà*, or whatever) and what he calls 'the codes of connotation – pathognomics, physiognomics, dress'. Every *Pietà* is a *Pietà*, Bryson argues, but each one will deploy the codes of connotation quite differently.[22] He therefore regards these latter codes as harder to pin down, and the ambiguities which they open up are of course very largely centred on the image of the body.

A parallel with the historical instability of the animal body is easily drawn. The iconographic codes by which, say, the bald eagle is recognized as the national animal symbol of America will offer virtually no control over the slippery codes of connotation which will be brought into play in interpreting the nuances of any given depiction of that eagle. This longstanding difficulty has been exacerbated as adherence to an unquestioning patriotic heraldry has fallen away. In its place, it seems, is either a cultural fragmentation (in which symbols are hijacked in desperation by extremist nationalist groups) or else a debilitating uncertainty (why else hang a sash labelled 'Canada' across the beaver's chest or a Union Jack tag from the bulldog's collar?).

The picture is not entirely negative, however. It is increasingly common to come across cases of animal symbolism where all the features which I have described as 'problems' are turned on their head and presented as advantages, and as the whole point of the image. Facial expression and bodily posture count for everything in these images; the heraldic is pushed aside by the pathognomic. They make deliberate and generally well-judged use of comic effect, of connotations and of contemporary references. They still involve seeing-as, but a form of seeing-as which has a history and is firmly *in* history. The work of two individuals, one British and one American, will suffice as examples.

Up to the time of the paper's closure, the regular political cartoon in the short-lived British *Sunday Correspondent* newspaper was drawn by Chris Riddell. Like Charles Livingston Bull, Riddell has made something of a speciality of drawing animals, and they are frequently incorporated across the range of his work. His iconography is generally traditional – the Chinese dragon, the British lion, the Russian bear – but these players seldom take quite their expected role. In the background of a 1990 cartoon the Russian bear stands in the woods alongside the huge 'One Party State' teapot which it has just smashed apart with its hammer. In the foreground, meanwhile, to the evident bemusement of this bear, about a dozen identical bears with their own teapots and plates of sandwiches are already enacting a sometimes fractious parody of The Teddybears' Picnic.[23] An expression of something like bemusement is seen crossing the faces of a number of the national animal symbols in Riddell's cartoons, and with good reason. It is the expression which perhaps communicates most clearly these animals' hypothesized recognition of their own redundancy. As meaningful symbols they have been overtaken by events, by history.

When the animal symbol does pursue its old national role in Riddell's cartoons, it does so in an enfeebled state. In an uncaptioned cartoon from April 1990, several months prior to the Iraqi invasion of Kuwait which was to lead to the Gulf War of early 1991, he showed the British lion confronting Iraq's Saddam Hussein (fig. 6). The figures clutched in Hussein's hand are a journalist and a nurse from Britain who had been held by Iraq on charges of spying. The British government regarded the charges as spurious, and had tried unsuccessfully to negotiate the release of the two; the journalist, Farzad Bazoft, had already been executed when the cartoon was published. I am certainly not anxious to praise the politics of this cartoon. It seems uncomfortably close to a jingoistic article which appeared in the *People* on the same day, on the same subject, under the headline 'A nation that roars like a mouse!' The article was more concerned that Britain had been somehow humiliated by Iraq than that an individual had been unfairly executed, and it concluded despondently that the British lion 'has lost all its teeth'.[24] The cartoon, however, is in my view doing something rather more complex, and this complexity lies almost wholly in the fact that it is a specific depiction of the enfeebled symbol and not a generalized reference to it.

6 The face of the British lion in the 1990s, where much depends on
the viewer's interpretation of the animal's expression. Chris Riddell's
reworking of this tired symbol is from the *Sunday Correspondent*, 1 April
1990, p.19.

The animal body is again at the centre of all this. The *miaow!* is quite redundant in this respect; the work of the cartoon is done by the lion's unkempt mane, by the slack set of its jaw and by its wide-eyed unbelieving stare. To use such specific adjectives in the interpretation of a graphic image is inevitably to court objections. Quite apart from the presumptious anthropocentrism involved in any such claims, who is to say that a certain distribution of ink lines will convey the idea that the animal is 'astonished' – as opposed, say, to its being 'appalled' or 'baffled'? This difficulty is real enough, but it is more than compensated for by the fact that the reading of facial expression is fully within the competence of the public (whatever minor disagreements it might entail), and can operate independently of a knowledge of specific iconographies. The point is echoed by Bryson: 'recognition of a Nativity, a Betrayal, a Madonna Enthroned, is taught and learned as a specific skill to be applied to *images* . . . The codes of connotation, by contrast, operate within the general social formation'.[25] What Riddell's work does, and does rather well on account of his considerable graphic skills, is to open a particular kind of space for the continued use of animal symbols. It is a space which builds on what viewers do automatically, which is to read for pathognomic and physiognomic clues, and not on what they do notoriously badly, which is to keep in mind the original meanings of politically-outdated symbols. There is thus at the very least the possibility of reading the Iraq cartoon as more subversive than jingoistic. Such a reading would argue not that the enfeeblement of the lion is regrettable, but that the demise of such symbols of nation is irreversible.

The irreversible shift in symbolic meanings is dealt with more cynically and more explicitly in the American example, which comes from a book called *Brought to Light*. Broadly following the format of the graphic novel, the book announces itself as 'a graphic docudrama' which uses the findings of the Christic Institute to present evidence of '30 years of drug smuggling, arms deals and covert operations that robbed America and betrayed the Constitution'.[26] One half of this two-part book is written by Alan Moore and drawn by Bill Sienkiewicz: called 'Shadowplay', it imagines an encounter in a seedy New York bar between a silent and anonymous listener and the American eagle. In a lurid pink and blue check suit, this is a foul-mouthed, xenophobic, coke-snorting eagle, an eagle which doubts neither its power nor its patriotism, but which reveals its true allegiance at the start: 'I represent The Company'.

7 Silencing its appalled companion with its bar-room tale of corruption and derring-do, Bill Sienkiewicz's American eagle is no longer the symbol of a nation but rather the self-appointed spokesbeast of the CIA. A detail from p.18 of the 'Shadowplay' side of *Brought to Light*.

Graphically Sienkiewicz establishes the loathsomeness of this personification of CIA corruption by similar means to those used in Bull's
First World War depiction of the enemy German eagle: the attention is
held by its body, and by its own acute awareness of that body (fig. 7).
'We never die! ... snfnff ... we just start to smell funny after a while is
all' – this is clearly no sentiment for the elevated abstraction of a
national symbol. The bird's physical grossness is however perfectly
fitted to its tale of institutionalized wrong-doing. If the image works as a
commentary on rather than just a travesty of that which is deemed
appropriate to a national symbol, it is partly because the text eventually draws attention to the issue of the invisibility and taken-for-
granted-ness by which such symbols more usually operate. Symbols
don't get their own claws dirty; as the eagle tells its listener at the end of
its shadowy history of the CIA:

> S'like, that whole story I just told ya; forget it! It didn't happen. Wuzza
> joke, okay? As for what really happened ... Well, earlier you asked what I
> wuz sellin', right? Okay. It's like this ... We never assassinated anybody,
> never smuggled drugs, laundered money or conspired with criminals an'
> dictators. What really happened, America protected the world; the CIA
> protected America; Shackley, Clines, anna rest protected the CIA an'
> that's why they're goddamn heroes! That's it. That's what I'm sellin'. You
> buy that, doncha? [27]

Both Sienkiewicz's eagle and Riddell's lion suggest that the contemporary relevance of the national animal symbol lies, if anywhere, in a
certain potential for further undermining an already unstable sense of
nation. This is perhaps the only role such symbols can now play with
conviction and credibility. It is not only that the firm centre, the symbolic element itself, has been dislodged and marginalized in cases such
as these; the very things they symbolized are losing their centrality or
succumbing to changing definitions. With nationalist values losing
ground to corporate and multinational considerations in many parts of
the world, the shift in the besuited eagle's loyalties reflects the eye it is
keeping on history. As it points out half-way through its harangue:
'Anyway – Nixon worked for Pepsi, goddammit! Ain't no better symbol
of the American way than Pepsi!'.
   This is not to suggest that in the hands of a few of the more imaginative contemporary image-makers the essentially reactionary role of the
national animal symbol can be transformed to any very significant

degree. In the end the symbol's function outweighs its form, and the form can be shed like a skin if necessary. The eagle isn't irreplaceable. It has long been recognized that Disney characters, for example, have served the broad interests of America's imperialist ambitions. More specifically than this, however, it is now sometimes claimed (both in the Disney hagiography and in the more critical literature) that Mickey Mouse has achieved the status of 'a national symbol in America'.[28] The coming of Euro Disneyland to Marne-la-Vallée in France will no doubt continue to consolidate the internationalization of that status. The rhetorical gesture of putting a bald eagle into a sharp suit and giving it a cocaine habit hardly looks subversive when set alongside that bizarre reality.

The arbitrariness of animal symbolism

> Of course, the behaviour of lions may be the least interesting thing about them. In the way of symbols, lions are pretty near the top of the tree. But would anyone have followed Richard the Lionheart if they had known how similar lions' behaviour is to that of tomcats?
>
> Justin Cartwright[29]

The example of Mickey Mouse leaves little doubt that just about anything will do as a national animal symbol. The qualities deemed appropriate to such symbols evidently do not stop at dignity and steadfastness. The purposes they serve are clearly more diverse, less obvious and less predictable than has been indicated so far. The symbolism itself is seldom very clearly defined, and it is open to manipulation: it is a rough-and-ready symbolism. It is in no way hindered by the fact that its meanings need owe *nothing* to the characteristics of the animals it employs. To understand more fully how it actually operates, both visually and at other levels, we will have to take a more imaginative perspective.

A fictional example will get us under way. The dodo, extinct since around 1740, survives in small numbers for rather longer on the un-named tropical island described in Tony Weeks-Pearson's novel *Dodo*. Some time after it has finally died out even there, an English teacher working on the island puts considerable effort into excavating a complete set of the birds' scattered bones; these are dispatched to a London

museum for the reconstruction of a dodo skeleton, which is then returned to the island's Gallery of Arts and Sciences. As an indirect result of
the general interest aroused by the teacher's enterprise, the dodo is
adopted by the inhabitants as the island's symbol. At this point Weeks-
Pearson devotes some pages to describing how he imagines the new
symbol to pervade the island's culture. Initially it does so in conventional enough ways. It is given the authorities' blessing by its incorporation in a new crest for the island, and a dodo stamp is also issued.
Versions of the dodo's image appear in prints and carvings sold on
market stalls, in expensive jewellery and in sweetmeats. Its effect, however, is soon more profound and far-reaching:

> Birds benefited. Certain attitudes developed towards them. In the absence
> of dodos to be honoured all species became popular. Once the story be-
> came known of its ancient fate, people felt regret and a late indignation
> against passers-by in their history who had meddled with their unique
> bird.
>
> Hens and ducks found themselves fussed over and became brazen; wild
> parrots were spoken to, with courtesy; people went into woods and
> thickets to observe the birds – chided one another if noise disturbed them.

These enthusiasms had further consequences for the inhabitants.
'Crops went undefended: scarecrows disappeared'. There were also
varying and unpredictable degrees of identification with the new symbol in the forms of bodily display:

> Ladies ... who had never suffered insult, felt threatened by hard looks at
> hats or fans. Feathers were among the early taboos. ... Whatever van-
> ished did so only to be replaced by fresh invention. Delicate dresses with
> separated, feather-like panels were all the rage. There were shoes and
> sandals with divided toes.
>
> In humble and politer circles fashions favoured the quicker, the more
> flighty styles of dance. At all levels new creations appeared, many drawn
> from courtship movements of particular birds.
>
> Hence, the 'Moorhen', the 'Pigeon', the 'Greenshank', and the 'Para-
> keet'. The most popular, they were replete with bobbing and bowing,
> delicate little runs or changes of place and sideways posturing of the bird
> ladies, bird gentry. The dancing classes were full.

Eating habits changed, and 'there was an edge to the debate whether
sympathy shown by eating food favoured by birds did not deprive
them'. Language changed: terms of verbal abuse which incorporated

birds' names were abandoned. And tastes changed: 'one curiosity was how young men and women, their longer, pointed noses despised before, now found their powers of attraction increased'.[30]

This account may seem excessively fanciful, but each element in it can find substantiation outside fiction in relation to the animal symbolism of one nation or another. The island's symbolism shows a certain mutability: any species of bird can apparently stand in for the missing dodo, and there is little evidence of a firm boundary being maintained between birds and humans. A parallel could be drawn here with the British national figure of John Bull, for instance, who in the course of his long symbolic life has variously been depicted either as human or as a bulldog.[31] The idea of the pervasiveness of the dodo symbolism, with everyone on the island contributing to it in their own small way, is hardly preposterous either. It is not so far removed from the recruiting poster's demand that each individual 'Be an American eagle!' (fig. 2), nor from Webster's cartoon image of the American boys spontaneously kicking the German dachshund (fig. 3).

The novel's account of how the bird's symbolic meanings became entangled in the practicalities of everyday island life calls for a more complex parallel. Clifford Geertz's essay 'Deep play: Notes on the Balinese cockfight' – which was briefly referred to in the previous chapter – offers opportunities for comparison at several levels. Although Geertz cautions that the cockfight is not 'the master key to Balinese life', its symbolic centrality in the island's culture allows the people one of their distinctive ways of 'being Balinese'. He describes the 'deep psychological identification' of the male owners with their birds, suggesting that the cocks may be seen as 'surrogates for their owners' personalities, animal mirrors of psychic form'. He also notes the effects of this identification on the forms of daily life. A 'large majority of Balinese men' spend 'an enormous amount of time' in the daily care of these fighting cocks: 'grooming them, feeding them, discussing them, trying them out against one another, or just gazing at them'. Beyond this role in the expression of individual identity, the bird also figures in national self-perception: 'Even the very island itself is perceived from its shape as a small, proud cock, poised, neck extended, back taut, tail raised, in eternal challenge to large, feckless, shapeless Java'.[32] It might be noted in passing that the thoroughgoing nature of the symbolism is something that Geertz as a Western outsider clearly found just as satisfying as the Balinese themselves.

Peace emblem ... Swapo's president, Mr Sam Nujoma, releases a white dove at a rally in Swakopmund to symbolise the end of the armed struggle

8 The problematic visual conjunction of the 'real' and the symbolic, the universal and the specific: for a short moment a single living bird is invested, quite arbitrarily, with a considerable weight of symbolic meaning at a Swapo rally in Namibia in 1989.

The other main point which both Geertz's anthropological and Weeks-Pearson's fictional example bring to our attention is one which has not really been touched on as yet in this chapter, despite its considerable importance. It is that animal symbolism makes frequent use of actual living animals, and that this may well have uncomfortable consequences either for the symbolism or for the animals themselves when they are called on to act out their unwitting role as the random bearer of a 'universal' meaning or as the arbitrary totem of some group or other. Here is one such example: in 1989 in Namibia the Swapo president, Sam Nujoma, is photographed at a rally releasing a white dove which he describes as 'a symbol of peace and reconciliation' (fig. 8). The image of this dramatic gesture, this living symbolism, is somehow hard to believe in; the specificity of the image seems to undermine the universality of the symbolism, and only calls attention to its arbitrariness. I'm reminded of the passage in Julian Barnes's irreverent retelling of the Noah's Ark story where the narrator says of the dove:

> You have elevated this bird, I understand, into something of symbolic value. So let me just point this out: the raven always maintained that *he* found the olive tree; that *he* brought a leaf from it back to the Ark; but that Noah decided it was 'more appropriate' to say that the dove had discovered it. ... The dove ... began sounding unbearably smug from the moment we disembarked. She could already envisage herself on postage stamps and letterheads.[33]

When ravens themselves are enlisted, not entirely metaphorically, in the symbolic battle of good versus evil, the meanings which are seen as 'appropriate' to them are perhaps too strident for the postage stamp. In 1990, in the months leading up to the Gulf War, Radio Baghdad is said to have announced to its Muslim listeners that 'the famous white pigeons from the holy city of Mecca have been replaced by ravens which will join the fight against the infidel Western armies ranged against Iraq'.[34] These last few examples, I hope it is clear, have not been chosen to characterize some notion of exotic difference in the construction of symbolic meanings. For some of the most extraordinary and contentious uses of the living animal in the context of animal symbolism, there is certainly no need to look so far afield.

Representing 'the British love of animals'

> I happen to think animals are important, even if they're not British animals.
>
> — John Selwyn Gummer[35]

The notion that one of the distinguishing characteristics of the British is that they are a nation of animal lovers has a wide currency, and not only in Britain itself. In *Men, Beasts, and Gods*, for instance, the American author Gerald Carson writes: 'The English have long enjoyed a reputation for exhibiting an exceptional devotion to animals ... The supporting evidence for this national fondness is totally convincing'.[36] This is not the place to consider whether or not Carson's certainty is justified. What is clear, however, is that by this or by other means, animals have long figured prominently in the public display of 'being British'.

Since the publication of John Berger's 'Why look at animals?' in 1980, at least, it has become something of a commonplace to say that the spectacle of the zoo animal must be understood historically as a spectacle of colonial or imperial power. Harriet Ritvo's more recent and more extensive treatment of this theme documents precisely how this rhetoric of power operated in Britain during the nineteenth century, when menageries and zoological gardens were growing in popularity. She suggests that in this 'grand appropriative enterprise' the captive wild animals served as 'simultaneous emblems of human mastery over the natural world and of English dominion over remote territories', and that the Regent's Park Zoo, for instance, became 'the symbol, for a large segment of the populace, of Britain's spreading global influence'. She explains part of the attraction of the spectacle as follows: 'Few English citizens were likely ever to wield the kind of power represented by the animals' captivity, but since that power was exercised by their countrymen over nature or the human inhabitants of distant lands, all could take vicarious pleasure in the evidence of its magnitude'.[37] This may seem to have little to do directly with expressions of a national fondness for animals. However, Ritvo's description of the animal's place in this pattern of associations prompts comparison with a quite different contemporary phenomenon, and one to which a spurious notion of fondness is central.

Along with subjects like royalty or sex scandals, the contemporary tabloid press cannot get enough of animals, but it naturally uses them for its own particular ends. The scenario described here by Tom Bussmann will be familiar:

> Front pages in full colour rammed home the horrors of entire Japanese families turning out to slaughter hundreds of beached dolphins. Once again the whole world had the chance to feel that extra sense of superiority that comes with the vindication of a racial prejudice.[38]

If there is a fault with Bussmann's analysis it is only that it is not specific enough. Stories such as these, in which vile foreigners mete out cruelty to lovable animals, are a staple of the right-wing press in Britain (and needless to say, the animal-loving reader's horror at these atrocities is an index of his or her Britishness). Headlines such as these abound: '£400,000 baby gorilla stars "sold illegally"' (Japan, Spain); 'Slaughter of the ocean innocents' (Japan); 'A tragic end for Sanny the tiger' (Spain); 'Zoo chains up "rescued" chimps' (Tenerife); 'Dogs slaughtered in clean-up for tourists' (Peking).[39] There is usually no need for the countries responsible to be identified in the headlines, since readers will take it for granted that such things seldom happen in Britain. So while there are admittedly one or two favourite locations, examples of animal abuse from anywhere abroad will do to get this basic message across. The racism implicit in these stories from the 'respectable' right-wing press is made spectacularly explicit in the appalling *Sunday Sport*'s hyperbolic interpretation of the genre. One such report begins thus:

> SICKO Spaniards are TOSSING helpless goats to their death from 100ft church towers during blood-soaked fiestas, we can reveal. The evil Dagoes gather in their HUNDREDS to watch the beasts SPLATTER on the pavement below.[40]

Just as any non-British location will do in the consolidation of this image of Britishness, it is also clear that any animal will do. The examples so far mentioned use gorilla, dolphin, tiger, chimp, dog and goat for essentially the same purpose. The relation between the animal and its meaning in these narratives of national identity is therefore entirely arbitrary.

This may seem a perverse perspective to take on these stories, since they are reporting on actual cases of animal abuse, and the newspapers rightly expect that their readers will be appalled by that abuse. Further, it is clear that these readers do not *pretend* to a concern for

animals simply to bolster their patriotic pride. There is a tension between their genuinely-felt concern and their readiness to see it manipulated in this simplistic manner – a contradictory state of affairs
which will call for fuller exploration in a later chapter. Other examples
of such stories do however attest to the thoroughness with which the
animal is implicated in the construction of nationhood.

Much as with the nineteenth-century zoo visitor, a proprietorial
attitude is everything. One's own identity is inscribed in the display of
the animal. This can be a simple pride in patriotic achievement: 'New
British bid to save the whales', and suchlike. A little more complex is
the prospect of a common fate, as in 'Turtle rescue team faces death
threats', the team being British and the threats both to it and to the
turtles coming from Greek islanders. An even closer identification is
evident in those stories where a nationality is attributed *through
ownership* to the animals themselves. 'British pair sent to a "better life"
may be destroyed' bewailed the subheading in the *Mail on Sunday*'s
'Scandal of bears on zoo death row', describing the fate of the 'British'
polar bears Pipaluk and Mosha which had been moved from London
Zoo to one in Poland.[41]

Identity through nationality is a more profound matter even than
this, however. British horror at the slaughter of dolphins turns to open
revulsion (in 'Dolphins made into sausage') as the story unfolds of how,
at the behest of the Mafia, the lovable creatures are 'served up as
sausages to unsuspecting British tourists' (fig. 9). The rhetoric is not
dissimilar to that of the front-page shocker 'Dogs butchered for Sunday
roast', which juxtaposed photographs of ('From this:') a row of cuddly
puppies and ('To this:') a line of carcasses hanging from meat-hooks, in
a story revelling in the threat posed to 'millions of British meat-lovers'
by 'yen-hungry sicko Chinese'. The anticipated form of the reader's
identification with the animal in this situation can perhaps best be
described in words used by Clifford Geertz in an only slightly different
context: it is 'a mixture of social embarrassment, moral satisfaction,
aesthetic disgust, and cannibal joy'.[42]

With so much riding so precariously on the image of the animal, it's
not surprising – to return to our starting-point – that it should be
Norman Tebbit's awkwardly proprietorial approach to the bulldog
'Duke' (fig. 1) which finally puts paid to any last glimmer of the dog's
credibility as a symbol. With potentially negative connotations crowd-
ing in on all sides, the animal looks in retrospect to be among the least

UGH! Our girl Jo with a dolphin sausage

NEWS OF THE WORLD INVESTIGATES

9 The dreadful prospect of unwittingly devouring the very thing by which you have defined your humanity, your generosity of spirit and your patriotic identity. An exposé of British tourists duped by Mafia bosses into eating dolphin sausages, from the *News of the World*, 22 July 1990, p.2.

secure images for carrying messages about human identity. Given the character of many of those messages, this may be no bad thing. But there is a more positive aspect to the examples discussed in this chapter. They show nations having chosen (and continuing to choose) to depict not only other or rival nations but also *themselves* in animal form, or else to define themselves by means of an identification with animals. There is thus a certain equilibrium, or balance of power, in the distribution and operation of these symbols. They serve to remind us that the clichéd notion that our culture always sees animals as inferior need not simply be taken for granted; the notion is certainly not manifested in overt form at *every* level of the culture. Even if, as suggested earlier, these supposedly positive animal images have been drained of much of their animality, they are still the culture's chosen iconography. It is too easy to forget this, or else to give insufficient consideration to its significance.

Notes

1 Elaine Scarry, *The Body in Pain: The Making and Unmaking of the World* (Oxford: OUP, 1985), p.46.
2 On the equation of the spatial and the moral, see for instance Rodney Needham (ed.), *Right and Left: Essays on Dual Symbolic Classification* (Chicago: University of Chicago Press, 1974), and Barry Schwartz, *Vertical Classification: A Study in Structuralism and the Sociology of Knowledge* (Chicago: University of Chicago Press, 1981).
3 See Christopher Prendergast, 'Flaubert: Writing and negativity', *Novel*, 8, no.3 (1975), p.206, and Roland Barthes, *Mythologies*, translated by Annette Lavers (London: Jonathan Cape, 1972), p.78.
4 Elaine Scarry, *The Body in Pain*, p.126.
5 Paul Wombell has suggested in a brief but fascinating article that this convention is one of the ways by which the Western world generally has tried to maintain its sense of superiority and 'civilization'. See his 'War, the body and distance', *Camerawork*, Gallery Special Issue: El Salvador, August 1983, p.32. In the context of the First World War, Sue Malvern has detailed the censorship of the dead British soldiers in C.R.W. Nevinson's paintings in '"War as it is"', *Art History*, 9, no.4 (1986), p.506.
6 Mary Douglas, *Natural Symbols* (London: Barrie & Jenkins, 1973), p.98.
7 Philip B. Meggs, *A History of Graphic Design* (London: Allen Lane, 1983), p.295.
8 Anonymous, 'Recruiting by poster: A remarkable patriotic campaign', *The Windsor Magazine*, no.246 (1915), p.6.
9 Roger Myrhum, 'The war and "advertising attention"', *The Poster*, July 1918, p.43.
10 See R.W. Scribner, *For the Sake of Simple Folk: Popular Propaganda for the German Reformation* (Cambridge: CUP, 1981), pp.1–7 and 69; E.H. Gombrich, *Meditations on a Hobby Horse* (London: Phaidon, 1963), p.134; Roy Porter, 'Prinney, Boney,

Boot', *London Review of Books*, 20 March 1986, p.19; and the anonymous article 'Poster theme of timely interest', *The Poster*, November 1918, p.30.

11 See my 'Describing images of the national self: Popular accounts of the construction of pictorial identity in the First World War poster', *Oxford Art Journal*, 13, no.2 (1990).

12 Sue Malvern, '"War as it is"', p.488.

13 Frank E. Huggett, *Cartoonists at War* (Leicester: Windward, 1981), pp.130–1.

14 Whitney Davis, 'Finding symbols in history', in *Animals into Art*, edited by Howard Morphy (London: Unwin Hyman, 1989), p.182.

15 Young & Rubicam, Inc., *How to Make Posters That Will Help Win the War* (Washington, D.C.: US Government Printing Office, 1942), p.1.

16 Young & Rubicam, pp.1, 10, 11 and 12.

17 The source of this information is the FA press release 'Bulldog Bobby helps youth football' (3 December 1981) and personal correspondence with Admiral Sportswear and the FA Press Officer.

18 The press reports included Jeff Powell, 'Dog's life for El Bruto', *Daily Mail*, 21 December 1981, pp.30–1; Steve Curry, 'Bulldog Bobby rules OK', *Daily Express*, 22 December, p.28; Robert Armstrong, 'Bulldog Bobby is in the doghouse', *Guardian*, 22 December, p.14; Donald Saunders, 'England sharpen up on Dutch for World Cup', *Daily Telegraph*, 22 December, p.16; and Brian Glanville, 'A load of old bulldog', *Sunday Times*, 27 December, p.30. All the quotations given below concerning the logo are drawn from these particular reports.

19 This is a summary of what might be called the 'popular' history of the symbol, as the information is drawn entirely from a variety of standard dictionaries and encyclopedias.

20 See David Lacey's 'Shake a leg for England', *Guardian*, 13 February 1990, p.14, which describes the 1990 logo as 'deeply unprovocative'!

21 On the increased importance of humour in the Allies' propaganda during the Second World War (as opposed to the First), see for instance Joseph Darracott and Belinda Loftus, *Second World War Posters* (London: Imperial War Museum, 1972), especially the Introduction.

22 See Norman Bryson, *Vision and Painting: The Logic of the Gaze* (London: Macmillan, 1983), especially chapters 3 and 4.

23 See the *Sunday Correspondent*, 11 February 1990, p.19.

24 John Smith, 'A nation that roars like a mouse!', *People*, 1 April 1990, p.6.

25 Norman Bryson, *Vision and Painting*, p.68.

26 *Brought to Light: A Graphic Docudrama*, edited by Joyce Brabner (Forestville, California: Eclipse Books, 1989).

27 *Brought to Light*, 'Shadowplay' side, p.27.

28 On Disney and imperialism see Ariel Dorfman and Armand Mattelart, *How to Read Donald Duck: Imperialist Ideology in the Disney Comic*, translated by David Kunzle (New York: International General, 1975); and Martin Barker, 'Deconstructing Donald', in his *Comics: Ideology, Power and the Critics* (Manchester: MUP, 1989). On Mickey Mouse as a national symbol, see Elizabeth A. Lawrence, 'In the Mick of time: Reflections on Disney's ageless mouse', *Journal of Popular Culture*, 20, no.2 (1986), p.65.

29 Justin Cartwright, *Look At It This Way* (London: Macmillan, 1990), pp.98–9.

30 Tony Weeks-Pearson, *Dodo* (London: Viking Salamander, 1986). All quotations are from pp.118–19 and p.124.

31 See Jeannine Surel, 'John Bull', in *Patriotism: The Making and Unmaking of British National Identity*, Vol. III: *National Fictions*, edited by Raphael Samuel (London:

Routledge, 1989), especially pp.6–10. For a broader account of how the forms and meanings of a particular animal symbol will characteristically shift in the course of its history, see for instance Alain Boureau, *L'Aigle: Chronique politique d'un emblème* (Paris: Cerf, 1985).

32 Clifford Geertz, 'Deep play: Notes on the Balinese cockfight', in *The Interpretation of Cultures* (London: Hutchinson, 1975). The quotations are from pp.452, 445, 417, 436, 418–19 and 418 respectively.

33 Julian Barnes, *A History of the World in 10½ Chapters* (London: Jonathan Cape, 1989), pp.25–6.

34 Shyam Bhatia, 'Saddam calls up holy birds to join his air force', *Observer*, 11 November 1990, p.15.

35 John Gummer, speaking in his capacity as Minister of Agriculture, interviewed on the BBC Radio 4 *Today* programme, 6 March 1991, about the export of animals to Europe for slaughter, and the conditions under which they are exported. The minister seemed unaware that his statement might be open to misinterpretation.

36 Gerald Carson, *Men, Beasts, and Gods: A History of Cruelty and Kindness to Animals* (New York: Charles Scribner's Sons, 1972), p.43. Also see Dix Harwood, *Love for Animals and How It Developed in Great Britain* (New York: Columbia University, 1928).

37 Harriet Ritvo, *The Animal Estate: The English and Other Creatures in the Victorian Age* (Cambridge, Mass.: Harvard University Press, 1987), p.209. The earlier quotations are from pp.210, 205 and 214.

38 Tom Bussmann, 'They're not human', *Weekend Guardian*, 10-11 November 1990, p.3.

39 These are from the *Mail on Sunday*, 15 April, 29 April, 12 August and 14 October 1990, and the *Sunday Express*, 19 August 1990, respectively.

40 'Sickos toss goats off tower', *Sunday Sport*, 25 March 1990, p.6. In 1990 this paper had a weekly circulation of around half a million copies, not much below that of 'quality' papers such as the *Observer* or the *Sunday Telegraph*.

41 Headlines in this paragraph are from the *Mail on Sunday*, 1 July, 12 August and 1 April 1990.

42 The stories are from the News of the World, 22 July 1990 and the *Sunday Sport*, 20 May 1990. Geertz's words are from 'Deep play: Notes on the Balinese cockfight', p.421, where he uses them to describe the mixed feelings of the owner of the winning cock as he takes the carcass of the loser home to eat.

Part II

Hatred
and pleasure

3

Mad dogs and half-human beasts: the rhetoric of animality

It was as a comment on *human* nature that the concept of 'animality' was devised.

Keith Thomas[1]

In the Introduction to her recent book *Humans and Other Animals*, Barbara Noske writes of the conflict between her personal feelings about animals and what she perceives to be her culture's dominant attitudes towards them:

> As I grew up I became more and more bewildered by the way people used to speak and think about animals, and I began to wonder, first in childish terms and later as a university-educated adult, how on earth our society had arrived at its subject–object attitude towards animals ... Contrary to current notions about humans and animals I never once felt myself to be a superior human subject dealing with an inferior and passive animal object.[2]

Noske clearly regards 'the object-status animals have been assigned' by human subjects as a bad thing, and in all probability a majority of readers of the present book will be in broad agreement with her. This agreement does not achieve much in itself, but it does raise an important question. If certain readers or writers believe that their own view of animals differs significantly from that held by their society at large, what are the forms in which they recognize or identify both that society's dominant attitude and their own dissension from it? Any answer will be tied directly to a further question: how is the evidence of our culture's 'subject–object attitude towards animals' presented or described in the current critical literature? These issues need to be considered in some detail before this chapter's main concern – the objectifying *image* of the animal – is addressed directly.

77

A rhetoric of opposition

> The purpose of the cognitive relations of opposition ... is not to resolve contradictions but rather to precipitate them. Meaning then emerges as the final product of the tension between opposed aspects of experience ... Animals would seem to be specially apt to this ultimate symbolic role ...
>
> Roy Willis[3]

Recent writings looking at animals from a predominantly historical and anthropological perspective make considerable use of binary oppositions such as *subject:object* in their accounts of the relation between humans and animals. Some of the oppositions they discuss are admittedly more current than others, but this is no great problem in itself; the writers generally call attention to the historical, geographical and cultural specificity of their evidence, and they have frequently been alert to the ways in which that evidence might enhance the understanding of contemporary Western attitudes.

Harriet Ritvo notes in The *Animal Estate* that 'anthropocentric binary distinctions, such as edible–inedible, useful–useless, wild–tame, and beautiful–ugly' were often invoked 'to organize discussions of specific kinds of animals' in medieval and later bestiaries, and she refers the reader to Keith Thomas's fuller discussion of the workings of these same oppositions in early modern England in *Man and the Natural World*. Thomas describes the religious, legal and scientific importance that these distinctions held, and occasionally still hold, but it is clear from his evidence that their classificatory function was not neutral. He explains, for instance, that Edward Topsell's 1607 *Historie of Foure-Footed Beastes* judged that 'the body of an ape is ridiculous', 'by reason of an indecent likeness and imitation of man'. The classification of species as beautiful or ugly was evidently in part a matter of maintaining the distinction judged necessary between animals and humans.[4]

Recognizing that the use of oppositions as a basic classificatory system in Western thought can be traced back at least to Aristotle, Thomas characterizes the *human:animal* opposition as one part of a larger coherent set of rhetorical oppositions operative within the culture. Thus, in the course of his historical account of theories of human uniqueness, he is able to assert that the Cartesian doctrine of the beast–machine in fact did no more than push 'the European emphasis on the gulf between man and beast' to its logical conclusion, presenting a view of human experience in which 'man stood to animal as did heaven to earth, soul to body, culture to nature'. It is clear to Thomas that the purpose of such distinctions must be understood anthropologically, as part of a continuous process of self-definition (in which, of course, that self is defined in opposition to an animal other or an animalized other). He refers to the views of Raymond Firth, Mary Douglas and Rodney Needham, respectively, in reminding the reader that sentiments about animals are typically projections of attitudes to humans; that the contrasting of humans and animals invariably serves as an analogy for the relation of those regarded by a particular society either as insiders or as outsiders; and that some societies have arrogantly appropriated the name 'human' for themselves while giving neighbouring groups derogatory animal names.[5]

The kind of oppositions to which Thomas refers in his description of the Cartesian position – especially that of culture and nature – are echoed (though not always approvingly) in the writings of other anthropologists, who share the view that the opposition *human:animal* has generally been given a variety of purposes and resonances. Elizabeth Lawrence argues in her book *Rodeo: An Anthropologist Looks at the Wild and the Tame* that the ritual display of the animal's subjugation by the human in American rodeo 'can be thought of in terms of the force of "culture" reaching out to dominate "nature"'. She laments, however, the fact that this abstract if inescapable formulation inevitably detracts from more concrete forms of understanding of the interaction of humans and animals in this context. Barbara Noske, calling in fact on some of Thomas's and Lawrence's evidence, presents her objections to the continuation of dualistic thought more forcibly:

> It seems that modern Western society more than any other emphasizes the 'Otherness' of the non-human. By drawing a sharp dividing line between human and non-human, a vast gap is created between *subject* (the free acting human agent) and *object* (the passive acted-upon *thing*). This division is related to the notion that we, as Homo sapiens, are unique among the natural species (as if not every species were unique in itself!). We perceive ourselves as belonging to a totally different order: the realm of *culture*, while all other beings and inanimate things are only *nature*.

Noske suggests that the *culture:nature* opposition also entails assumptions about gender inequality: 'in as far as humanness is equated with the shaping of culture and history, men are made to appear more

79

human than women. Women are commonly thought of as more biological than cultural, and are taken to be closer to animals than men'. For all that both Lawrence and Noske disapprove of these interrelated oppositions, they appear to grant the terms a certain continuing usefulness in their analyses of contemporary society.[6]

In an invaluable recent essay called 'Animality, humanity, morality, society', the anthropologist Richard Tapper attempts to put Western prejudices into context by presenting a cross-cultural perspective on the evidence of totemic thought. Like Thomas, he notes the use of animals in relation to questions of self-definition, observing that one widely accepted premise (forwarded by such as Edmund Leach) 'is that in every society children have to learn how to distinguish Self from Other; and "people like me" (kin and friends) from "people not like me" (strangers, enemies and witches); and "people" from "not people" (usually animals)'. Tapper suggests, though not as convincingly as he might have done, that this process of distinction and opposition need not invariably present a negative image of the animal:

> For example, the straightforward Cartesian dualism familiar to the West, yielding the series of homologous oppositions culture:nature::people:animals (::male:female::reason:passion) is perhaps historically rare – and indeed the denial of it is currently popular: people are animals, animals have rights like people. In other cultures a continuum may be constructed, or a more complex series of distinctions. For example, 'people' are divided into some that are 'like us' and others that are 'like animals'; or 'animals' are divided into 'tame animals' that are 'like people' and 'wild animals' that are not; or 'tame animals' are divided into 'pets' that are 'like people' and 'livestock' that are not. The various distinctions may be treated as analogies: each Other may be likened to each other: 'strangers' are 'wild animals' and 'witches'.[7]

At this point Tapper quotes the same phrase from Mary Douglas as had Thomas: 'in each constructed world of nature, the contrast between man and not-man provides an analogy for the contrast between the member of the human community and the outsider'.[8]

Tapper concludes, however, that 'these analogies remain metaphoric, they are not identifications'. On the face of it this is an odd judgement at the end of a passage dealing specifically with the cross-cultural role of the animal in constructions of selfhood. What he appears to mean is simply that people don't *really* mistake some animals for humans, or themselves for animals. We risk becoming a little confused by the terminology here, however, because alongside the various commentaries on the conceptual status of the animal in Cartesian dualism is another commentary (often in the same texts) about the role of the animal as metaphor. It will be well to distinguish these issues.

Animals as metaphor

It has become commonplace to talk of the role of animals as metaphor. The opening section of Berger's 'Why look at animals?', indeed, was first published under the title 'Animals as metaphor' in 1977. In it he wrote that 'it is not unreasonable to suppose that the first metaphor was animal'. He refers to Rousseau's *Essay on the Origins of Languages* and to Lévi-Strauss's *Totemism* in support of his views, but his fullest illustration deals with examples from the *Iliad*. Part of his explanation reads as follows:

> Book 17 of the *Iliad* opens with Menelaus standing over the corpse of Patroclus to prevent the Trojans stripping it. Here Homer uses animals as metaphoric references to convey, with irony or admiration, the excessive or superlative qualities of different moments. *Without the example of animals*, such moments would have remained indescribable. 'Menelaus bestrode his body like a fretful mother cow standing over the first calf she has brought into the world'.[9]

The idea that animals are metaphorically indispensable to humankind has certain attractions, because it proposes a relation between humans and animals which is not necessarily an exploitative one, nor one which necessarily works by denigrating the animals. Certainly it is anthropomorphic, attributing through carelessness or convenience all manner of human motives to the animals, but its motivations do not seem to be inherently selfish when seen alongside the self-defining oppositions discussed earlier. The spirit of amicable exchange implied in this relation is caught nicely, though somewhat incongruously, in the cartoon frontispiece to a French book of political caricatures, *Ces Animaux qui nous gouvernent*. In the cartoon the eighteenth-century naturalist Buffon says to his companion, an improbable composite creature, 'Si les animaux n'éxistaient pas, l'homme serait encore plus incompréhensible à lui-même', and the creature (which is evidently of more recent origin) responds with a quotation from Jacques Cousteau to much the same effect (fig.10).

10 Buffon and the beast:

'If animals did not exist, man would be even more incomprehensible to himself'. (Although ...)

You talk as if in a book, Monsieur Buffon! Cousteau himself says that 'the observation of animals is an inexhaustible source for the understanding of human nature ...'

I don't care, I was there first!

Richard Tapper's essay, which opens with an interdisciplinary selection of quotations dealing directly or indirectly with the animal as metaphor, also recognizes a distinction between positive and negative uses of the convention:

> Animals, or rather cultural constructions of them, are used as metaphors ... in two rather different, even contradictory, ways. Sometimes certain animals are idealized and used as models of order and morality, in animal stories and myths ... The animals are treated as agents and social beings, with motives, values and morals; and differences between them and people are implicitly denied. By contrast animals are sometimes represented as the Other, the Beast, the Brute, the model of disorder or the way things should not be done. Animals are ideal for both of these purposes ...[10]

The positive connotations of animal narratives will be explored in some detail in the next chapter; my main concern for the moment is to understand more fully the negative and demeaning and objectifying constructions of animality. I want to put forward the hypothesis that the dualistic thinking expressed in binary oppositions is the main problem here, if 'problem' is the right word. When animals figure, or can easily be thought of as figuring, in binary oppositions, *they invariably represent the negative term in the opposition:* 'the Other, the Beast, the Brute'. The occasions on which they serve a more positive metaphoric role (as in Berger's examples from the *Iliad*) are generally ones which cannot be cast so readily into binary terms.

To explore the hypothesis further, some tightening up of the terminology is called for. Most references to the animal as metaphor use the word *metaphor* very loosely; the terms analogy, image or symbol would do just as well and are often used interchangeably.[11] I propose to use the word in this loose everyday sense hardly at all in what follows, but instead will use it specifically as one of the terms in the rhetorical opposition of metaphor and metonymy – an opposition first applied to the question of animals by Lévi-Strauss.

The exploration of these terms which follows is not at all a mere technical digression, nor is it a case of piling yet another binary opposition on to the problematic set already encountered. The *metaphor:metonymy* opposition has quite specific advantages as an analytical tool which, I shall argue, are nowhere more evident than in the study of animal images of human identity.

metonymy:
crown for king

Metaphor and metonymy

Some historical background to the terms is called for at the outset. Their use in a binary opposition is principally associated with writers working in a semiological or structuralist tradition, such as Roland Barthes or Lévi-Strauss. Such writers have employed the opposition of metaphoric and metonymic modes of figurative expression in order to characterize a distinction between those forms of substitution in which one thing is likened to another (metaphor), and those in which a thing is used to stand for another by reason of its being uniquely associated with it (metonymy). My intention is to propose a correspondence between this *metaphor:metonymy* opposition and some of the visual strategies typically used in our culture to articulate the distinction between self and others, subject and object, humanity and animality.

It is easy enough to demonstrate that such a correspondence is feasible in the area of visual communication. To take an example from the preceding chapter, the Bulldog Bobby logo was designed with the intention that it be *uniquely associated with* the England football team (a positive metonymic reading), whereas its appearance was *likened to* that of a football hooligan by several critical viewers (a metaphoric reading with thoroughly negative connotations). However, before any systematic analysis can be begun along these lines, the extent to which it is justifiable to employ these rhetorical terms outside literature and linguistics must briefly be explored.

The first account of the *metaphor:metonymy* opposition to influence semiological theory is generally taken to be the closing section of the linguist Roman Jakobson's essay 'Two aspects of language and two types of aphasic disturbances', first published in 1956. There, based on his observation of the distinction between linguistic *similarity* and *contiguity* in aphasic disturbances, he ventured the more general proposition that 'the development of a discourse may take place along two different semantic lines', which he termed 'the metaphoric way' and 'the metonymic way' respectively. Jakobson's main examples of the opposition are drawn from the discourse of literature – he notes that 'in verbal art the interaction of these two elements is especially pronounced' – but the essay also includes examples drawn from the discourses of painting and film and from those of psychoanalysis and anthropology. From the start, therefore, this particular opposition was envisaged by Jakobson as having applications beyond the purely verbal, despite its linguistic origin.[12]

Lévi-Strauss recognized its usefulness in the description of structural relations in anthropology as early as 1962 in *The Savage Mind*. His rather idiosyncratic use of the opposition is important in the present context not because I propose to follow it in detail but because he uses it to structure his discussion of human relationships to animals, and because that discussion is itself couched partly in terms of the opposition of subject and object. His analysis is prompted by speculations on the kind of 'pet' names which are respectively given to birds, dogs, cattle and racehorses in Western (or rather, French) society. More generally, he proposes that we 'think of the bird world as a metaphorical human society: is it not after all literally parallel to it on another level?'. He considers the reverse to be true of dogs: 'Not only do they not form an independent society; as "domestic" animals they are part of human society', and therefore have a metonymic relation to it. He then takes the case of cattle, 'the social position of which is metonymical (they form part of our technical and economic system) but different from that of dogs in that cattle are more overtly treated as "objects" and dogs as "subjects" (this is suggested, first, by the collective name we use to designate the former and, secondly, by the taboo on the eating of dogs in our culture; the situation is different among the African pastoral peoples who treat cattle as we treat dogs)'. Finally these positions are distinguished from that of racehorses, which 'cannot be said to constitute an independent society after the manner of birds', but which in Lévi-Strauss's view 'do not form part of human society either as subjects or as objects' owing to the peculiar condition of their 'desocialized' life 'as isolated individuals' on stud farms. The tortuous argument finally permits a kind of diagrammatic elegance:

> If, therefore, birds are *metaphorical human beings* and dogs, *metonymical human beings*, cattle may be thought of as *metonymical inhuman beings* and racehorses as *metaphorical inhuman beings*. Cattle are contiguous only for want of similarity, racehorses similar only for want of contiguity.[13]

The lasting worth of this exercise lies in Lévi-Strauss's parenthetical declaration, half-way through the argument, that 'we need not in this work regard ourselves as bound by grammarians' refinements'. Consequently he avoids entangling himself in the traditional rhetorical distinctions of metaphor and simile, of metonymy and synecdoche, and so on.[14]

This seems to be very much in the spirit of Jakobson's original essay, which itself implied that much of the usefulness of the *metaphor:metonymy* opposition is as an organizing structure which can be applied, by analogy, to things *already intuited to be opposed*: poetry and prose, realism and symbolism, or, as in the present book, representations of selfhood and of otherness. This approach appears to differ significantly from the various historical arguments about the relative merits of different rhetorical figures – arguments which might be characterized as part of a search for the elusive 'true' or 'real' nature of rhetoric. In non-linguistic applications of the *metaphor:metonymy* opposition, what is in question is not so much the nature of rhetoric as the nature of opposition, and this is why Lévi-Strauss seems justified in his claim that rhetorical refinements are of little concern here. The opposition offers a flexible means of conceiving and describing complex relationships – as, for instance, in this statement from Roy Willis's book *Man and Beast*:

> The distinctive peculiarity of animals is that, being at once close to man and strange to him, both akin to him and unalterably not-man, they are able to alternate, as objects of human thought, between the contiguity of the metonymic mode and the distanced, analogical mode of the metaphor.[15]

It is metaphor's connotations of distance and otherness, and its contrast to metonymy's sense of familiar proximity, which gives the opposition its evident relevance in accounts of any *self:others* relation. It is far more than a tautological statement of that relation, however, as in the present context it will enable us to describe far more effectively the specific strategies by which that relation is given visual form, and to account for the place of animal imagery in that process.

A visual rhetoric

Given this lack of concern for the niceties of rhetoric, it must be shown at this stage that the proposal to discuss visual images in terms of rhetorical relations is more than merely a random strategy by which to investigate visual oppositions – and, following from this, that it is not a complete travesty to speak of a visual metaphor or of visual metonymy.

It won't really do to begin with Jakobson's own token visual example – metonymic Cubism versus metaphorical Surrealism – because that example is already as much concerned with opposition as it is with rhetoric. E.H. Gombrich provides a better starting point. In his essay

'Visual metaphors of value in art' he is concerned to show what the visual and the verbal may have in common. He suggests that metaphors, visual or otherwise, are derived from 'traditional lore' and that 'it is this lore which defines what may be called the area of metaphor'. In 'The cartoonist's armoury' he goes further, suggesting that 'In cartooning, as in language, there are metaphors which are so widespread that one may call them universal or natural metaphors. The contrast between light and darkness as a symbol for that between good and evil is perhaps the first that comes to mind'. Reservations over Gombrich's notion of a natural metaphor may be put to one side here, for what matters at present is his concern to show that certain visual and verbal strategies may have a similar rhetorical structure.[16]

Metaphor is the main rhetorical figure discussed by Gombrich in this way, but similar points are made in Stephen Bann's *The Clothing of Clio* in relation to both metaphor and metonymy. This is a book which explores the ways in which history itself has been represented in the past; at one point, contrasting the methods employed by two nineteenth-century French historians, Bann specifically addresses the relation of image to text in their books. He argues that in early editions of Barante's *Histoire des Ducs de Bourgogne* the illustrations (simple portrait-bust engravings of the dukes) can be said to stand in metonymic relation to the text, whereas in the 1838 edition of Thierry's *Histoire de la Conquête* the illustrations (of dramatic scenes drawn directly from the narrative) stand in metaphoric relation to the text – and, more importantly, that in both cases this is consistent with non-visual aspects of the rhetorical structure of those texts. He handles this sensitive and potentially difficult transition from the verbal to the visual as follows:

> Already, in examining the implications of the different usages of the reference or footnote in Barante and Thierry, we have made the assumption that the text mobilizes a system of references which exists outside itself, and that this dimension is an integral aspect of its meaning. We might well expect that not only footnotes, but line drawings, engravings and maps, and whatever other types of illustration are employed, participate in the unified effect of historical discourse ... Once we move from the simple consideration of 'words on a page' to the examination of signifying procedures like the relation of text to source, we are obliged to take into account a much wider field of analysis. It is no longer so much a question of the individual historian and his proprietary text, as of 'history' being

communicated throughout a particular society according to a special set of rules and protocols.[17]

This 'set of rules and protocols', though historically more specific than Gombrich's notion of 'traditional lore', is not entirely unrelated to it. The important point about both concepts is that they encompass both the visual and the verbal. If, as Bann and Gombrich suggest, they also constitute the area from which rhetorical structures can be said to be drawn, then it is indeed reasonable in principle to speak of a visual rhetoric.

What would such a rhetoric be, and what sort of things could it describe? In Stephen Bann's examples, it describes the relation of image to text, of one sign to another. It always necessarily concerns a relation. It is not, for instance, that a thing (an image, an animal, or whatever) somehow simply *is* metaphoric, but rather that it stands in a metaphoric relation to another thing. A little more needs to be said about the character of such relations. Gombrich suggests that visual metaphors typically involve 'visual qualities that lend themselves to symbolic use', as opposed, presumably, to qualities which are likely to be taken literally. Jakobson himself argued that the play of metaphor and metonymy characterized 'any symbolic process',[18] and crude as the distinction between the literal and the symbolic may be, it is rather important here. Barante's and Thierry's illustrations, regardless of their metaphoric or metonymic relation to their texts, were intended to be taken literally. An engraving of a duke represented a duke, and was in that sense quite different from, say, a First World War poster in which the lithographic image of a lion represented Britain or the British Empire.

Many of the examples discussed in the present study are of this latter non-literal type. They typically involve some kind of projected equivalence: the devising of a graphic image which will *somehow* connote certain non-visual qualities; or the construction of a visual identity which is in *some* sense equivalent to the 'actual' identity it is desired to communicate. It is the questions of *how*, and in *what* sense, which I hope will be elucidated through the application of the *metaphor:metonymy* opposition. One of the clearest and most common forms of substitution by which this 'equivalence' is attempted involves the symbolic use of animal imagery, a practice which has been described as 'the favourite means of metamorphosis'.[19] Such metamorphoses will be evident in the visual examples which follow shortly, and a major part of our purpose will be to assess their relation to the question of the object-status of animals.

Animals and cultural expressions of contempt

In language, it is generally held that animals figure in the unfavourable characterization of others principally through the crude tactic of name-calling. In colloquial French, as it happens, to 'call someone names' is already *donner à quelqu'un des noms d'oiseau*. But the immediate concern here is the term *animal* itself, and the following is a typical description of how it figures abusively in English:

> In everyday speech, the term animal is associated with uncivilized behaviour and socially disapproved behaviour. Criminals, hoodlums and punks are described as animals that deserve to be punished if justice is to prevail. In these usages, animal behaviour is contemptible behaviour and is used to express the view that important social norms have been violated.

Another writer puts it even more forcefully: 'To suggest that someone or some group has behaved *like* an animal (or wild beast) is to accuse them of plumbing the very depths of moral degradation: no description could be more damning'.[20] Leaving aside for now the more complex connotations of calling someone either a 'beast' or any particular species of animal,[21] there seems only one exception to the negatively metaphoric connotations of the term *animal*, and even that is only superficially an exception. I have in mind the connotations of sexual predation which the term sometimes carries, as in examples such as these: a poster for a 1950s American film called *The Female Animal* proclaiming 'When a woman wants a man she is like an animal'; or, in the 1980s, an advertising executive proudly explaining that 'we developed the idea of the urban animal – a guy out on the prowl'.[22] Even in these male fantasies of sexual predation, however, the term *animal* still appears to serve 'to express the view that important social norms have been violated'.

A major difficulty here is how to assess the significance of this rhetoric of moral and social regulation. Are its overwhelmingly negative connotations evidence that animals are generally held in contempt in the contemporary imagination, and, if so, is it the same contempt which is more dramatically apparent in the culture's toleration of such practices as vivisection and factory farming? A parallel could certainly be drawn between rhetoric and practice in this respect; though while the structural purpose of the contempt has fairly clearly to do with issues of self-definition and of identity in the case of the rhetoric, it may need to be described in quite different (though no less selfish) terms in the case of the practices.

As emphasized in previous chapters, there is of course a danger in setting, as it were, an 'underlying' rhetoric against the stark and imme-diate 'reality' of such practices. The rhetorical and the symbolic are once again likely to be taken as less than, or as secondary to, the real and the literal and the practised. The point is not to reverse the priority, which might lead to the absurd proposition that the verbal abuse was somehow worse than the animal abuse. It is rather to suggest that the two are held in a quite complex relation: in the present example, for instance, the contemptuous rhetoric is quite openly employed by the public, while at the same time much care is taken to conceal the con-temptible practices from the view of that same public. It would be unwise to be more specific at this stage. It *may* be that the practice somehow accounts for the rhetoric; it *may* be that the rhetoric sustains and substantiates and consolidates the practice, leading us to continue to hold animals in contempt; I contend only that they run parallel, and that it is rash to assume that the parallel is without significance.

Beyond name-calling

In this attempt to get under the culture's carapace in order to under-stand more fully the workings and the logic of the rhetoric of animality, it will help at this point to focus on its visual expression. A brief example will explain why. On the release of the 'Birmingham Six' after sixteen years of wrongful imprisonment for the 1974 IRA pub bombings, the cartoonist Trog addressed the issue in an uncaptioned cartoon. It showed the bronze personification of Justice which tops the Old Bailey law courts, her outstretched arms holding the familiar attributes of the sword and scales, but her head replaced by that of an ass. Any caption would have been redundant; the sole purpose of the image was to call to the viewer's mind the appropriate *verbal* idiom as a comment on the fiasco.[23]

The point about this example is that (while it was a perfectly good political cartoon) it is far from typical of how the visual rhetoric of animality operates. First, the rhetoric is very seldom simply a matter of the visual rendering of verbal clichés. Secondly, the comparison of an individual or an institution to an animal, to their disadvantage, is frequently achieved by means far more subtle and circuitous than the crude visual juxtaposition of a human head and an animal body, or vice versa. It will call on common knowledge and received ideas, certainly, but it can be more than a visual form of name-calling. It may therefore offer unexpected insights into embedded but unstated cultural assumptions regarding the object-status of animals, and into how such assumptions are deployed either to bolster our own sense of identity or to undermine that of others.

'We saw the beast!': How animals figure in visual stereotyping

After this lengthy preamble it is time to consider a fairly detailed example, and it is worth explaining its purpose at the outset. It cannot be claimed that it is a representative case study: it concerns the role of the animal in the visual articulation of political opposition, and it has been selected precisely for the unusual clarity and directness with which it presents that opposition.

It will be described at some length, partly because much of its interest lies in points of detail, but more particularly because it will offer evidence to support the following five claims: (1) that visual stereotypes do indeed draw on cultural assumptions; (2) that they nevertheless work largely independently of the culture's relevant verbal clichés; (3) that these visual workings are 'approximate', working mainly by a simple process of juxtaposition; (4) that the clear purpose of these visual stereotypes is to distinguish between identities; and (5) that the visual strategies used in the characterization of those regarded as 'other' display metaphorical rather than metonymic characteristics.

As noted above, our central concern in this example is the role of the animal in the visual articulation of political opposition. The historical setting is Britain in 1983; the Conservative Party was in power, as it was throughout the 1980s, under the premiership of Margaret Thatcher. In the wake of the Falklands War with its attendant patriotic hysteria the previous year, the national press (unhampered by the 'objectivity' expected of the broadcast media) was overwhelmingly behind her. Correspondingly, that press was also generally hostile to Labour as the main opposition party. This was a time when the Soviet perestroika of the later 1980s was of course as yet unheard of, and some British newspapers saw (or claimed to see) little to distinguish Labour's socialism from Eastern-bloc communism. Under the leadership of Michael Foot, Labour's policies were at their most uncompromising. When, on 10 May 1983, a General Election was called for 9 June, the political opposition of Thatcher and Foot was as stark as it could be. It is therefore hardly surprising that the visual rhetoric of the press was to be largely articulated around a straightforward opposition of the Conservatives and Labour, the good guys and the bad guys, the natural and the political, with no doubt as to the preferred outcome.

Animals figured in the media coverage of the election campaign in ways which could not have been predicted in any detail at the outset. Before explaining exactly how they did so, it is worth remarking on a significant difference between British and American conceptions of the 'political' animal. In American party politics and electoral politics, the main parties are frequently and conveniently referred to through the pictorial image of their respective animal symbols. The elephant stands metonymically for the Republicans, the Grand Old Party; the donkey stands metonymically for the Democrats. For the most part this is a comfortable and uncontroversial symbolism, as an example by the renowned American cartoonist Herblock will demonstrate. In the early days of the 1980 presidential campaign Herblock drew a cartoon showing the elephant and donkey in anthropomorphic form as besuited gamblers at a roulette wheel labelled 'early caucuses and primaries', with one animal lamenting to the other 'We know it's cockeyed, but it's the only roulette wheel in town'. He had no need to refer to the parties by name, of course, because his *Washington Post* readers would have been in no doubt as to the identity of the two rather desperate-looking characters he had depicted.

In this instance the treatment of these symbols is comparatively respectful, good-natured and even-handed. The two creatures find themselves in the same fix, and visually it's not even clear which of them is speaking. From a cartoon such as this, readers would hardly guess the less impartial origins of this symbolism. Both symbols are generally agreed to have first appeared in the cartoonist Thomas Nast's work for *Harpers Weekly* in the 1870s. An 1874 cartoon called 'Caught in a trap' shows an elephant labelled 'The Republican vote' blundering

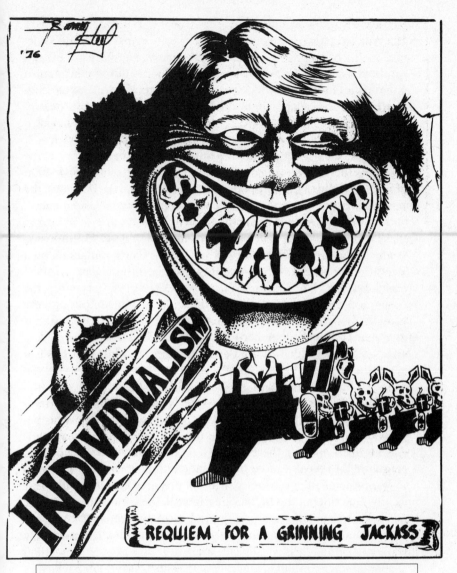

11 In this American cartoon from 1976 it is the unstable boundaries of animal identity which are manipulated to political effect. The Democrats' chosen symbol almost invites the unsympathetic cartoon transformation of the party leader into the image of an idiotic-looking 'jackass'.

towards the 'third term trap', while the donkey in the same cartoon is portrayed, altogether less sympathetically, as Aesop's 'ass in a lion's skin'.

In the century or more of their use, both symbols have maintained their potential for unflattering characterizations of the parties, especially when it is the parties' individual leaders who are caricatured in semi-animal form. In 1976 the right-wing libertarian cartoonist Barney Steel drew a vicious caricature of Jimmy Carter, with donkeys' ears and a broad grin revealing teeth which spell out the word 'socialism'. From the corner of the cartoon a fist labelled 'individualism' speeds towards these unsightly teeth, intent on delivering what Steel's caption describes as a 'Requiem for a grinning jackass' (fig. 11). Cartoonists from the political mainstream have been capable of putting these symbols to equally cruel effect, of course. Paul Conrad's much-reproduced *Los Angeles Times* cartoon from 1980, 'The end of an ERA', caricatured Ronald Reagan's face as (or on to) the wrinkled rear end of an elephant.[24]

There is an important point to be made about the contemporary operation of both of these party-political symbols. Once their invention at the hands of Nast, a Republican sympathizer, had been largely forgotten, and the donkey had been as willingly accepted by the Democrats as the elephant by the Republicans, they could be said to have acquired a kind of neutrality. As Herblock's characteristically tame treatment of these creatures might reasonably be thought to show, the animal qualities of either symbol need not in themselves be regarded as demeaning in any way. At the same time, even when the imagery seems harmless enough, there is often a residual awareness that close scrutiny might reveal a more problematic and politicized animality. The *Washington Post*, for instance, was not prepared even to countenance my reproducing the Herblock cartoon in the context of the present book. And as the Steel and Conrad cartoons demonstrate, this 'neutral' symbolic iconography needs little manipulation to regain its full potential for aggressive political caricature.

The situation in Britain is quite different. British party politics has no equivalent of the elephant and donkey to influence or regulate the symbolic role which animals might play in an election campaign. In the British context the intrusion of *any* animal into the public consciousness of the election campaign will be both political and arbitrary: 'political' in the negative sense, as opposed to 'natural'; and arbitrary in the sense that there will have been no reliable way of predicting its intrusion. The British political animal is therefore a dangerously unstable sign.

The image of the animal turned out to be central to the entire national press's characterization of the Labour Party in the 1983 British General Election campaign.[25] In terms of its visual expression, this unfavourable stereotype of Labour can be seen in retrospect to have stemmed from photographs of Michael Foot which appeared on 11 May, the second day of the campaign. Seven of the ten national dailies carried photographs of Foot walking his dog Dizzy on Hampstead Heath the previous morning. The image appeared in several different versions, and the photographs seemed innocent enough, offering a legitimate glimpse of a political leader in relaxed mood prior to the onset of political campaigning proper. The version used on the front pages of the *Guardian* and *Telegraph* and inside two other papers (fig. 12) was the classic image from which the stereotype ultimately derived – though in its later more baroque elaborations the stereotype needed to make no direct reference to the characteristics of this original image. Manipulated and transformed in a variety of ways throughout the weeks of the campaign, the stereotype became so pervasive that even the Labour-supporting *Mirror* was sometimes unable to avoid it.

The politicization of this original news photograph followed two distinct but related paths. The first associated Michael Foot with madness; the second associated him with animality. Since the theme of madness is to be taken first, it is important to understand its connection and continuity with that of animality. Michel Foucault has famously described the complex interrelation of these two themes in an earlier age in his *Madness and Civilization*, and has even pointed to their iconographic connection, writing that 'It has doubtless been essential to Western culture to link, as it has done, its perception of madness to the iconographic forms of the relation of man to beast'.[26] If the national press can be taken as any kind of reflection of the contemporary popular imagination, it is clear that at least in a general sense such associations still hold good.

So, to madness. By the time the *Sun* re-used a cropped but page-high version of the classic Hampstead Heath photograph on 2 June, in a centre-page spread under the screaming banner headline 'Do you seriously want this old man to run Britain?', what had started as a topical

12 The photograph that launched a stereotype: Michael Foot waves to the photographer, oblivious to the fact that the innocent presence of his dog Dizzy is soon to give the media its visual *raison d'être* for representing both the man and his party as less than wholly human.

SUNDAY EXTRA

" *Re-nationalise every-thing! Soak the rich! S p e n d billions! ... Dizzy! Come back Dizzy. You're not a taxpayer!"*

13 The visual stereotyping of the Labour Party: stage one, insanity. Without needing to take too many liberties with the form of the Hampstead Heath photograph, the cartoonist provides Tory sympathizers with an entirely plausible reading of its iconography. From the *Sunday Express*, 15 May 1983, p.1.

if ephemeral news photograph had become a relatively timeless politically motivated icon. This is how it happened.

Among the different versions of the Hampstead Heath photograph in which Foot's face is visible, the one reproduced here, which I'm describing as the classic image, was the only one in which he was not clearly smiling. Instead, caught at an unfortunate instant by the photographer, his mouth is open in an expression it is difficult to describe, but which is not particularly flattering. Given the news value of the original photograph, this presumably mattered little. However, two of the subsequent cartoon images which draw on it pick up this small feature and exaggerate it to show Foot ranting wildly, in one case scaring his dog (fig. 13) and in the other driving it to sleep. The message is clear: the dog is saner, or at least has more sense, than the man. The unreasoning animal's 'reasonable' reaction is a necessary visual foil here for what is shown as Foot's intemperate gesticulation.

The impression of imbecility and senility was further encouraged by a small photograph in the *Express* showing an old man waving a walking stick with his right hand and dragging not a dog but a shopping trolley in his left. He was described as a seventy-eight-year-old election candidate whose mind 'has finally cracked'. The comparison with Foot is unstated but is iconographically clear. It is therefore the pose itself which comes in the course of the election campaign to signify both madness and Foot, at one and the same time. The emphasis on senility, apparently prompted by the walking stick, recurred in a cartoon in the *Mail* which combined Foot's raving gesture with a distinctly unsteady stance – this feature of the developing stereotype evidently stemming from popular notions of infirmity rather than from Foot's stance in the original photograph. Given this background, the *Sun's* re-use of the photograph on 2 June did little more than state openly in its headline what these other variations had none too subtly implied.

Accusations of lunacy were admittedly not employed exclusively against Labour. A press advertisement opposing the privatization of British Telecom made play of the fact that the only parties in favour of its privatization were the Conservatives and the Monster Raving Loony Party. More ambiguously, a *Mail on Sunday* cartoon showed a man at his front door asking an eccentrically-dressed canvasser: 'Which Monster Raving Loony Party?'. But these are the only exceptions. A Hector Breeze cartoon in the *Guardian* commented ironically on the stereotyped characterization of the parties. It showed a member of the public evidently taken aback by the opinion poll question 'Do you intend to vote for: The Government; a crowd of loonies; or a few deadbeats who have no chance of winning anyway?'. There could have been no doubt in readers' minds as to which party was being referred to as 'a crowd of loonies'.[27]

It is important to understand that the use of references to the Hampstead Heath photograph in order to reinforce the association of the Labour Party with madness (or, as below, with animality) occurred against a background of more 'innocent' reference to that same image. In some press images Foot seems to have been shown with his dog and stick not with any clearly malicious intent but simply to make him more recognizable, more like his visual stereotype.[28] With this as the norm, very little inflection of such images was necessary to show Foot in an unfavourable light.

Running alongside the strand of imagery depicting Foot as physically and mentally unstable was another strand, drawn from that same classic Hampstead Heath photograph, in which the image of Foot's dog Dizzy was fused with that of either Foot himself or Denis Healey (who was then deputy leader of the party). Thus, intentionally or not, and jokingly or not, an image of Labour as less than human began to develop.

The earliest example was Garland's cartoon in the *Telegraph* from the day after the publication of the photograph (fig. 14). Here the oversized dog is given Healey's facial features, notably the distinctive bushy eyebrows. Foot's supposed instability is again referred to by this giant dog causing him to lose his balance, but here the intention seems not personally vindictive but political. Overpowered by an animal which presumably stands not only for Healey but for the party as a whole, Foot as the leader is shown not to be in control of it; interpreting the cartoon's space politically, the symbolic dog is doing its best to tug Foot away from the left.

Three further Garland cartoons during the campaign showed Healey as Foot's dog,[29] while most other references to Dizzy cast Foot in this other-than-human role. This was done with the utmost ingenuity, if not subtlety. Only one cartoon resorted to the direct depiction of Foot as a dog (in the sense of putting his head on to a dog's body); this was in the *Daily Mail*, and showed him being walked on the heath by a stick-waving Denis Healey. Elsewhere the visual strategies varied. Foot was shown cowering on all fours towered over by an upright and thus human Margaret Thatcher (by Garland again). A photographic juxta-position drew an analogy between Foot's shaggy hair and that of Dizzy; this was on the front page of the *Guardian*, which should perhaps have known better. The *Mirror*, struggling to turn this whole damaging tendency to Foot's advantage, ascribed an aggressive canine reaction to him in its prominent front-page headline 'Foot bites back'. Franklin's cartoons in the *Sun* were less sympathetic. One, for no very clear reason, was a simple reversal with Foot on the leash being taken for a

14 Stage two, animality. The style of Garland's cartoon is far from vicious, but in it Healey undergoes that 'favourite means of metamor-phosis' and the precedent is set: the Labour Party is seen as a political animal, with all that that entails. From the *Daily Telegraph*, 12 May 1983, p.8.

walk by an upright Dizzy. Another had Foot as a fox being chased by a pack of dogs representing opinion polls whose results did not bode well for Labour. This last example may seem something of an exception to the Foot-as-dog stereotype, though its conformity to the stereotype can be recuperated with the knowledge that in the euphemistic language of bloodsports, the dogs are called hounds and it is the fox which is known as the dog. Conformity to a dominant stereotype also appears the only adequate explanation of the *Mirror* headline's acceptance of the unfavourable equation of Foot and a dog.[30]

While all the foregoing instances of comparison with Dizzy work to the disadvantage of the Labour Party, dogs themselves could be said to have had a very good press during the election campaign. They were variously depicted with Prince Charles, with Sir Alec Douglas Home, with John Bull and with policemen. Such images, along with the original Hampstead Heath photographs, would not generally have been regarded as political in the context of the largely right-wing sympathies of the press. The *Sunday Express* cartoon from 22 May with one dog saying to another 'I just feel dogs are better off not getting mixed up in politics' can only be a reference to the subsequent politicization of the classic image, and more importantly, it acknowledges that a process of politicization was in fact occurring.

While the general status of the dog in the 1983 election press was therefore somewhat problematic, the emotive word *beast* was fairly consistently used to convey disapprobation. It certainly had no positive connotations to redeem it. Its first openly political (though hardly serious) use in the campaign was in a brief item in the *Express* attributing the sobriquet 'the Beast of Bolsover' to the Labour MP Dennis Skinner on account of 'his mad rantings'.[31] It was not until the end of May that the word was applied more frequently in a political context, however.

At that time considerable publicity was being given to an unidentified creature wandering Exmoor, which the media dubbed 'the Beast of Exmoor'. Tabloid papers like the *Sun* and the *Star* took a particular interest in the story. On 31 May, for instance, the *Star* carried a large feature headlined 'We saw the beast!' (fig. 15), and the *Sun* that day called the same story 'Scared kids face the Beast of Exmoor'. The same day, reporting internal reorganization of Labour's campaign committee, the *Sun* ran a front-page caricature of Healey's face with the headline '"Beast" takes over Labour fight'. Both papers followed up this theme the next day. The *Star*'s Bill Caldwell cartoon made the connec-

WE SAW THE BEAST!

And this is what it looks like

The boys' drawing   ABOVE: Its paw print

Wayne Adams and Marcus White. They told of a large animal with bulging green eyes

THE hunt for the Beast of Exmoor was on again last night.

Police acted after two boys told of their "terrifying" face-to-face meeting with a large black animal with bulging green eyes.

They said it was the best sighting so far in the four-month search for the killer of 80 sheep.

The animal is four to

By TOM ROCHE

five feet tall and about 15 inches wide across the back, said Wayne Adams, 14, and his pal Marcus White, 12.

Isolated

They stumbled upon it while holidaying at an isolated farm on the Somerset - North Devon border.

Walking near a flock of sheep on Haltwoube Common they suddenly found themselves staring into the cruel eyes of a

powerfully built animal "bigger than any dog we've ever seen."

Wayne, of North Molton, Devon, said of their Sunday adventure:
"I looked over a gate and saw the animal about 10 yards away.

"It stared straight at me with bulging, greeny eyes just like a lion. It was jet black apart from white markings down its chest and had a head Like an Alsatian dog.

"I was dead scared and said to Marcus 'There's

the thing everyone is looking for' and it lolloped away.

"It moved like a cat, but I don't think it was a puma.

"We later found its footprints and claw marks. It must be very heavy because of the deep impression it left in the ground."

Marcus, of Exwick Exeter, added: "It did not move like a dog. It sort of pranced away."

Earlier this month, the Royal Marines joined the hunt. They spotted a "black and powerful" animal, but were unable to get a shot in.

---

15 Delighting in the horror of the unknown: the *Daily Star* reports a rare sighting of the mysterious 'Beast of Exmoor' and tells how Wayne and Marcus 'suddenly found themselves staring into the cruel eyes of a powerfully built animal "bigger than any dog we've ever seen"'.

tion between the two stories quite explicit: an investigating policeman shows the 'scared kids' a head-and-shoulders shot of a grinning Denis Healey and asks 'This "beast" you saw – did it look like this?'. The *Sun* carried both a headline and a Franklin cartoon labelling Healey as 'the beast' (fig. 16).

Several points need to be made about these images of Healey. The visual response to what the *Sun* had reported as virtually a change in the leadership of the Labour Party was to forge a stereotype of the new 'leader' which had as much as possible in common with the stereotype of the old one, and to do this from the very start. It is therefore no surprise that Franklin depicts 'the beast' as a puppet, reiterating the theme of the Labour 'leader' not being in control. It was also imperative

16 As if by complete coincidence, the day after the Beast of Exmoor story, Denis Healey finds that in the weird imaginings of the popular press he is no longer seen as Foot's amiable dog but instead as a sinisterly bushy-eyebrowed version of 'the beast'. From the *Sun*, 1 June 1983, p.6.

to establish some kind of animal connection. Healey's bestial qualities, beyond calling him 'the beast', are pointed to primarily through the fact that even the more 'human' head-and-shoulders images give considerable prominence to the hairiness or bushiness of his eyebrows. Hairiness is one of the qualities mentioned by Keith Thomas in his discussion of the relation of humans and animals, and although Thomas is of course writing of an earlier period, his comments still seem to apply to the conservative values of the modern press cartoonist. He writes:

> Wherever we look in early modern England, we find anxiety, latent or explicit, about any form of behaviour which threatened to transgress the fragile boundaries between man and the animal creation. ... It was bestial for men to have unduly long hair: 'Beasts are more hairy than men', wrote Bacon, 'and savage men more than civil'.[32]

The opposition of the savage and the civil may go some way to explaining a further aspect of the Labour stereotype which must be mentioned briefly: the association of the party with crime and with violence. The implied criminality of the politicians, it must be stressed, was intended to be taken no more literally than their supposed animality. When a cartoon showed them as squabbling protestors, or as bank raiders, or even compared them visually to IRA prisoners (as one Peter Brookes cartoon in *The Times* did), its purpose was of course more general: to show, for instance, that the party was divided, or that the 'criminal' actions of its own politicians were tearing it apart.

It should be clear by now that the stereotype of Labour which is being described here operated as a network of ideas and expressions, not all of which can be traced directly to the classic Hampstead Heath image, but all of which are ultimately consistent with the politicized form of that image. To recapitulate, the stereotype includes the themes of mental instability, physical infirmity, lack of control, internal strife, lawlessness, and a subhumanity which is expressed through representations of both domestic and wild animals. These diverse elements appear to have been united in contributing to the marginalization of Labour. The politicians were presented as unnatural or abnormal, as monstrous outsiders who threatened the firm boundaries of ordinary civilized society. They were stigmatized as less real, less human and less known than either that to which they were opposed or the viewers who witnessed that opposition. With its thoroughgoing connotations of distance and otherness, it is hard to imagine a more clearly meta-phoric (as opposed to metonymic) strategy.

The cartoonist who understood all this best and who exploited it to the full was Cummings, of the fervently Thatcherite *Daily Express*. One of his cartoons appeared the day before the election, and made refer-ence to a news story of the time concerning a family of nudists whose house was burned down by angry neighbours. The cartoon sets lead-ing Labour politicians as the 'nudists' (fig. 17), and in addition to giving due prominence to Foot's shaggy hair and Healey's eyebrows, it incor-porates many other elements of the Labour stereotype. Participating in their naked pagan ritual, the politicians show evidence not only of moral depravity but also of an underlying animality. As Keith Thomas observes, the audience which recognized the significance of hairiness would also have known that 'nakedness was bestial, for clothes ... were a distinctively human attribute'.[33] In casting off the 'Manners makyth man!' shirt, the politicians show themselves to be both uncivil-ized and less than human. Likewise, in discarding the shirt of natural and expected 'moderation', they demonstrate their political extre-mism. It is no accident that the attackers are ordinary outraged citizens rather than rival Tory politicians. And all this, it should be noted, is achieved without reference to dogs, walking sticks or Hampstead Heath.

It will now be shown that throughout the campaign these various elements constituted a distinctive Labour stereotype, which was understood to be antithetical to the Tories. The animal theme was crucial here: the image of animals was a polluting thing, and the Tories could not afford to come into metonymic visual contact with it. Aside from a single drawing in the *Sun* showing her as Britannia alongside the British lion, Margaret Thatcher consistently suffered as a result of coming into contact with animals. On the very first day of the cam-paign, the *Guardian* re-ran a photograph from the 1979 campaign showing Thatcher seated in a Suffolk field stroking a sleeping calf. Using a cautionary comment made by Denis Thatcher at the time, the piece was headlined ' "We'll have a dead calf on our hands", said Denis'. In another example the *Mirror*, again trying lamely to twist Labour's unfavourable animal image to the party's advantage, began its serialized 'Private life of Mrs Thatcher' with a centre-page illustra-tion and story about her once being attacked by an alsatian, which it headlined 'How a dog caused her downfall'.[34] As the *Guardian* headline also implies, the negative relationship of Thatcher and animals worked both ways – the principal aim of advertising from animal rights pressure groups during the election campaign was to suggest that animals would suffer at the hands of the Tories.[35]

Perhaps the most impressive evidence for the visual antithesis of the Tories and animals is this: among the hundreds of relevant political images in the national press in the course of the month-long election campaign, *there was only one image which showed Thatcher or indeed any Conservative politician in the form of an animal.* It was a less than wholly successful cartoon in *The Times* which sought to make the point that Francis Pym was then seen as something of a 'black sheep' among the Tories on account of his more moderate views on some issues. To get

" It's very odd! The neighbours don't seem to like OUR behaviour. . . ."

17 Political animals don't always need to take the form of 'Foure-Footed Beastes'. Cummings can see that in depicting the violation of social norms and niceties, he is implying quite enough about the politicians' underlying animality. From the *Daily Express*, 8 June 1983, p.6.

the point across, however, the cartoonist ended up depicting three other leading members of the party, including the prime minister, as 'ordinary' sheep. This animalization put them in dangerous proximity to the Labour stereotype, of course. The best that the cartoonist could do in this awkward situation to salvage a degree of conformity to the dominant stereotypes was to make Thatcher's depiction *less* bestial than the others. This was done by separating her entirely human head from the indignity and impurity of the ovine body by a distinct string of civilizing pearls.[36]

A more general point about the workings of visual stereotyping in this campaign can be proposed on the basis of this exceptional example (and it may in fact need little modification to be applicable in other circumstances too). Verbal clichés and commonplaces, it seems, will fail to translate into satisfactory visual form if they transgress the basic *visual* boundaries by which competing identities are kept separate and distinct. If the pictorial association of Labour with animals or animality is to work effectively, meaningfully and systematically within the dominant press discourse of the time, that discourse will and must preclude the possibility of depicting the Conservatives in that manner. It is hardly too glib to say that the exception demonstrates this rule. The exception failed to recognize that in this context the unflattering verbal or conceptual connotations of animality are almost beside the point; it is the visual image which is of overriding importance here, and its first purpose is simply to distinguish the rival groups. Since this visual rhetoric has no place for idioms which do not conform to its systematic organization, it offers rather convincing evidence that visual stereotyping is by no means simply a matter of finding crude pictorial equivalents for things that are already going on in the language.

None the less, as a final comment on this political case study, it says something clear and disturbing about the cultural attitudes on which the press was able to draw, that *everyone* risked a kind of contamination by visual contact with the politicized animal.[37] The Tories had to avoid such contact for fear of the harm and confusion it might cause, but Labour was certainly not benefiting from its own clear association with this imagery – witness the *Mirror*'s attempts to subvert this inescapable stereotype in order to get it to work to Labour's advantage once in a while. The imagery only reiterated what the culture evidently believed. Animals are dangerous; *cave canem*.

Drawing distinctions

A review of the theoretical distinctions available to us would now be helpful. So far it has been proposed that metaphorical strategies will be evident in the characterization of 'others' through animal imagery in order to convey a sense of their distance, strangeness and difference. The examples discussed above seem to bear this out: Labour politicians were *likened to* animals in order to discredit and marginalize them. To find convincing equivalent cases of the metonymic relation of humans and animals in the positive visual presentation of the self, however, it would be easier to think back to examples discussed in the previous chapter. The way in which the image of the lion *stands for* Britain, or in which the image of the bald eagle *stands for* the United States, is almost a textbook case of a metonymic relation.

It will be useful to introduce another distinction here: the distinction between theriomorphism and therianthropism. A theriomorphic image would be one in which someone or something (in the words of the *OED* definition) was presented as 'having the form of a beast'. Therianthropic images, in contrast, would be those 'combining the form of a beast with that of a man'. It will be immediately apparent that these terms, though very seldom used, are actually far more appropriate for our purposes than the over-used and frequently misused notion of anthropomorphism. What is being discussed, after all, is the casting of humans into animal form, and not the reverse.

One of the attractions of this form of classifying and distinguishing images is the way it seems to complement and elucidate the oppositions which are central to this chapter: those of metonymy and metaphor, and of self and others. It may be unduly schematic, but it would certainly not be misleading, to suggest the following formula. Where animal imagery is used to make statements about human identity, *metonymic representations of selfhood will typically take theriomorphic form, whereas metaphoric representations of otherness will typically take therianthropic form.* In other words we tend to represent ourselves as wholly animal, but our others as only half-animal. There is nothing particularly surprising about this, and it can be explained at a number of levels.

Consider the case of caricature. Caricatures are usually of others: we are understandably reluctant to see the symbolic violence of this technique turned against ourselves or those we support. When the caricaturist employs that 'favourite means of metamorphosis' so that a

recognizable individual's human head 'becomes gradually transformed into the head of an animal without losing the portrait note, the
likeness', the resulting therianthropic image will far more often be the
depiction of a rival than of an ally.[38]

Because of the negative connotations of this imagery in the public
imagination, there are in fact rather few occasions on which the depiction of an individual friend or ally or hero in this semi-animal form
will even be attempted. When, on the tenth anniversary of her premiership, Margaret Thatcher likened herself to a tigress, the comment
was taken up with enthusiasm in the tabloid press.[39] Even the most
sympathetic Conservative cartoonists, however, were distinctly unen-
thusiastic about *depicting* her in this form. The few who tried to do so
seemed already aware that the results of their efforts to portray this
'good' animal would be somehow unsettling and anomalous (fig. 18).
Here there was little choice but to put her head, or at least her facial
features, on to the tigress's body, but the therianthropic result is flawed
by a strangeness – a metaphoric distance – which is at odds with the
cartoonist's political intention.

It is quite a different matter, of course, to depict whole groups favourably in animal form. As the previous chapter explained, auth-
orized images of the collective self are already *known*; there is no need to
put the current president's head on the body of the American eagle,
and no need either to call attention to its animality. The symbol of the
eagle simply stands for the nation; it is uniquely associated with it; and
because of its familiarity, and the immediacy with which it is recognized, the symbol is effectively invisible – effectively drained of its
animality. In all these respects such symbols represent a strategy of
visual metonymy, and they will take a wholly animal, theriomorphic
form. This, at least, is how they ought to work. The last chapter included examples whose lesser success can now be put down to their
mixed, therianthropic appearance: the British lion walking on its hind
legs with a Churchillian cigar in its mouth, for instance. As was seen
there too, the strategy of giving human attributes to animals works
best when they are meant to represent others rather than the self, as in
the case of the 'silly' French poodle with its beret and string of onions.

When whole groups such as rival nations are to be shown *unfavourably* in animal form, it is not always enough to put hats on their
heads, and suchlike. The more typical therianthropic strategy is to
show them as 'subhuman', which in the world of post-Darwinian

Labels in image: HEATH, SCARGILL, GALTIERI, Gale

How the tigress tamed her brood

Ferdinand Mount

MRS MARGARET Thatcher, as everyone knows, has no small talk. She has never been one for that cocktail of gossip — musty, slightly bitter, and not quite fizzy enough — with which politicians and journalists while away the waiting hours. On first meeting her 25 years ago, when I was a junior researcher in social security, her opening words were: "Are you sure you've got your figures right?" When I met her at a party last week, her first words were: "What are we going to do about the law of defamation?"

Mrs Thatcher's dedicated workaholic approach has scarcely made her 10th anniversary celebrations an unbuttoned carousal. We are constantly reminded that there is still a war on, strict black-out must be observed and the bar will close at eight sharp. More important, despite the reams of stuff we have had to plough through in books and news-

We remember William Tyndale school, the "snakepit" psychiatric hospitals, the thousands of men paid to do little or nothing in almost every nationalised industry, the corruption that nobody would admit to in local government, the thieving at the docks and airports.

What was (and alas in many cases still is) needed was for both Ministers and managers to have their tasks radically simplified to set achievable targets, to cut away the opaque layers of bureaucracy and make their performance transparent to the public. Managers who had to spend three-quarters of their time trying to placate trade unions — our own newspaper industry was the classic example — could not begin to formulate realistic plans beyond the following week. It is the Thatcher Government with all its faults that has made genuine planning possible again. This painstaking disentangling of the

18 'I'm a tigress', Margaret Thatcher announced in 1989, leaving the cartoonist Gale struggling to get a therianthropic image to work to her advantage and not, as the rules of caricature dictate that it should, to her clear disadvantage. From the *Daily Telegraph*, 5 May 1989, p.18.

stereotypes, at least, means depicting them as some kind of ape-like creature. The depiction of the enemy in Norman Lindsay's Australian recruiting poster from the First World War (fig. 19) is a case in point. Declining to use the enemy's own theriomorphic symbol, the eagle, Lindsay chooses instead to liken the 'Hun' to an ape, and invites his viewers to consider and appreciate the points of comparison. These metaphorical comparisons have little to do with zoological knowledge, of course. Lindsay and his viewers would not have expected real German soldiers to be that hunched, or that hairy, and certainly not to be naked; nor (had they troubled to think about it) would they necessarily have believed that real apes shared the 'blood lust' or 'murder lust' widely attributed to the 'Hun', and referred to in the reddened arms of Lindsay's creature. Like all such ape-like inventions it is, rather, the focus of a variety of entrenched cultural stereotypes which serve to characterize that which is threatening, or despised, or other. The metaphorical task which Lindsay asks his viewers to undertake is therefore one of no great difficulty. The image *is* distinctly metaphorical, however, because its visual details remain important. The prognathous features, bared teeth, and hands dripping blood are meant to be noticed, and to be disconcerting. In contrast to the complacent silence of a metonymic response, it is recorded that when this poster appeared in 1918 it 'was a great surprise to the public and caused much discussion'.[40]

The perfect container and the polluting mixture

Having considered these examples, it is now possible to comment further on the appropriateness of theriomorphism and therianthropism as strategies for the respective depiction of self and others. The idea of the 'wholeness' of theriomorphic creatures has already been touched on, and its logic may well derive in part from Western culture's acceptance and internalization of the rules for the classification of animals proposed in the Old Testament book of Leviticus. In the chapter of *Purity and Danger* dealing with the Levitical abominations, Mary Douglas observes that 'the idea of holiness was given an external, physical expression in the wholeness of the body seen as a perfect container'. More generally, she goes on: 'We can conclude that holiness is exemplified by completeness. Holiness requires that individuals shall conform to the class to which they belong. And holiness requires that different classes

19 The mark of the beast: the blood-drenched arms of Norman Lindsay's ape-like 'Hun' drip across the world in this savage Australian recruiting poster from 1918. Lindsay spoke of his belief in the importance of preserving 'the killer in man' and 'the instinct to kill'.

of things shall not be confused.'[41] This is certainly one reason why therianthropism is regarded as unsettling, and why from a propagandistic point of view the technique is best restricted to the depiction of others. It exemplifies Julia Kristeva's notion of *abjection*, which is characterized principally as a threat to the certainty of self's identity. In Leviticus the classification-threatening animals are described as 'unclean'; Kristeva plays on the connotations of the term *l'impropre* to signify both the unclean and that which is not of the self. What is at stake here is not only the self's identity but also the assumed superiority and moral righteousness of the self. As Mary Douglas puts it later in her book, 'a polluting person is always in the wrong'.[42]

It is clear that these prejudices translate readily enough into visual imagery, and that the pictorial form of 'a polluting person' will be characterized by the troubling in-between-ness of therianthropism. Here, however, there is one further distinction which calls for attention: the distinction between what have been called conceptual metaphors and sensual metaphors.[43] The casting of a hated or despised human into the role or image of an animal is, as we have seen, a very frequent and effective means of stereotyping them, of objectifying them, and of rendering them inferior. It is hardly an attractive practice, but it is of course a mere convention. The metaphorical relation which the caricaturist proposes is in this sense a conceptual one: we are not meant to believe that the politician so depicted is in fact subhuman. This would seem to be very different to the sensual metaphor recognizable in the convention employed by a long tradition of racist imagemakers. There, a whole other national or racial group will be depicted as subhuman, sometimes in the apparent belief that the depicted group is genuinely on a lower rung of some evolutionary ladder.

Lewis Perry Curtis's book *Apes and Angels* is an invaluable documentation of the way many prominent English cartoonists in the late nineteenth century systematically portrayed the Irish as simian subhumans. As Curtis points out, however, this was an instance of what was then a widespread metaphoric practice: 'Virtually every country in Europe had its equivalent of "white Negroes" and simianized men, whether or not they happened to be stereotypes of criminals, assassins, political radicals, revolutionaries, Slavs, gypsies, Jews, or peasants'.[44] While the acceptability of these visual stereotypes has diminished in the mass media in more recent times, they can still find vitriolic expression in extremist propaganda, where, in Britain and America at least, it

20 Sticker printed for the National Front or a similar neo-fascist organization, *c.* 1978. A contemporary photograph of an NF rally shows young white boys with a number of these stickers plastered on their clothes or their bare chests, alongside other stickers asking 'Who needs niggers?'.

has been blacks who have typically been the object of such undiluted hatred. The openly racist material associated with the National Front in Britain in the late 1970s included leaflets warning that 'Racially mixed couples pollute White Race', and stickers making a simian comparison explicit (fig. 20).

These preposterous 'Independence for Brixton NOW' stickers should alert us to an important feature of therianthropic image-making which might otherwise be overlooked. In employing the half-human simian stereotype to signal both a horror of racial impurity and a blind adherence to the notion of one race's inferiority, the image itself does not need to be literally therianthropic. The image on this sticker is not some vicious animalizing caricature but rather an apparently straightforward photograph of a gorilla's head: here, as elsewhere, it is only the context which renders the image therianthropic.

Much as with the treacherously slippery meanings of animal photographs, the distinction drawn here between conceptual and sensual metaphors needs to be treated with considerable caution. As Kris and Gombrich noted in the 1930s, the satisfyingly malicious animal caricature of a rival depends just as heavily on 'the dogma of physiognomy' as does the discredited 'scientific' illustration of racial or mental inferiority.[45]

From lion to mad dog to beast: A last word

Earlier in the chapter I distinguished John Berger's identification of the 'positive' use of animal metaphors, which are an invitation to thought and understanding, from the 'negative' use of the animal in an oppositional rhetoric, which is characterized by the conceptual closure of stereotyping. Most of the subsequent examples have been pictorial, but parallels can certainly be found in verbal rhetoric, drawing as it does on a common set of cultural assumptions.

A clear demonstration of the shift from the positive to the negative can be seen, for instance, in the language chosen by the British media to characterize Saddam Hussein in the days following his invasion of Kuwait in August 1990. The day after the invasion, his position in relation to the neighbouring Arab countries could still be explained as that of 'A lion among the gazelles'. Within days, however, any interest in explanation disappeared, and he became to those headline writers who still chose to employ animal references first a 'wild dog' and then a 'mad dog': 'World can tame Iraq's mad dog' and 'Inside mad dog Hussein's torture chamber' were typical examples. When some days later it became known that British citizens in Kuwait were to be taken hostage, the press had to dredge deeper in its rhetoric of contempt: 'Beast cages 4,000 Brits' announced the front page of the *Star*. The implication here that Hussein must be an animal because he's treating 'us' like animals was made even clearer when this was seen alongside the same day's front-page headline in the *Mirror*: 'Brits herded up like cattle'.[46] It says something about the values of this nation of self-proclaimed animal lovers that it is automatically considered 'beastly' to be treated like an animal.

What conclusions could be drawn at this point concerning the way the culture articulates its rhetoric of animality? Certainly, as suggested earlier, it does seem that animals – and cultural constructions of 'the animal' – will invariably figure as the negative term when used in binary oppositions. This is perhaps why, in the post-Cartesian West with its continuing appetite for the dualistic and the oppositional, animals seem to figure so overwhelmingly negatively in our imaginative and our visual rhetoric. From these provisional findings it should be possible to go on to make a rather stronger statement about how and why our visually-oriented culture objectifies the animal and keeps that animal object at a distance, but to do this convincingly it will be necessary to contrast this chapter's concerns with the quite different evidence of the next.

Notes

1 Keith Thomas, *Man and the Natural World: Changing Attitudes in England 1500–1800* (London: Allen Lane, 1983), p.41.
2 Barbara Noske, *Humans and Other Animals: Beyond the Boundaries of Anthropology* (London: Pluto Press, 1989), p.vii.
3 Roy Willis, *Man and Beast* (London: Hart-Davis, MacGibbon, 1974), p.128.
4 See Harriet Ritvo, *The Animal Estate: The English and Other Creatures in the Victorian Age* (Cambridge, Mass.: Harvard University Press, 1987), pp.12–13; and Keith Thomas, *Man and the Natural World*, pp.53–7.
5 On the importance of oppositions in Aristotelian thought, see Mark Cousins, 'Men and women as polarity', *Oxford Literary Review*, 8, nos 1–2 (1986); Thomas's account of 'Human uniqueness' is from *Man and the Natural World*, pp.30–6, and his references to anthropologists' views are from pp.40–1.
6 See Elizabeth Atwood Lawrence, *Rodeo: An Anthropologist Looks at the Wild and the Tame* (Knoxville: University of Tennessee Press, 1982), p.7, and Barbara Noske,

Humans and Other Animals, p.40.

7 Richard Tapper, 'Animality, humanity, morality, society', in *What is an Animal?*, edited by Tim Ingold (London: Unwin Hyman, 1988), pp.49–50.

8 Mary Douglas's statement is from her *Implicit Meanings: Essays in Anthropology* (London: Routledge & Kegan Paul, 1975), p.289. The circularity of these references will be becoming evident to the reader. Tapper uses this phrase of Douglas's to sum up an analysis which draws heavily, though he doesn't say so, on the equivalences which Edmund Leach proposed between particular categories of humans and of animals in his celebrated 1964 essay on animal categories and verbal abuse (cited in note 21 below). In that essay Leach had acknowledged his own debt to the then-unpublished ideas of Mary Douglas on anomalous animals, ideas which were later to appear in her 1966 book *Purity and Danger*.

9 John Berger, 'Animals as metaphor', *New Society*, 10 March 1977, p.505. Other recent writings pursuing the metaphor theme include Maureen O. Paley's essay 'The animal as metaphor', in *The Animal in Photography 1843–1985*, edited by Alexandra Noble (London: The Photographers' Gallery, 1986), and the section 'Animals as metaphors' in David Harper's article 'Gentle giants caught by the cruel sea', *Magazine of Cultural Studies*, no.2 (1990).

10 Richard Tapper, 'Animality, humanity, morality, society', p.51.

11 Mary Douglas makes some apposite criticisms of indiscriminate references to metaphor in her essay 'The pangolin revisited: A new approach to animal symbolism', in *Signifying Animals: Human Meaning in the Natural World*, edited by Roy Willis (London: Unwin Hyman, 1990).

12 See Roman Jakobson, 'Two aspects of language and two types of aphasic disturbances', reprinted in his *Selected Writings II: Word and Language* (The Hague: Mouton, 1971), pp.239–59. For a fairly thorough survey of the many later writings which have developed these ideas, see Willard Bohn, 'Roman Jakobson's theory of metaphor and metonymy: An annotated bibliography', *Style*, 18, no.4 (1984), pp.534–50.

13 Claude Lévi-Strauss, The *Savage Mind* (London: Weidenfeld & Nicolson, 1966), pp.204–7.

14 In a 1970 essay called 'Rhetoric restrained', Gérard Genette provides a convenient summary of the complex and problematic history through which the number of rhetorical terms used or favoured by linguists and rhetoricians has been pared down, and he himself argues in favour of the retention of 'the exemplary figurative pair, the irreplaceable bookends of our own modern rhetoric: metaphor and metonymy'. The essay is reprinted in Genette's *Figures of Literary Discourse*, translated by Alan Sheridan (New York: Columbia University Press, 1982).

15 Roy Willis, *Man and Beast*, p.128.

16 Both essays appear in Gombrich's *Meditations on a Hobby Horse and Other Essays on the Theory of Art* (London: Phaidon, 1963); the quotations are from p.12 and p.138.

17 Stephen Bann, *The Clothing of Clio: A Study of the Representation of History in Nineteenth-Century Britain and France* (Cambridge: CUP, 1984), pp.42–3.

18 See E.H. Gombrich, *Meditations on a Hobby Horse*, p.13, and Roman Jakobson, 'Two aspects of language', p.258.

19 Ernst Kris and Ernst Gombrich, 'The principles of caricature', *British Journal of Medical Psychology*, 17 (1938), p.334.

20 See Arthur G. Neal, 'Animism and totemism in popular culture', *Journal of Popular Culture*, 19, no.2 (1985), p.16, and Anthony Wootton, *Animal Folklore, Myth and Legend* (Poole: Blandford Press, 1986), p.9.

21 Examples of the rhetoric of 'the beast' are discussed later in the chapter. On the arbitrary use of particular species in terms of verbal abuse, see Edmund Leach, 'Anthropological aspects of language: Animal categories and verbal abuse', in *New Directions in the Study of Language*, edited by Eric H. Lenneberg (Cambridge, Mass.: MIT Press, 1964).

22 The 'urban animal' example, devised for the Pure New Wool 'Beware a wolf in sheep's clothing' campaign from the mid–1980s, is quoted in *Male Order: Unwrapping Masculinity*, edited by Rowena Chapman and Jonathan Rutherford (London: Lawrence & Wishart, 1988), p.33. Commenting on the model used in the campaign, Rutherford observes without apparent disapproval that 'he still retains that animal predatory sexuality that is proof of his manhood' (p.32).

23 The cartoon appeared in the *Observer*, 17 March 1991, p.20.

24 As with many other such examples, Conrad's cartoon is far more than merely an abusive animal caricature of Reagan. For an indication of the complex range of issues which would need to be taken into account in a more thorough reading of this particular cartoon, see Martin J. Medhurst and Michael A. DeSousa, 'Political cartoons as rhetorical form: A taxonomy of graphic discourse', *Communication Monographs*, 48, no.3 (1981), p.219.

25 Surprisingly, this fact went largely uncommented upon in the two main British studies of the election: David Butler and Dennis Kavanagh's *The British General Election of 1983* (London: Macmillan, 1984), and *Political Communications: The General Election Campaign of 1983*, edited by Ivor Crewe and Martin Harrop (Cambridge: CUP, 1986).

26 Michel Foucault, *Madness and Civilization: A History of Insanity in the Age of Reason*, translated by Richard Howard (London: Tavistock/Routledge, 1989), p.77. The quotation is from Chapter 3, 'The insane', which deals at length with notions of animality.

27 The images referred to in the last three paragraphs are from the following sources, respectively: *Sunday Express*, 15 May 1983, p.1 (fig.13); *Sun*, 30 May, p.2; *Daily Express*, 19 May, p.19; *Daily Mail*, 17 May, p.15; *Sun*, 2 June, pp.16–17; *News of the World*, 5 June, p.19 (British Telecommunications Unions Committee advertisement); *Mail on Sunday*, 22 May, p.31; *Guardian*, 28 May, p.12.

28 See for instance the *Daily Mail*'s photograph captioned 'Dogged pair: Foot and pet', 21 May, p.9; and the same paper's drawing of Foot on 1 June, p.25.

29 They appeared in the *Daily Telegraph* on 25 May, p.21, and 31 May, p.17, and in the *Sunday Telegraph* on 5 June, p.20.

30 The sources of the examples referred to in this paragraph are as follows: *Daily Mail*, 1 June, p.13; *Daily Telegraph*, 19 May, p.2; *Guardian*, 24 May, p.1; *Daily Mirror*, 31 May, p.1; *Sun*, 8 June, p.6, and 6 June, p.6. The bloodsports terminology is referred to in Edmund Leach's 'Anthropological aspects of language', p.52.

31 Relishing the fact that the Tory candidate at Bolsover had chosen mockingly to give his black labrador the same nickname, the paper juxtaposed photographs of the dog and of Skinner with the respective captions 'Canine beast' and 'Political beast', and closed its report by explaining to its readers 'That's Dennis on the right'. See the *Daily Express*, 18 May, p.13.

32 Keith Thomas, *Man and the Natural World*, pp.38–9.

33 *Man and the Natural World*, p.38.

34 See the *Sun*, 9 June 1983, p.1; *Guardian*, 10 May, p.19; *Daily Mirror*, 17 May, pp.16–17.

35 Advertisements paid for by the International Fund for Animal Welfare (IFAW)

were used quite widely in the press in the final days of the campaign. They addressed several forms of animal abuse – vivisection, bloodsports, and the killing of animals for their fur – and suggested that the Tories had no commitment to bring such practices to an end. Most of them depicted a single cat, dog, fox or seal and carried the uncompromising headline: 'Vote to save us. Stop the Tories. Please, please end our torture'. Independently of these, the Animal Protection Alliance (a temporary alliance of animal rights organizations including the BUAV) produced press advertisements specifically advocating a Labour vote.

36 The cartoon, by Peter Brookes, appeared in *The Times* on 24 May, p.5.

37 While I don't propose to extend my own analysis in this direction, the notion of the harm or shame which such images can provoke might usefully be viewed in relation to theories of 'image magic'. On this subject see for instance Ernst Kris and Ernst Gombrich, 'The principles of caricature'; and David Freedberg, *The Power of Images: Studies in the History and Theory of Response* (Chicago: University of Chicago Press, 1989), especially chapter 10, 'Infamy, justice, and witchcraft: Explanation, sympathy and magic'.

38 The quotation is from Kris and Gombrich's 'The principles of caricature', p.334, though they do not use the term therianthropism.

39 See for instance the following articles and editorials, all from 4 May 1989: 'I'm a tigress and the fight's not over', *Sun*, p.2; 'I'm so proud of being a tigress', and 'Britain with a "tigress" in its tank', *Daily Express*, p.1 and p.8; 'The tigress defending Britain', *Daily Mail*, pp.22–23; 'The tigress in me', *Daily Mirror*, p.2.

40 Joseph Darracott and Belinda Loftus, *First World War Posters* (London: Imperial War Museum, 1972), p.41.

41 Mary Douglas, *Purity and Danger: An Analysis of Concepts of Pollution and Taboo* (London: Routledge & Kegan Paul, 1969), pp.51–2 and 53.

42 See Julia Kristeva, 'Approaching abjection', translated by John Lechte, *Oxford Literary Review*, 5 (1982), pp.125-49; and Mary Douglas, *Purity and Danger*, p.113.

43 This distinction is briefly discussed in J. David Sapir's essay 'The anatomy of metaphor', in *The Social Use of Metaphor: Essays on the Anthropology of Rhetoric*, edited by J. David Sapir and J. Christopher Crocker (Philadelphia: University of Pennsylvania Press, 1977), pp.6–7.

44 Lewis Perry Curtis, Jr, *Apes and Angels: The Irishman in Victorian Caricature* (Newton Abbot: David & Charles, 1971), pp.13–14.

45 Ernst Kris and Ernst Gombrich, 'The principles of caricature', p.334. For a concise historical account of physiognomy in relation to pictorial practice, see also the opening chapter of Curtis's *Apes and Angels*.

46 The sources of these animal references are as follows: *Guardian*, 3 August 1990, p.17; *People*, 12 August, p.6; *Sunday Sport*, 12 August, pp.10–11; *Daily Star*, 17 August, p.1; *Daily Mirror*, 17 August, p.1.

E

4

Of *Maus* and more: narrative, pleasure and talking animals

If you want to clear the room of derrideans, mention Beatrix Potter without sneering.

Ursula Le Guin[1]

Forget, for the moment, all the contempt, condescension and hatred described in the last chapter in regard to animals and animal imagery. It is possible – and it will now be useful – to think about animals quite differently: to begin, for example, from the assertion that our culture is replete with the evidence of the pleasure which people take in animals, and that this is a pleasure which is taken unselfconsciously and apparently quite genuinely. Taking pleasure in animals and taking pleasure in *depictions* of animals may seem two quite separate matters, of course, but it will not be helpful to draw that distinction too sharply at the outset. For one thing, much of the pleasure which people seem to take in animals is not the result, say, of direct contact with their pets; instead it's to be found in the animal toys they buy their children, or in their choice of greetings cards populated by animal characters, or perhaps in their deriving a vague sense of satisfaction (pride may be too strong a word) from believing that they belong to an animal-loving nation. This risks being too wide a front on which initially to approach the question of pleasure, however, so I propose to give the chapter a rather narrower focus.

What follows is an exploration of something which started as little more than a hunch. The previous chapter was concerned for the most part with hostile representations: static images encapsulating and immortalizing the inflexibility of the attitudes they described. The rectangular frames of the images themselves seemed to operate as a form of conceptual closure – an echo or reminder of stereotyping's own immutability. In contrast to this fixity and closure, I wondered if the relative openness and continuity of a *narrative* structure might more often permit or even invite more enjoyable encounters with or identifications with the image of the animal. These speculations necessarily take us into the field of animal stories, of comic-strip and animated imagery, and consequently into all the problems occasioned by what Ursula Le Guin characterizes as the 'critical terror of Kiddilit'.

This change of subject-matter entails a change of approach: for the most part the material to be considered here will not be cases of animal imagery used to identify humans (theriomorphism) but examples, instead, of human characteristics imposed on the images of animals (anthropomorphism), whether those images be visual or verbal. We are moving, in other words, from the realm of the animal symbol and the animal caricature into that of the talking animal. As will be seen, however, issues of identity and of 'identification' loom large here too, and these must be dealt with before the question of narrative can be tackled.

Identifications

It is important to appreciate the extent of the continuity between the theriomorphic material dealt with in earlier chapters and this new anthropomorphically-inclined subject matter. The idea of a pleasurable identification with the image of an animal is perfectly feasible in both areas. The question in both cases is this: how are we to account for the pleasure genuinely taken in representations of animals, and for people's readiness to identify themselves with and through such images? I am not talking here about representations of power – identifying oneself with the fierce image of the British bulldog, and so on – but rather about an apparently simple pleasure. People, it seems, just like looking at the image of animals. This may seem too simplistic an assertion but, before moving into the domain of animal comic-strips and the like, some of its implications can be explored by considering a tale of such 'liking' on more familiar theriomorphic territory. It concerns the use and meaning of the animal in that flourishing modern medium, the corporate logo.

Liking the look of animals

In the early 1970s the British design consultancy Wolff Olins took on the task of clarifying and improving the corporate image of the civil engineering and construction firm Bovis. The result was a corporate identity programme which made widespread use of colourful and realistically-rendered images of a humming-bird. The logo appeared on everything from bulldozers to company stationery. It was a far from obvious choice of image, being most unlike the graphically-macho imagery of other construction companies at that time, and having no very clear relevance to Bovis's work or history. Nevertheless, in his book *The Corporate Personality*, Wally Olins emphasized the popularity of the logo: 'Bovis site workers put stickers of the humming-bird on their cars, not because they are asked to but because they think they look nice and they want to associate themselves with the company'. On grounds such as these he also claimed, reasonably enough, that 'the design scheme is popular in the sense that people like it'.[2]

More recently Olins has explained the thinking behind the image of the bird. In trying to devise a logo which would play its part in a more comprehensive improvement and brightening-up of the construction site environment, the design consultants were seeking a visual image which the workers would understand, enjoy and with which they could somehow identify. The condescending view was taken, it seems, that in the case of a 'typical' construction site worker this narrowed the options to images of half-naked female pin-ups on the one hand, or of Disney cartoon characters on the other. The humming-bird solution, though far from Disney-esque in style, emerged from an exploration of that second option. Along the way, and apparently much to the disappointment of Olins's partner, Michael Wolff, a similarly realistic image of a goldfish was rejected for the Bovis logo. When Wolff later left Wolff Olins to set up his own design firm, Addison, he took the goldfish image with him and used it unchanged as the Addison logo.[3]

The story of these logos raises three issues which are of general relevance here: pleasure, identification and arbitrariness. According to Olins, the Bovis workers took pleasure in the humming-bird image and they chose to identify with it; and Wolff did exactly the same with the image of the goldfish. In both cases, however, the relation of the image to what it identified was entirely arbitrary; the goldfish makes this particularly clear, having been designed to identify a construction firm but being finally used to identify a design firm. I would suggest that it is far from obvious what is going on in examples such as these. It may indeed be that people take pleasure in their use of animal imagery. But there remains the question of what it is that they are doing, and what exactly it is they think they are looking at, when they engage in this pleasure. What, in other words, is the status of these representations, and what is invested in human identification with them?

Identifying with the talking animal

Received wisdom has it that the tendency to like, to care for and to identify with animals is essentially a childhood phenomenon, or, as it might often be more condescendingly expressed, a childish thing. Examples abound, and range from the deliberate sentimentality of the mass media ('Children were raiding their piggy banks to save the animals of London Zoo last night after the Government insisted: "No more money from us" ') to the apparently serious opening statement in a recent book on animal welfare: 'It is said that the British never really grow up and that this is why they are animal lovers'.[4]

Some of the more serious attempts to understand the particular characteristics of this widely accepted child–animal sympathy have tended to focus on childhood animism. Bruno Bettelheim provides a concise explanation of this phenomenon:

> To the child, there is no clear line separating objects from living things; and whatever has life has life very much like our own. If we do not understand what rocks and trees and animals have to tell us, the reason is that we are not sufficiently attuned to them. To the child trying to understand the world, it seems reasonable to expect answers from those objects which arouse his curiosity. And since the child is self-centered, he expects the animal to talk about the things which are really significant to him, as animals do in fairy tales, and as the child himself talks to his real or toy animals. A child is convinced that the animal understands and feels with him, even though it does not show it openly. . . . In animistic thinking, not only animals feel and think as we do, but even stones are alive; . . . And since everything is inhabited by a spirit similar to all other spirits (namely, that of the child who has projected his spirit into all these things), because of this inherent sameness it is believable that man can change into animal, or the other way around . . . [5]

This is convincing enough in its own way, and as the reference to fairy tales indicates, it can also account for the believability of the whole tradition of talking-animal stories. But such a line of argument presumes a clear-cut distinction between the value and belief systems of the sophisticated adult, who is ultimately always in the right, and those of the ignorant child – the child who intuitively, which is to say *wrongly*, holds open the possibility of an identification with the animal and the inanimate. This prejudice constructs the animal as absolutely *other*, and by association those who identify with the animal themselves come to be seen as other.

The literary conventions of the talking-animal story are perhaps the clearest case in point. These conventions are very widely treated as built-in safeguards to hold the adult safely aloof from all that which is other. The exceptional cases where the principles of childhood animism are allowed to figure in the experience of the adult are only there to catch out the unwary: those who are insufficiently sophisticated, insufficiently adult. This is something like the literary equivalent of the empowered white male gaze, which was discussed in an earlier chapter. Unlike the child, whose misapprehensions are temporarily indulged, those adult others who are still persuaded by the child's naive identifications will be at least implicitly stigmatized: they will be marked out from the 'norm', typically by demeaning reference to their race, their class or their gender.

A brief example of each will clarify the point. Dorfman and Mattelart's classic Marxist study, *How to Read Donald Duck: Imperialist Ideology in the Disney Comic*, exposes the racist assumption behind those comics that the 'savages' of the Third World will be easily taken in by a duck-populated narrative which is pitched at the mental level of the young Western child. Wally Olins, in the example cited earlier, refers to an amused acceptance and perpetuation of the class stereotype of the thick construction site worker who cannot get beyond the simplistic narratives of the tabloid press or Disney.[6] And on the question of gender, Ursula Le Guin has drawn particular attention to the stigmatization of childhood values in relation to questions of narrative. In the introduction to *Buffalo Gals*, a recent collection of her animal stories, she writes:

> Critical terror of Kiddilit is common. People to whom sophistication is a positive intellectual value shun anything 'written for children'; if you want to clear the room of derrideans, mention Beatrix Potter without sneering. With the agreed exception of *Alice in Wonderland*, books for children are to be mentioned only dismissively or jocosely by the adult male critic. ... In literature as in 'real life', women, children, and animals are the obscure matter upon which Civilization erects itself, phallologically.[7]

Apart from the slighting reference to Derrida, which I will challenge a little later, this is very much to the point. The aesthetic and the political dimensions of the power to discriminate are not easily separated. Le Guin's stereotypical 'adult male critic' is distinguished by the sophisticated pleasure he is able to take in his recognition that the only worthwhile animal stories are the ones which are not really for children. These are the stories in which things are not as they seem, where surface appearances are deceptive, and where irony and metaphor abound. They are the stories in which the only good animal, one might say, is the one that is not *really* an animal at all.

Le Guin suggests that it is precisely this denial of the animal, this edgy avoidance of embarrassment, of contamination, which the talking-animal story has the potential to subvert. It is this insight – the idea that somehow, in narrative, the animal might be a spanner in the workings and self-identifications of the dominant culture – which the present chapter is concerned to explore and elaborate.

Tensions in the text

Even within the bounds of contemporary Western culture, the talking-animal story has many different forms, different purposes and different audiences. Some stories are manifestly subversive in intention; others appear to be quite the opposite. Initially, in the descriptions that follow, these differences will be overlooked. In particular, the temptation to distinguish between the human–animal interactions characteristic of children's stories and those found in adult narratives will be resisted. The point of this deliberately naive approach is to work towards the location of certain tensions, certain awkwardnesses, which may be present throughout the genre. If the talking-animal story can indeed be considered unsettling in and of itself, its power to perturb needs to be evident in some form in even the most conservative examples. Nevertheless, even with the knowledge of this objective, those who are easily embarrassed by the prospect of Rupert Bear stories and the like being discussed *as though we might learn something from them* may find that a certain grim determination is called for if they are to suppress for the moment their desire to leave Ursula Le Guin's proverbial room.

Two tales of Noah's Ark

In 'The stowaway', the chapter which opens Julian Barnes's novel *A History of the World in* $10\frac{1}{2}$ *Chapters*, the 'true' or inside story of Noah's Ark is revealed. It is told in retrospect by one of 'the humble, the discreet, the disregarded yet sensible *anobium domesticum*' – the stowed-away woodworm – which had been unwittingly taken on board by one of the ship's carpenters. And unlike this woodworm's medieval descendents, who are put on trial in a later chapter for infesting the leg of a throne used by Hugo, Bishop of Besançon (the collapse of which throne led to the bishop's fall, injury, and subsequent imbecility) and who are eloquently defended in a *plaidoyer des insectes* where the counsel attempts 'to make my speaking tongue do service for their silent tongue' – unlike those poor dumb insects, the Ark's secretive narrator has no problem speaking up for itself and for the whole of the Ark's non-human inhabitants.

The woodworm reports a solidarity among the various non-human species, and a shared contempt for the greed of Noah and his family, for whom 'we were just a floating cafeteria'. The family's voracious appetite had accounted for the demise of everything from the behemoth (salted, on account of its size) to the unicorn (casseroled). The reader is told, for instance, of Noah's reaction to the moulting of the pair of Arctic plovers:

> As soon as he saw the plovers turning white, he decided that they were sickening, and in tender consideration for the rest of the ship's health he had them boiled with a little seaweed on the side. He was an ignorant man in many respects, and certainly no ornithologist. We got up a petition and explained certain things to him about moulting and what-have-you. Eventually he seemed to take it in. But that was the Arctic plover gone.[8]

There are certain features here which sophisticated readers, well-versed in the conventions which allow for the playful or ironic deployment of the talking-animal genre, are not supposed to be troubled by – if indeed they notice them at all. To spell them out is to engage in a deliberate or even perverse refusal to suspend disbelief, at least for a moment. The problem is not that the narrator is supposedly a woodworm: readers' collective eagerness for a good story will generally let them pass unconcerned over the precise identity or status of the storyteller. Instead, it is *within* the story that difficulties arise once the fanciful reader steps back from the narrative flow. The animals 'got up a petition'. What would this have involved? The various species were evidently able to compose, or at least to sign, a document in a language which they all shared and which even Noah – for all his doltishness – was able to read and eventually to take in. Which of them (not the stowaway woodworm, clearly) handed the petition to Noah, and was Noah taken aback by this? What size was the woodworm's writing instrument, and how did it hold it? And so on, and so on. The whole incident glossed over in the five-word phrase 'we got up a petition' might in fact present a fitting challenge to the apprentice book illustrator.

By a considerable coincidence, the narrative convergence of Noah's Ark, extinct species, and the disruptive effect of an excessive appetite is to be found in another story, contemporaneous with Barnes's, where the illustrator's role is very much to the fore. The story involves Rupert Bear, the tiresomely well-behaved creature whose adventures have been chronicled in cartoon-strip form in the pages of the *Daily Express* since the 1920s, and in the famed *Rupert Annuals* since the 1930s. This particular adventure is called 'Rupert and Terry's Return', and is from the 1989 annual. The unlikely starting point for the story – told as ever in the cloying couplets which accompany every frame – is Terry the baby pterodactyl's rapid depletion of the village of Nutwood's supply of sardines. As the closing couplet of the earlier story in which Terry was discovered puts it:

He tried spaghetti, crisps and beans
But all he likes are tinned sardines.

Now, however, as Nutwood's resident birds are too scared by Terry to play with him,

All he can do is hang around
And gorge on sardines by the pound.

Rupert's friend the Wise Old Goat suggests that the only kind solution is to use his History Clock to transport the bored pterodactyl back to its own age. Rupert must go first, of course, to check that the clock is set to the right era.

Waking, after his time travel, Rupert finds himself on the deck of Noah's Ark. The scene is thus set, more acutely than almost anywhere else in the bear's adventures, for some searching questions about the nature of his identity. When Noah appears, quite as bumbling as in Julian Barnes's version, his first question to Rupert is 'Where's the other bear?' (fig. 21). Evading the question, Rupert initially manages to sidetrack him into a conversation about pterodactyls and dragons. It is only with the arrival of Noah's son Japheth that things take an ominous turn: 'Father dear! You know we don't let the animals out here! This bear should be in with the others'. Rupert has little choice but to make an uncharacteristically clear declaration of his ambiguous identity: 'B-but I'm not that sort of bear!'.[9]

A voice asks, "Where's the other bear?
On my Ark there must be a pair."

21 Transported to the deck of Noah's Ark, Rupert Bear encounters a befuddled Noah, who for some unaccountable reason takes him to be a bear. Beyond the secure bourgeois surroundings of Nutwood village life, it seems that even the most obvious of comic-book conventions can no longer be quite relied on. From the 1989 *Rupert Annual*, p.82.

There can be no clear ruling on what this declaration means. It c⟨_⟩ be taken to mean that he's not a real bear but a toy, a teddybear: it has been observed that in Mary Tourtel's earliest Rupert stories from the early 1920s 'there are lines on the head which might indicate the joins where a toy's head is sewn together'. There are clear arguments against such a view; perhaps most obviously, that on the occasions when Rupert's adventures are neither with humans nor with his animal 'chums' but with things that are clearly toys, those toys are depicted on a consistently smaller scale than Rupert himself. Alternatively, his declaration could be taken to mean that he is somehow, fundamentally, a boy rather than a bear, whose bear-form is little more than a convenient device enabling him to communicate with animals, thus giving a far freer rein to the storyteller. Certainly, a number of commentators have noted an increasing humanization of the faces, expressions and actions of Rupert and his animal friends over the years, but there is no possibility of these characters being confused visually with the humans in the stories.[10]

The undecidability of Rupert's identity is compounded by the fact that it has been entrusted to a variety of people in the course of his history: up to 1935 the official *Daily Express* stories and drawings were principally by Mary Tourtel; from then until his recent death it was Alfred Bestall who was most closely associated with Rupert in the public mind; and many of the most recent stories (including 'Rupert and Terry's Return') have been written by James Henderson and drawn by John Harrold.[11] Despite the discontinuities such changes inevitably involve, one of the shared if only occasional themes running through the different writers' storylines is this: *animals can be threatening*, and threatening to whatever sort of bear it is that Rupert is. Both Tourtel and Bestall had stories in which Rupert was attacked by wolves, for instance, and on occasion even dogs would suffice; as one couplet from the 1973 *Rupert Annual* puts it:

'Woof, woof!' How frightened Rupert feels,
To find a rough dog at his heels.

And on Noah's Ark (see fig. 22), despite the fact that he is not in any imminent danger, it is clear that he is distressed by the very animalness of the 'jolly crowded zoo' into which he finds himself packed by the condescending Japheth:

RUPERT QUITS THE ARK

"Now back you go with all the rest,"
The boy says. "Folk like me know best."

Thinks Rupert, "I'm not staying here.
The time has come to disappear!"

"Well," Rupert says. "That wasn't long!
But I'm afraid the time was wrong."

"Still, Noah helped more than he knew.
Something he said gave me a clue."

This Japheth really is an unpleasantly bossy youth. "Now don't argue," he snaps. "Can't think what gets into you animals. Remember, folk like me know best!" And he bundles Rupert into what looks like a zoo, a jolly crowded zoo! Something bangs on Rupert's chest. Of course! The Returner. And plainly now's the time to use it. At once Rupert presses the button. He feels a buzzy sensation, then the drowsiness. The cries of amazement around him fade away . . .

"Thank goodness, you're safe!" The first voice Rupert hears when he opens his eyes again is the Professor's. He's back in the Wise Old Goat's castle. He doesn't seem to have been gone for any time at all. "Whew!" he gasps. "That wasn't long!" "Well, what did you find?" clamour his old friends excitely. How they groan when they hear that the History Clock only goes back to Noah and the Flood. "But," Rupert grins, "Noah said something that's given me an idea!"

22 Rupert gets a brief taste of how it feels to be treated like an animal, and decides he's having none of it. Fortunately the science fiction technology is at hand to rescue him from the threat of a severe identity crisis in this 'jolly crowded zoo'. From the 1989 *Rupert Annual*, p.84.

Thinks Rupert, 'I'm not staying here.
The time has come to disappear!'

He wastes no time in returning to the present, and to the altogether less threatening animal presence of the Wise Old Goat.

The difference the image makes

The most obvious basis for discussing the relation of these two Noah's Ark episodes, and the role of the animals in them, might be thought to lie in a comparison either of their very different intended readerships or of the relative self-consciousness of their telling. I want instead to focus on an even more glaring difference: the difference it makes that one is an illustrated narrative and the other is not.

In *Animaux en cases*, the only authoritative survey of animal comic strips (including *Rupert*) to date, Thierry Groensteen argues that in contrast to literature and even film, 'it is ... in the *bande dessinée* that animal fiction has found its chosen territory'. He goes on to claim that while there are inevitably some difficulties in constituting contemporary animal comic strips as a unified or coherent field of inquiry, 'it is easier to understand why animals have proliferated at this time in the *bande dessinée*. The *bande dessinée animalière* has seen this expansion because it is situated at the confluence of two traditions: that of children's literature on the one hand and that of satire and fable on the other'. The particular advantage of the genre lies precisely in its adaptability and its slipperiness. In neither its childhood strand nor its satirical strand is it bound by the 'rules' of orderly, rational narrative. Since its examples are linked by little more than the fact that 'animals figure in them', it is, Groensteen suggests, almost an 'anti-genre'.[12]

It may be that Groensteen overstates the cultural importance of this anti-genre – though in Britain, in contrast to much of Europe and even America, it is certainly generally underestimated. Nevertheless, there is good reason to concentrate on the *bande dessinée animalière* in searching for evidence of animals' disruptiveness in narrative. As the Noah's Ark examples showed, while the verbal narrative can to some extent glide over the surface of its own inconsistencies, the visual imaging of an animal character has always to deal with the stubborn ineradicable trace of its animal identity.

In pursuit of the meanings of whiteness

How is Rupert's distinctively ambiguous identity – a bear, but 'not that sort of bear!' – established visually? The answer, though not altogether clear in the regular black and white drawings in the *Daily Express* nor in the two black and white reproductions from the 1989 annual shown here, but which is taken for granted by readers of the annuals and other full-colour versions of Rupert's adventures, is that Rupert's hands and face are not coloured in. The visible parts of his body, in other words, are simply *left white*. The same technique is used in the depiction of most of Rupert's established animal friends.

Before considering the significance of this, a little more description of the evidence will be helpful. In the top two frames of figure 22, showing the inside of Noah's Ark, Japheth's skin is given a suitable flesh tone and the various animals are all shown in their naturalistic colours. Apart from the aura of light around Rupert as he begins to disappear in the second frame, his head, hands and feet are the only sections left pure white in either frame. In the two frames below, however, where Rupert has returned to the Wise Old Goat's workroom, things are rather different because the Goat – another Nutwood regular – is also shown with hands and head left white. The pictorial logic of these last two frames therefore seems to be as follows. The Professor, although a regular character, is given a flesh-coloured skin like all humans in these stories; Rupert and the Goat, as explained, have their distinctive white features; but Terry the pterodactyl, as no more than a temporary visitor to Nutwood (at the end of the story he's packed off to China with the Pekinese dog Pong-Ping's pet dragon), is given a passably authentic pterodactyl colour.

What then does whiteness signify here? The few readily available published writings on Rupert have little to say on this question. For more detailed and attentive readings it is necessary to search out *Nutwood*, the journal of the somewhat secretive association called The Followers of Rupert. Founded by Tony Shuker in 1983, this slim publication considers such things as the printing processes used for the early annuals, the artistic merits of the latest stories, and inconsistencies in the depiction or description of aspects of Nutwood life. It also monitors the standard of the Rupert industry's merchandise – everything from duvets to porcelain to bendy toys – and rails against the modern world whenever Rupert is represented satirically in the mass media, or when the question of racism in some early stories is raised yet again by interfering do-gooders.

Since a major part of the journal's purpose is the surveillance and policing of Rupert's image, it is not surprising that the problem of whiteness is openly addressed in its pages. It was in fact only with the publication of the first full-colour annual in 1940 that the whiteness of Rupert's features was established beyond doubt as a characteristic of the stories (though even in Mary Tourtel's days Rupert's face was free of any shading or modelling in the daily drawings). The question of whiteness is more often raised in *Nutwood*, however, in relation to what was apparently regarded – by those to whom these things matter – as a highly controversial change to Alfred Bestall's cover painting for the 1973 *Rupert Annual*. Part of a letter from W.O.G. Lofts, one of the most dedicated Rupert scholars, will give a flavour both of this extraordinary journal's style and of its treatment of this particular question:

> My mental image of Rupert has always been that of a *white* bear. It was with some surprise, therefore, that I learned from Alfred Bestall that he was so annoyed that Rupert was portrayed with a white face on the cover of the 1973 Annual that he refused to do any more cover paintings. It was true that in previous years Rupert had been shown with a brown face and this broke with tradition, but in my opinion millions of readers have probably assumed that he was a white bear by reading his adventures in the *Daily Express*. After all, white bears do exist – polar bears – and in any case, Rupert is fantasy. He acts like a boy, so why the need to make him a real bear? ... When in late 1974 I saw the new *Rupert Annual* with the hairy brown face on the cover, I was dismayed. A small niece to whom I later presented the book, on seeing the cover exclaimed: 'That's not Rupert, is it, Uncle Bill?'. I think most Followers would agree.[13]

Be that as it may, an article in the same issue of the journal meticulously tracing family relationships among Nutwood residents describes Rupert's Uncles Grizzly and Polar (who seldom appear) as 'exotic' and 'far-flung', so the idea that Rupert *himself* is some kind of polar bear does not seem a plausible way forward.

Where Lofts's frantic reasoning clearly *is* right, however, is in his belief that Rupert's identity is inextricably bound up with his whiteness. But what neither Lofts nor any other contributor to *Nutwood* appears to have acknowledged is the operation of the graphic device of whiteness as a means of making distinctions and maintaining order within the Rupert narratives. In Rupert's diverse iconic forms outside the stories – the enamel badge, the bendy toy, and so on – this is of no concern. It is only within the more complex narrative settings that this unremarked detail becomes both significant and potentially obtrusive. Glancing at a typical *Rupert Annual*, it is the whiteness of Rupert, of his animal chums (Bill Badger, Algy Pug, Edward Trunk and others), and of a few select adult animals like the Wise Old Goat and Rupert's parents, which appears to work as the visual marker by which they are collectively distinguished from the various human characters – like the Professor – who share their narrative space. What the Noah's Ark episode clarifies, however, is that those creatures which might for want of a better term be called *proper* animals are in fact depicted naturalistically, so whiteness is not the marker of animality at all. Instead it marks out all those – the central characters, after all – who are in-between, neither human nor properly animal: the clothed and upstanding misfits who populate the stories so apparently 'naturally'.

The question remains as to why whiteness should be the signifier of this interstitial state. More than anything else, it seems to signal the narrators' failure of nerve. (The term *narrators* is used here for convenience, but it must encompass the collective responsibility of the numerous story writers, couplet writers, illustrators and colourists who have worked on Rupert's adventures.) This whiteness – or better in this context, this *blankness* – may be taken to represent the narrators' continuing refusal to commit themselves as to the precise form of Rupert's identity. And while it thus seems conveniently to fudge the problem of how to depict a bear who is a boy who is a bear who is 'not that sort of bear', the tiny expanse of blankness that is Rupert's face serves in turn to create its own graphic problems and interpretive anxieties. *Nutwood* reports two small but telling examples. When Mary Tourtel's eyesight began to fade in the early 1930s, one of the illustrators drafted in to work on the Rupert drawings reported the greatest difficulty 'in placing that wretched dot of an eye in the right place'. And Lofts, again, is frustrated in his attempt at a naturalistic resolution of the same dilemma:

> The question of Rupert's eyes always mystified me. True, a bear's eyes, like an elephant's, are small compared with the rest of his body, but I always thought that something more elaborate than a dot would have made Rupert more human.[14]

The desire for Rupert to be more human, or the insistence that he is 'really' a boy rather than a bear, is found throughout the Rupert literature, and is all of a piece with the explicit claim by several commentators that as children (and even sometimes as adults) they *identified* with him. Whiteness's connotations of cleanliness, of course, are entirely consistent with the propriety of identity – an identity characterized and rendered secure primarily by its avoidance of animality. In contrast, *l'impropre*, that which is neither clean nor of the self, is precisely the property of the classification-threatening interstitial animal; it is also encountered, in Julia Kristeva's words, in those 'fragile states where man wanders in the territories of the *animal*'. Even the purity of whiteness seems a slim defence against the dangers of that kind of uncertainty.[15]

There is of course the possibility of another, rather literal, reading of Rupert's whiteness. In much the same way that the 'scandalous point' has recently been made 'that Mickey Mouse is black; indeed, a minstrel performer', Rupert's whiteness *could* be read as the apt outward sign of the white middle-class values which he epitomizes. For many Rupert enthusiasts and 'Followers', we may feel, these dominant values will appear as transparent and as natural as Rupert's skin colour. To question the natural is to be unwarrantably political: Tony Shuker thus quite consistently gave the title 'Political animals' to the *Nutwood* editorial in which he denounced the Inner London Education Authority for complaining of racist elements in some of the old Rupert stories.[16]

An attention to the iconographic is important here, for there are significant discrepancies between word and image in relation to matters of race in these stories. George Perry's book on Rupert remarks that a 'problem that often arises is the changed modern attitude to matters of race', since it is clearly no longer acceptable to refer, as for example certain pre-war stories had done, to a troupe of 'nigger minstrels' giving a beach concert at the seaside.[17] In fact, however, there is scant evidence of this 'changed modern attitude' in the Rupert stories currently available. In the late 1980s Express Newspapers published a facsimile edition of *More Adventures of Rupert*, the second Rupert annual, which initially appeared in 1937. It includes one story which both depicts and describes 'a jolly nigger minstrel who is playing on the front'. In 1989 the same story reappeared in an issue of *Rupert Fun*, a publication which recycles and 'modernizes' stories from the older Rupert annuals by replacing the traditional rhyming couplets with speech balloons inside each frame. There is no open reference to nigger minstrels in the rescripted version, of course, but the image itself is iconographically unchanged. The black-faced white-lipped character wearing a boater, white gloves, striped blazer and flannels, a banjo tucked beneath one arm, obligingly points the way exactly as he had done in 1937.[18] Rupert's whiteness, it seems, continues to operate in condescending contrast to the image of a servile blackness.

Denying the animal

The matter of Rupert's whiteness has been dealt with at such length only because it may serve as the basis for a more general interpretive model of a disruptive animality. Across the range of the critical literature on the talking-animal story, there recurs a fascinating and perplexing motif. It is the assertion that in these stories the animal, and most particularly the *pictorial image of the animal*, does not signify 'animal' at all. Instead, it is treated as the transparent signifier of something quite different.

In the Rupert literature, the motif takes the form of the widely-held view that the central character is not really a bear at all – merely an ordinary boy who happens to have a bear's facial features. If that trace of animality signifies anything at all, it is the childhood *innocence* of the stories.

In the case of Bruno Bettelheim's psychoanalytical study of fairy tales, *The Uses of Enchantment*, the animal characters in the tales are again presented as not really being animals in any meaningful sense – they are merely there to facilitate, for example, the child's coming to terms with its own sexuality. The wolf is the girl's father in the story of Little Red Riding Hood; it is 'a projection of the child's badness' in that of the Three Little Pigs. The 'animal-groom' cycle of fairy tales, which includes stories such as Beauty and the Beast, operates 'by making animal existence a chrysalis from which a most attractive person emerges', and by giving the child 'the strength to realize that his fears are the creations of his anxious sexual fantasies'. Animal presence is consistently explained away; the animal is the appropriate medium for these messages solely because, in Bettelheim's words, 'children have a natural affinity to animals'.[19]

Dorfman and Mattelart's *How to Read Donald Duck* also operates this double standard – on the one hand locating the animal as a source of natural innocence, and on the other refusing to grant it any significance.

They write that 'it is, of course, true that children tend to identify with the playful, instinctive nature of animals', but that the Disney industry's cynical construction of 'a facade of innocence' founded on the 'animal-like traits' of the characters is in fact a 'perversion of the true nature of animals'. A perversion of the true nature of animals? This high-minded regard for the 'truth' of the animal is short-lived. They berate Disney for the fact that 'once the little readers are caught within the pages of the comic, the doors close behind them. The animals become transformed, under the same zoological *form* and the same smiling mask, into monstrous human beings'.[20] Having established this as their contention, they are then able to proceed for almost the entirety of their analysis to ignore the persistent animal appearance of Donald Duck and the others. Their concern is solely with human relations; the animal is really the child, or rather the narcissistic middle-class adult's fantasy of the child. *How to Read Donald Duck* is indeed about the *reading* of narratives: appearances are simply overlooked. The visual, at least in so far as it concerns the animal, does not signify.

Of these three examples, it is only Bettelheim's book which does not have the pictorial image of animal characters as its main object of study. Nevertheless, he is just as concerned to *avoid* coming to terms with the pictorial image as are the writers on Rupert and Donald Duck. He explicitly proscribes the illustrated fairy tale: 'illustrations are distracting rather than helpful'; 'pictures divert from the learning process'; 'the illustrated story is robbed of much content of personal meaning'. In contrast to the diversity of a child's interpretation of some creature encountered in the text, the animal or half-human monster 'as painted by the artist in a particular way' may have 'nothing of importance to tell us'.[21]

Culturally and politically, it would be difficult to find much to link the views of Shuker, of Bettelheim, and of Dorfman and Mattelart beyond their common concern to deny or to displace the animal. What might explain the force of this taboo? Could it be that they have themselves glimpsed that insight of Le Guin's: that something in the structure of the talking-animal story makes it inherently subversive of patriarchal culture? If so, their particular concern to avoid the image of the animal is easily understood, for it is that image rather than the text which carries the constant and undeniable trace of a character's animality.

It must be emphasized that this critical displacement of animal content does not appear to be motivated by the conviction – and it would be an entirely justifiable conviction – that the meanings of any particular animal representation will be arbitrarily constructed, and will by no means necessarily be 'literal'. Instead, quite wrongly, the displacement has the effect of ruling out one whole area of potential meanings by assuming that whatever else they may have to do with, the meanings prompted by these representations are *not* to do with animals.

The notion that talking-animal narratives are not really about animals – that the worthwhile ones, at least, must surely be about something more important than mere animals – is quite consistent with the far wider cultural trivialization and marginalization of the animal. The animal content of literary, artistic and other cultural productions is seldom regarded as a serious or proper field of inquiry, and all those coffee-table volumes on 'Animals in Art' do little to counter such a view. It is probably in deference to this received wisdom that Groensteen felt obliged to concede that the *bande dessinée animalière* could probably only really be called an anti-genre. Genre or not, its workings deserve to be more fully understood.

A supplement to the text

In a rather obvious sense, the illustrated image of the animal character might be regarded as supplementary to the main narrative of the talking-animal story – a mere optional extra, as it were. The knowledge that these stories can take forms other than those of the *bande dessinée* or the animated film, that plenty of the stories have no illustrations at all, and that many of them have their historical origin in a long-established oral tradition, would seem to support the idea that the pictorial image plays, at best, a supplementary role in this tradition. I want to contradict this common-sense assumption, but to do so without abandoning the notion of supplementarity itself.

In her mocking comment about 'derrideans', Ursula Le Guin in fact does Jacques Derrida a great disservice in suggesting that his approach to cultural and textual analysis would dismiss out of hand the serious study of texts which have been marginalized by the dominant culture. The opposite would be nearer the truth. Whether the object of his attention has been a single philosophical work or, say, a 'text'in the much looser sense of any system of cultural representation, he has usually set out to demonstrate that deconstruction is always already at work in the text – that the text is unwittingly engaged in the undoing of its own dominant assumptions. The concept of the supplement is among the most useful of the various strategies which he has exploited for this purpose. Its effect is to throw into question the self-containment of the text and its meanings.

Derrida's double-edged sense of the word *supplement* has often been explained by reference to the example of a supplement to a multi-volume dictionary. Such a dictionary will have been generally considered to be a complete work in itself, but as soon as the first supplement is produced, the self-containment of the work is no longer assured. In one sense the supplement is outside the original work, a later addition to it. But in another, of course, its new words and definitions are an essential and integral part of the revised totality of the dictionary. The supplement exposes a lack or a gap in the completeness of the original, a gap which it purports to fill. Nevertheless, once that original incompleteness has been pointed to by the existence of the supplement, there must remain an awareness of other potential gaps which other later supplements could only provisionally fill. The notion of a complete text, secure in its regulation of its own meanings, has been jeopardized for good by the worrisome effect of the supplement.[22]

My proposal here is that the visual image of the animal, however minimal or superficial the degree of its 'animality', invariably works as a Derridean supplement to the narrative. It is apparently exterior to that narrative, but it disturbs the logic and consistency of the whole. It has the effect of *bringing to light* the disruptive potential of the story's animal content. It limits the extent to which the narrative can patrol and control its own boundaries.

The example by means of which this proposal will be considered is Art Spiegelman's book *Maus*. This may seem a far remove from the Rupert stories, but they have one highly significant thing in common: in both cases the nominal animality of the central characters has been generally regarded as being restricted to their facial features. These animal 'masks' serve either as an enjoyable or else as a useful graphic device for making more palatable a narrative which is essentially about *human* values and identities. Or so the story goes.

Mice, masks, and the metaphor that cannot hold

Maus was published in the United States in 1986 and in Britain a year later. Subtitled *A Survivor's Tale*, the book is Spiegelman's account of his father's harrowing experiences as a Polish Jew from the mid-1930s up to 1944. Each of the book's six chapters opens with Art visiting his father Vladek at his home in Rego Park, New York, and getting him to recall episodes from his years in Europe. The chapters follow Vladek through his early romances and marriage to Anja in the period immediately before they became aware of the Nazi threat, up to the point where they pass through the gates of Auschwitz in the winter of 1944. As many readers will be aware, there are two highly distinctive features to *Maus*. One is that it is told entirely through a comic-strip format. The second and more striking feature is that the panels of this comic strip are 'peopled' entirely with animals; with Art, Vladek and many of the other main characters taking the form of mice. Or, to be more precise, in exactly the way that Rupert may be described as a bear *simply because* he is depicted with a 'sort of' bear's head on a generally human body, Art Spiegelman depicts himself and his father with the sketchily drawn heads of mice stuck on to their otherwise entirely human bodies.

Although widely admired, the book has attracted criticism on a number of grounds. It has been said that the style of presentation is not in good taste, and is perhaps even offensive. Further, the book's adventurous style has been accused of having 'more to do with the cultural ambitions of comics than with the Holocaust'. Spiegelman has been seen as trivializing the Jewish experience of fascism by his mode of presentation – the Holocaust is 'reduced to' a comic strip. It has also been suggested that to portray social or racial groupings in animal form is inherently insulting, and unwittingly lends credence to fascist views on racial superiority. Despite the considerable importance and complexity of this final objection in particular, these criticisms are not to be the focus of attention here.

Instead, the main questions to be addressed in what follows are these. On the one hand, why should Spiegelman choose to depict his real human characters, himself included, with animal characteristics? And on the other, what can be learned from the iconographic disorder that this animal imagery occasionally creates within the logic of his story? The book's only direct clue to the *why* question is in its epigraph, a statement by Hitler: 'The Jews are undoubtedly a race, but they are not human.' Sympathetic reviewers, following a hint on the book's dustjacket, have also offered variants on the idea that the animal imagery creates a 'radical defamiliarization of a kind of story that has been told so often during the past forty years that it requires the shock of the new to keep it fresh in our memories and imaginations'.[23] The point, however, is that this imagery, like Rupert's whiteness, is not neutral. It has its own narrative consequences. And this is where the questions of *why* and *to what effect* come together.

Let us begin, therefore, to read *Maus* not for its historical but for its animal content: to read it against the grain, as it were, and to see what emerges from such a reading. In the early part of the book all the characters appear to take the form of mice. There are in fact two exceptions, easily overlooked, where non-speaking background figures who are irrelevant to the story appear as animals other than mice. These aside, it is not until page 27 in the second chapter that pigs are introduced into the plot: as uniformed Polish police. Pigs? Police? The reader will probably be inclined to make the obvious connection in terms of American colloquial speech, but it does look rather a gratuitous visual gibe in a story where all the other characters seem to be mice. After all, turning over to page 28 where these police enter the apartment of a mouse seamstress, a tailor's dummy is seen in the corner of the apartment with a head which is unambiguously mouse-shaped. This looks as clear a sign as any that within the visual conventions of this story a body with a mouse-shaped head is simply an *ordinary* body.

It is only later – with the appearance first of a smiling pig nurse, then of some vaguely cat-like German soldiers in swastika armbands, and then of a quite exceptional frame of a café dance in Czechoslovakia featuring mice, pigs, cats, rabbits and what I think is meant to be a toad – that we begin to grasp that the various animal species are meant to stand for different human nationalities, or races, or other significant identity-groupings. The basic operative distinctions, as is fairly clear by the third chapter, are that the mice stand for Jews, the cats for the Nazis, and the pigs for non-Jewish Poles. The pig/police connection was presumably just a hiccup, an accident, though one that in its own small way has impeded the intelligibility of the early part of the story. The cultural cliché which looks most relevant to the book as a whole is that of the game of cat and mouse, the Jewish victim tossed from one prison camp to the next by the Nazi persecutor, with plenty of opportunity for unimaginative commentators to get in facetious quips about this not being Tom and Jerry. It is altogether less clear how the Poles fit in as pigs. As one reviewer complained in the face of this unsatisfactorily partial logic, 'however you look at it, drawing Poles as pigs is basically an ethnic insult'.[24]

Returning to the question of 'ordinary' bodies, there are more general consequences to depicting humans in semi-animal form or vice versa. Exactly as with Rupert, there is a rather obvious inconsistency in showing a character with an animal head but with human hands, but since these are typically kept at some distance by an intervening stretch of clothing, this much-used pictorial convention will seldom seem problematic. The smallest expanse of naked flesh other than head and hands, however, may invite the reader to focus directly on the awkward conjunction of these bodily parts. *Maus* is full of such instances: Vladek as a prisoner bathing naked in the river; Anja sponging herself in a tin bath while on the run; Art sitting on his bed dressed only in his Y-fronts; or even Vladek studying Art's palm and saying 'Like you, Artie, my hands were always very delicate'.[25]

The earliest of these disconcerting instances has Vladek at home in Rego Park, pedalling his exercise bicycle, while Art talks to him about the book he's proposing to draw. One frame shows a close-up: Vladek grips the handlebars, his shirtsleeves rolled up to the elbow to reveal his concentration camp number tattooed on his thoroughly human left forearm. In the background Art's mouse-shaped head is visible. I take it that this is a quite deliberate move: the artist-narrator acknowledging, in passing, his conscious use of the convention, and refusing to pass it off as 'natural' in the way that the Rupert stories might.

This is something of a high-risk strategy, for it can easily be misjudged and allow the reader to look *too* closely, breaking the narrative flow entirely. Later in the same episode, still on his exercise bike, Vladek recalls that in his youth 'People always told me I looked just like Rudolph Valentino' (fig. 23). Not only is this a direct invitation to study Vladek's features in detail, but there too, for purposes of comparison, is a convenient back-projection of a Valentino film poster, with Valentino also as a mouse, his mouse-heroine expiring languorously in his arms! This, the reader may feel, is really too much. We may not know what the 'real' Vladek looks like, but we do have an idea what Valentino looks like, and Spiegelman will be hard pressed to pass that mouse off as any kind of an image of him.

23 Art's father Vladek, at home in New York, recalls with some nostalgia his life in Poland in the mid-1930s. Valentino's view on the matter of their alleged resemblance is not recorded. A frame from Art Spiegelman's *Maus* which puts more strain than intended on the story's unspoken animal metaphor.

It is not immediately clear how this kind of 'jarring' effect is to be understood. Some implicit boundary seems to have been overstepped, so that the standard explanation that the effect is unproblematic within the flexible and essentially arbitrary conventions of the comic book is no longer quite convincing enough. It may be that a good deal depends on the notion of a certain generality – on something like the narrators' refusal-to-commit-themselves which was noted in relation to Rupert. Readers will be quite prepared to go along with the obviously non-literal so long as things are held within certain bounds of generality: the indirect report of speaking animals on Barnes's Ark; the absence of detail or colour or modelling in Rupert's features; the overall sketchiness of Spiegelman's mice. It is a strategy devised to minimize the risk of giving 'wrong information'.[26]

Is it therefore the case that the strange hybrid creatures of *Maus* and the Rupert stories can *only* convince us if we are not forced to look at them, to think about them, too closely? This sounds feasible, but as a generalization it does not stand much scrutiny, as an example from an historical period more enamoured of graphic detail will demonstrate. It is from the work of Charles Henry Bennett, who worked in Britain in the 1850s and 1860s on periodicals such as *The Illustrated London News*, *The Cornhill Magazine* and *Punch*, alongside other illustrators and caricaturists like John Tenniel, Richard Doyle, John Leech and 'Phiz'. Historically Bennett has been judged something of a minor figure in this company; he has been described, for instance, as a man 'whose comic invention usually outstripped his drawing ability'.[27] None the less, he had already gained a wide popularity with his magazine work by the time his first book was published in 1857. This was *The Fables of Aesop and Others Translated into Human Nature*.

The book's engravings show none of the stylistic coyness of Spiegelman and of Rupert's illustrators. The direct human relevance of these beast-fables is signalled clearly in a vignette on the title page. A high-collared and bewhiskered Victorian gazes with some alarm into his dressing table mirror where he is met by the reflection of a wolf, as sharp-featured *and sharply drawn* as the man himself. This kind of graphic doubling of identity is in fact something Bennett seems particularly to have relished. In his illustration to the fable of 'The ass in a lion's skin' (fig. 24), the visual contradictions of the disguise are certainly not disguised from the viewer. The ass's head, his lion's-head mask, and his otherwise human frame clad in the uniform of a Guards

24 'The Ass in a Lion's Skin'; or, how to stay cool in the face of being unmasked. An exemplary image from Charles Henry Bennett's 1857 *The Fables of Aesop and Others Translated into Human Nature*, illustrating something rather more complex than the stated moral: 'It is not the cocked hat that makes the Warrior'.

officer are each drawn with equal attention to detail. And while the human moral may have more to do with the dangers of trying to pass oneself off as a Guards officer or whatever, it is clear enough to the viewer that it is the revelation of the ass's true *animal* identity which offends the lion who is seen entering the room. The animals' human frames and uniforms might as well be invisible; and yet, of course, it is the human frames they have in common which permit the ambiguity of the moral in the first place, and which allow the lion's-head mask to pass as a total disguise.

In tales such as those described in this chapter, even the flimsiest disguise may be taken to be total. Much of the viewer's or reader's pleasure in such stories comes from the playful relation of seeing and not seeing – of realizing but choosing to disregard – the thin-ness or preposterousness of these disguises. This would appear to be as true of prose as it is of visual imagery. There's a passage in Kenneth Grahame's *The Wind in the Willows* where Toad, having disguised himself as a 'washerwoman', begs a lift on a barge and ends up (through his rash claim never to be so happy 'as when I've got both arms in the wash-tub') having no option but to struggle with a tubful of the barge owner's dirty washing. When eventually she openly laughs at Toad's manifest ignorance of laundry skills, he comes clean: ' "Washerwoman indeed! I would have you know that I am a Toad, a very well-known, respected, distinguished Toad!." ' Only at this point, having been *told* Toad's true identity, is she able to *see* it: 'The woman moved nearer to him and peered under his bonnet keenly and closely. "Why, so you are!" she cried. "Well, I never! a horrid, nasty, crawly Toad!" '.[28] The reader is invited to enjoy a doubly visual joke, since the barge owner had simultaneously seen and not-seen through Toad's disguise. She had spotted from the start that he wasn't a washerwoman, but to discover that he was an *animal* she had needed to peer 'keenly and closely'.

This kind of playful failure to see through disguises is also found in *Maus*, where the pictorial disguising of identity takes some peculiarly complex twists. In an interview given shortly before the book's publication in the United States, Spiegelman described his characters' animal heads as 'masks' or 'mask-like'. He referred specifically to certain episodes where identities are doubly masked (see fig. 25), and insisted that these showed the characters' animalization to be a metaphor which inevitably broke down from time to time:

There's a point where my father's travelling from a prisoner of war camp, sneaking across the border to his own part of Poland, the Poles feeling rather antipathic towards the Germans, although they also bore no love t'the Jews. My father never mentioned he was Jewish, he was just wearing a Polish army uniform and said he'd escaped from a prisoner of war camp and was trying to sneak back and some Poles helped him. Now in my comic book if I did that straight I would have been in a bind in that the Pole pig looking at the mouse in uniform would be aware that he was a

25 Spiegelman on his deliberate doubling of identities: 'Now in my comic book if I did that straight I would have been in a bind in that the Pole pig looking at the mouse in uniform would be aware that he was a mouse. So I had my father wearing a pig mask, that's a mask on top of a mask . . .'.

mouse. So I had my father wearing a pig mask, that's a mask on top of a mask, and it's obviously there as a way of calling attention to the fact that this metaphor can't hold.[29]

The metaphor cannot hold, and yet that metaphor is at the heart of the story and of the identities with which it is concerned. In one sense of course it is outside the story: the story is about people, not animals; the animal 'masks' are a mere conceit, as the viewers' privileged glimpse of the string holding the second mask in place makes clear. But it is inside the story too: inscribed in its title, evident in every frame, the whole basis of what makes this story of the Holocaust distinct from all the others. This animal 'metaphor' is a supplement in the full Derridean sense of the word, always already pointing to the fact that word and image are at work against each other.

The fact that Spiegelman deliberately puts the metaphor under strain does not mean that he is in full control of it. The written text of *Maus* is silent on the matter of its characters' animal look, but Spiegelman is given little choice but to address it directly in every published interview on the project. The metaphor's use becomes ever more wary and self-conscious. In an early chapter of the recent sequel, *Maus II*, it begins to look as though Spiegelman would rather be rid of it entirely. He draws himself no longer with a mouse's head, but with a stubble-chinned human head which is only partially covered by a tied-on mouse mask.[30] But as soon as he starts to 'shuck' the metaphor in one place, it appears in another: it has now insinuated itself in the dialogue, with characters beginning to quiz each other about their animal status, to which they were previously blind.

It was never going to be possible to sustain animal-ness as a metaphor which is somehow innocent – free of meanings and consequences for the identity and propriety of both the characters and the text. This is not only because the mice in *Maus* are periodically made to say things like 'I want to be treated like a human being'. As with Rupert, it's the confrontation with 'real' animals which provokes the greatest threat to the believability (the invisibility, the 'naturalness') of *Maus*'s principal characters. At one point Vladek and Anja are confined in a friend's dark cellar for several days while hiding from the Nazis. One night Anja calls out 'Aieee! Th-there are *rats* down here!'. Vladek, lying through his teeth to calm her down, says 'Those aren't rats ... They're just *mice*!'. It is fairly clear that Spiegelman relished the rich ironies in this little exchange.[31] But as so often, the image exceeds the artist's intention: the rat he draws in the foreground of the frame where Vladek is comforting Anja – its teeth and claws exposed – is as ugly and vicious a stereotype of rat-ness as one would be likely to find anywhere. Far from pointing to the essentially human status of the main characters, the image simultaneously highlights their interstitiality and reveals a malevolence in the metaphor.

The 'animal' is thus seen to be a thoroughly threatening category: in *Maus* as in the Rupert stories, the intrusion of this category not only upsets the consistency of these fragile narratives but also throws their main (animal) characters into a state of panic or terror. The characters admit to a fear of the animal as though on behalf of the writers. The disruptive work of the animal exposes the innocence of the metaphor in all its fraudulence. For when animal characters are substituted for humans (as in *Maus*) or when they constitute the ordinary players in a narrative (as with Rupert), it is the 'real' animals – the rat in the cellar, the animals on the Ark – which the narrative treats as anomalous beings, and not the hybrid humans. When Rupert protests 'B-but I'm not that sort of bear!', he displays or recognizes in himself a horror of the *inferiority* of animals and of animal identity: a horror which haunts the Rupert stories, however seldom it may surface.

Two kinds of pleasure?

Far from evoking the pleasure taken in animals, the evidence of these narratives seems close to putting the animal back into the realm of hatred and horror. A case has been made, certainly, that the animal can confound the priorities and propriety of the narrative which houses it, but this is not quite in the spirit of Ursula Le Guin's conception of a world in which one might 'mention Beatrix Potter without sneering' or being sneered at.

It would be unfortunate, however, if the preceding inspection of the Rupert stories in particular was taken as a simple attempt to strip them of their power to please. Pleasures are not so easily regulated or denied. The decision to take Rupert as key example, in preference to some Beatrix Potter or Walt Disney character, is itself the result of a continuing personal fascination with this imagery – a fascination which has its origin precisely in 'liking' the look of it. It has been suggested with regard to such pleasures that the power of cultural hegemony is seen most clearly in its ability to operate 'as the process whereby we not only consent to forms of domination which we know, rationally and politically, are "wrong", but even *enjoy* them'.[32] This idea is important because it is all too easy, especially from any position on the political left, to condemn or dismiss such enjoyment as nothing more than a form of false consciousness.

Some recent theoretical writings on pleasure have taken as their point of departure Roland Barthes's *The Pleasure of the Text*, the book which distinguishes two kinds of pleasure, *plaisir* and *jouissance*, in the experience of narratives. Barthes characterizes *plaisir* as the typical response to the easily-followed plots of the nineteenth-century realist novel, for example, where readers need not attend too closely to the text. If the mood so takes them, they can 'skip certain passages (anticipated as "boring") in order to get more quickly to the warmer parts of the anecdote'. He sees it as an essentially bourgeois, comfortable form of enjoyment: a 'readerly' pleasure. In contrast, *jouissance* (usually but rather inadequately translated as 'bliss') is described as 'writerly'. It is a more intensely personal pleasure, a more politically radical pleasure. It involves working with the text, paying close attention to its every move, to its complexities and ambiguities. Such work 'unsettles the reader's historical, cultural, psychological assumptions'. In the *texte de jouissance*, 'language is in pieces, and culture is in pieces'.[33]

Understandably enough, when such a model is considered in relation to the 'politicizing' of pleasure, it has been *jouissance* which has looked the only acceptable goal. It offers the ideal of a personal investment in the deconstruction of what Barthes had called 'the reactionary darkness'. *Plaisir*, in its wider cultural forms, tends to be presented in the politics-of-pleasure writings as the ignorant public's wholesale acceptance of the commodification of pleasure under capitalism.[34]

This is highly problematic when it comes to the question of animals, however. What many people experience as a conscious pleasure in the consumption of animal representations – reading a Beatrix Potter story to their child, watching a wildlife documentary on television, or simply admiring the fine profile of their dog or cat – will be denounced as inauthentic, worthless experience. The theoretical model, at least in its cruder formulations, does not allow for the possibility that *plaisir* might be experienced as real and satisfying pleasure. But in the case of animals, most people's sympathy for them and pleasurable experience of them is grounded entirely in these 'inauthentic' representations. The sources of more radical forms of human pleasure which would do animals themselves no harm are few and far between. The keen satisfaction experienced in learning of the success of a raid on an animal research laboratory, for instance, is likely to remain marginal to the culture as a whole; so too are the satisfactions of the kind of mischievous (though hardly radical) reading of the talking-animal story which has been practised in this chapter.

The question remains as to whether the image of the animal, this dangerous supplement to the text, can evoke its irreverent *pleasures* – as opposed to simply doing its disruptive work – even in those texts of 'reactionary darkness' which are usually read for the comforting warmth of their anecdotes. It seems entirely possible, and it has much to do with the routine conventions of the talking-animal story. A brief inspection of one such convention will show this. Across the range of animal fiction, the animals who stand upright are invariably the clothed ones. 'Four legs good, two legs bad', chant the sheep in Orwell's *Animal Farm*, as the slogan of the animals' solidarity once the farmer has been ignobly ejected. Later in the book, of course, it is the sight of Napoleon and the other pigs emerging shakily from the farmhouse on their hind legs and *dressed in the farmer's clothes* which turns the other animals' pride to horror. But the same phenomenon, the same transformation, is itself the source of the simple visual pleasures in other less 'demanding' texts.

Consider for example Jean de Brunhoff's popular book *The Story of Babar*, which charts the little elephant's progress from the Great Forest to the town and back again.[35] By page 10 of the book, still depicted on all fours, Babar has entered the town and stands in the street admiring the townsfolk: 'What lovely clothes they have got! I wish I could have some too!'. By page 13 he has entered one of the town's *grands magasins*, still on all fours, and is enjoying repeatedly riding up and down in the lift until the lift-boy loses patience with him and directs him towards the shop-walker to make his purchases. It's worth emphasizing that Babar is clearly no innocent abroad: he admires and craves human clothes and motorcars from the moment he sees them; he can communicate unproblematically with the humans he meets; and he has no difficulty handling the concept of the money which a rich old lady ('who understood little elephants') gives him. Despite all this, it is not until we turn from the lift sequence on page 13 to the clothes department on pages 14 to 15 that we first see a clothed Babar, who not only stands upright (as he will for the remainder of the book) but whose whole body shape is changed considerably by his new green suit.

The Story of Babar is perhaps unusual for the openness with which it displays and apparently delights in its improbable visual transformations. Having set himself up with a natty wardrobe, Babar was so 'satisfied with his appearance that he paid a visit to the photographer'. And there on the next page is the photograph: a three-quarter view, presumably so that his trunk won't obscure the view of his new winged collar and bow-tie. In a later scene (fig. 26) – with all the cool complacency of Charles Henry Bennett's unmasked ass in his Guards uniform – Babar leans on the mantelpiece in evening dress and regales the guests with tales of his former life as a real elephant! The transformation is almost a complete one. Driven out of the Great Forest in the first place by the hunter who shot his mother, it is as though Babar has here taken on the mantle of the arrogant yarn-spinning hunter or colonizer himself – and this even before his return to the forest to become king of the elephants, those simple elephants who are so easily dazzled by Babar's fancy clothes and car and human ways.

It may not be possible to redeem this story from its reactionary darkness, but whatever we may feel about its colonialist and speciesist assumptions, its playful graphic transpositions and ironies are likely to be regarded as a source of visual pleasure in the animal body. More to the point, the graphic forms of its joking may not be so far removed from those that prevail in the glorious tradition of the avenging cartoon animal, and which prompt altogether more malicious pleasures.

The pig's, rat's, penguin's and monkey's revenge

It goes without saying that talking animals lead thoroughly humanized lives. This is why they wear clothes, why they drive or ride in cars, why they eat the food they do ('spaghetti, crisps and beans' in *Rupert*, cakes in the tea-shop in *Babar*, even bacon for breakfast in *The Wind in the Willows*) – and why, of course, they sometimes fear animals. Unlike these gentle examples, however, the delicious irony of 'vengeance' cartoons is that they so often exploit precisely those same mundane signs of human-ness in order to turn the tables on the society which so readily marginalizes them. The havoc and violence they un-

In the evenings, after dinner, he told the old lady's friends all about his life in the Great Forest.

26 An after-dinner speaker with a difference: the worldly Babar treats his listeners to the story of his former life as a real elephant. His complacent stance and their rapt attention add a certain twist to the problem of deciding who's exploiting whom. From Jean de Brunhoff's *The Story of Babar*, p.23.

leash might be regarded as anthropomorphism at its least objectionable.

Within the conventions of the genre, animals' ability to read usually follows quite naturally from their ability to talk, and this is often an ideal site for an unsettling *renversement* of anthropocentric priorities. It is not restricted to cartoons, of course. In *Dirty Beasts*, one of Roald Dahl's books of illustrated comic verses for children, there is a rhyme called 'The pig'. It is the extensive reading of this 'wonderfully clever pig', we are led to understand, which enables him finally to grasp the meaning of his life:

> They want my bacon slice by slice
> To sell at a tremendous price!
> They want my tender juicy chops
> To put in all the butchers' shops!'[36]

And so on, through the list of his edible porcine potential. Without spoiling the ending for readers who do not already know it, they can be assured that the pig evades his fate in a most satisfying fashion. Almost equally satisfying is Quentin Blake's principal illustration to the piece. It shows the pig, unclothed but standing upright, in his study late at night, the deskful of books and notes in front of him illuminated by a single table lamp, as the sudden realization of the fate awaiting him – but perhaps also the glimmer of an idea of how he might take his revenge – begins to show in his taut features.

The well-read pig's grudge against humanity is a logical enough one, but the avenging animal really comes into its own when its delight is prompted by a pure and arbitrary spite – a spite which matches the mindlessness of human violence to animals. My own favourite example on the theme of reading is by Ptiluc, a French artist well known for a series of *bandes dessinées* featuring a cast of rats. This particular example is a single cartoon showing three rats on a rubbish heap, turning the pages of a discarded copy of Camus's novel *The Plague*. They are laughing so much that they are almost reduced to tears (fig. 27).

In Britain in recent years it has probably been Steve Bell's daily 'If . . .' cartoon strip which has developed the notion of the avenging animal most fully. Bell's marauding animals are neither conventional heroes nor even the central characters of the strip. Instead they weave in and out of his social and political satires, always getting the better of

27 An uncaptioned cartoon from Ptiluc's 1987 collection *Faces de rat*. Readers who are particularly taken with this spirited image may wish to head directly for the shop opposite the Louvre which sells a range of T-shirts emblazoned with Ptiluc cartoons, including this one.

humans, and often getting the last word. It is a reversal of the usual form of advocacy associated with animals, where, as in the *plaidoyer des insectes* described by Julian Barnes or the practices of contemporary animal rights organizations, we attempt to speak on behalf of – we *represent* – the animals themselves. Here instead the source of our pleasure comes from the fact that the animals represent us, they do our bidding, they take our revenge for us. This 'us' is very close to Ursula Le Guin's conception of the audience for the talking-animal story: women, children, 'unruly men', and – if they could only understand – animals too. It is all those constituencies, in other words, with something to gain from seeing the values of the dominant culture undermined. In Bell's work it is exactly right to say that the animal represents the unruly.

Few of his characters are more unruly than Raymond the yuppie rat. In the late 1980s the image of the striped-shirted Wall-Street-style yuppie came to serve Bell as the icon of much of what he loathed in the deeply right-wing values of the time. His stereotypical and identically-dressed (human) yuppie couple, Carl and Carla, spot Raymond the rat one morning while out driving their Porsche: 'Carl, dworling, look! A jogging rat!! How aspirational!!' Lured by the bribe of a great deal of cheese, the rat agrees to take up residence in their fashionable and minimally-furnished London Docklands apartment, where they regard him as their pet rat and he sees himself as their lifestyle consultant. Enthusiastically latching on to their values but respecting neither their rules nor their boundaries, he takes the place over in style; on their return home from work in the City one day, Carla shrieks to Carl above the noise of the booming stereo: 'Dworling – the rat is playing abominably loud Acid Hice music and sitting in my personal Bauhaus chair!!' Our pleasure in the discomfort of these appalling people is immeasurable.[37]

Such pleasures are only increased, of course, when the victim of the unruliness is not a mere stereotype but a living individual, and one whose association with the values of the time could not be closer. The episode in question is a slightly older one, but it shows Steve Bell at his most vindictive. It is from the summer of 1987, when to the despair of the British left and doubtless many others, Margaret Thatcher had just begun her third successive term as prime minister. She was Bell's (and Bell's readers') *bête noire*. There was little choice but to bring out the avenging animals in force.

The central players are John the monkey and Prudence the penguin, along with various other penguins and a couple of giant pandas.[38] Forced out of their squalid high-rise London flat by an exorbitant rent increase which will clear the way for a yuppie takeover of the building, they hijack a dustcart but are not sure what to do next. In line with the prevailing spirit of privatization, Prudence suggests that they 'opt out of the sewerage system' and instead 'all go and crap on Margaret Thatcher!!'. Anticipating timorous readers' qualms, John the monkey complains that such a course of action would be nothing but 'infantile anarcho-leftist gesture politics', but having got that small objection out of the way they speed off in the dustcart towards 10 Downing Street. John gets past the policemen at the door by pretending to be an upper-class twit from the Peckham Young Conservatives who has brought a consignment of cuddly soft toys (the penguins and pandas) as a present for the prime minister. Without further ado they are in.

The scene is thus set for the key frame of the episode (fig. 28) – Prudence jumps on to Margaret Thatcher's coiffured hair and promptly defecates all over it, John gets the whole thing on video, and the two of them make good their escape. The important thing here is not the infantile gesture itself but the fact that the animals get away with the *image* of it. From all points of view it seems to be the monkey's actions rather than the penguin's which call for the closest attention. Like the earlier examples of the reading pig and the reading rats, it is the monkey which turns its distinctly anthropomorphic accomplishments (operating a video) against the human characters. A clue in the dialogue also points to the monkey as the more disruptive influence on events. 'Where did that monkey with a video camera come from??' demands Denis Thatcher, irresistibly calling to mind the question asked of the man in the macintosh in Joyce's *Ulysses*: 'Where the deuce did he pop out of?'. This character of Joyce's – whose identity and whose significance are elusive – turns up in the text of *Ulysses* at unexpected moments to disturb the other characters and upset the progress of the narrative; the parallel with the unruly animal's role in the talking-animal story is striking.[39]

In terms of animal representations it is again the monkey's action which is the more significant, as all the participants are aware. The final frame of the episode has the prime minister looking in a mirror in horror: 'But what about my *image*?? That monkey had a *video*!! It's not going to *look good*!!' What the monkey has achieved here is quite simply the reversal of the empowered gaze. This exceptional episode shows the animal slipping out of its stereotypical role as 'the represented', the objectified other, fixed and distanced by the controlling look of the empowered human, and instead exploiting the flexibility of the narrative space to turn that look back upon the humans, rendering *them* 'other', dismantling their secure sense of a superior identity by attending to that fragile identity's investment in – and fear of – the visual.[40]

This is a more optimistic note on which to close the chapter. The satisfaction which Steve Bell offered his readers in this absurd little story may have achieved little if anything in direct political terms – it

28 In the image-conscious 1980s, for an image-conscious politician, there can have been few greater threats than that of an avenging animal using a video camera to treacherous effect. The first two frames from Steve Bell's 'If...' strip, *Guardian*, 8 July 1987, p.35.

was never intended as more than a venting of frustration – but it does lend further credence to Ursula Le Guin's views about the animal in narrative. The animal story's invitation to pleasure is invariably an invitation to a subversive pleasure. It is the simple fact that everyone, including quite young children, knows that animals don't really talk which prompts such genuine delight in the anomalous convention of the talking animal. As the foregoing examples have shown, this is far from being entirely dependent on either the politics of the narrator or the age and sophistication of the intended audience. And as the various forms of *illustrated* narrative have shown particularly clearly, it is the very instability of the anthropomorphized animal's identity which can make contact or even proximity with it so hazardous for those with an overblown sense of their own importance, power and identity.

Notes

1 Ursula K. Le Guin, *Buffalo Gals and Other Animal Presences* (London: Victor Gollancz, 1990), p.10.

2 Wally Olins, *The Corporate Personality: An Inquiry into the Nature of Corporate Identity* (London: Design Council, 1978), p.77.

3 Wally Olins related this story in the course of his paper 'The invention of tradition at Bovis', read at Middlesex Polytechnic on 7 February 1989. For general evidence of the ubiquity of animals in contemporary corporate imagery, see Paul Ibou (ed.), *Famous Animal Symbols*, vol. 1 (Zandhoven: Interecho Press, 1991).

4 See the *Daily Express*, 8 April 1991, p.1; and Valerie Porter, *Animal Rescue* (Southampton: Ashford, 1989), p.1.

5 Bruno Bettelheim, The *Uses of Enchantment: The Meaning and Importance of Fairy Tales* (London: Thames & Hudson, 1976), pp.46–7.

6 In this respect the enthusiasm of Olins for the humming-bird or of Wolff for the goldfish may appear to throw their own 'sophistication' into question. It is more likely, however, to be a further example of the widespread contempt for visual imagery – the refusal to take it seriously. On the surprising centrality of this theme in Olins's own writings, see my 'Re-reading *The Corporate Personality*', *Journal of Design History*, 2, no.4 (1989), pp.275–92.

7 Ursula Le Guin, *Buffalo Gals*, p.10.

8 Julian Barnes, *A History of the World in $10\frac{1}{2}$ Chapters* (London: Jonathan Cape, 1989), p.14.

9 *Rupert: The Daily Express Annual* (London: Express Newspapers, 1988), p.83.

10 See for instance George Perry, *Rupert: A Bear's Life* (London: Michael Joseph, 1985); and Margaret Blount, 'The Rupert stories of Mary Tourtel and Alfred Bestall', chapter 11 of her *Animal Land: The Creatures of Children's Fiction* (London: Hutchinson, 1974).

11 A more complete list would need to include not only the various lesser-known story writers, illustrators, couplet writers and colourists who have worked on the annuals, but also the many others unconnected with the *Daily Express* who have

produced Rupert imagery and stories for Ladybird Books, BBC Publications, and so on.

12 Thierry Groensteen, 'Le plus grand zoo du monde', in *Animaux en cases: Une histoire critique de la bande dessinée animalière*, edited by Thierry Groensteen (Paris: Futuropolis, 1987), pp.8–10 (my translation).

13 W.O.G. Lofts, letter, in *Nutwood: The Journal of 'The Followers of Rupert'*, no.8 (1986), p.15.

14 See Basil Reynolds, 'That wretched dot of an eye', *Nutwood*, no.5 (1985), p.10; and W.O.G. Lofts, 'Childhood memories of Mary Tourtel', *Nutwood*, no.1 (1983), pp.9–10.

15 On *l'impropre*, and the idea of animality as a threat to the wholeness of human identity, see Julia Kristeva, 'Approaching abjection', translated by John Lechte, *Oxford Literary Review*, 5 (1982), passim. On the cultural antithesis of physical cleanliness and animality, see Keith Thomas, *Man and the Natural World: Changing Attitudes in England 1500–1800* (London: Allen Lane, 1983), p.38.

16 See Susan Willis, 'I want the black one: Is there a place for Afro-American culture in commodity culture?', *New Formations*, no.10 (1990), especially the closing section, 'Minstrelsy: The Disney version', pp.95–6; and Tony Shuker, 'Political animals', *Nutwood*, no.6 (1985), p.1.

17 George Perry, *Rupert: A Bear's Life*, p.141.

18 See the story 'Rupert and Dog Toby' in *Rupert Fun*, no.2 (London: Express Newspapers, 1989). The book also includes a rescripted version of a 1938 story, 'Rupert and the Ruby Ring', in which this grossly stereotyped character reappears and is euphemistically referred to as a 'performer'.

19 Bruno Bettelheim, *The Uses of Enchantment*, passim. The quotations are from pp.44, 290 and 306.

20 Ariel Dorfman and Armand Mattelart, *How to Read Donald Duck: Imperialist Ideology in the Disney Comic*, translated by David Kunzle (New York: International General, 1975), p.41.

21 Bruno Bettelheim, *The Uses of Enchantment*, pp.59–60.

22 For Derrida's own account of the logic of the supplement, see his *Of Grammatology*, translated by Gayatri C. Spivak (Baltimore: Johns Hopkins University Press, 1976). Christopher Norris's *Derrida* (London: Fontana, 1987) also comments helpfully on the concept.

23 Peter Lewis, 'Recovering the past, uncovering the present', *Stand Magazine*, 29, no.2 (1988), p.36.

24 Marek Kohn, 'Paws and whiskers', *The Listener*, 10 September 1987, p.25.

25 See Art Spiegelman, *Maus: A Survivor's Tale* (London: André Deutsch, 1987), pp.53, 148, 97 and 51 respectively.

26 This is Spiegelman's own revealing phrase. He deliberately rejected the use of a sharper graphic style for this particular project, because early experiments led him to conclude that greater detail 'banalizes the information by giving too much information and giving too much wrong information'. The comment is quoted in Joseph Witek, *Comic Books as History: The Narrative Art of Jack Jackson, Art Spiegelman, and Harvey Pekar* (Jackson: University Press of Mississippi, 1989), p.104.

27 Simon Houfe, *The Dictionary of British Book Illustrators and Caricaturists, 1800–1914* (Woodbridge, Suffolk: The Antique Collectors' Club, 1978), p.120. The brief details given here of Bennett's career are also drawn largely from Houfe's book.

28 Kenneth Grahame, *The Wind in the Willows* (London: Puffin Classics, 1987), pp.166–7. The book was first published in 1908.

29 Graham Smith, 'From Micky to Maus: Recalling the genocide through cartoon'

(an interview with Art Spiegelman), *Oral History*, 15, no.1 (1987), p.32.

30 This chapter, 'Time flies', first appeared in Britain in the comics magazine edited by Spiegelman and Francoise Mouly: *Raw: Open Wounds from the Cutting Edge of Commix*, 2, no.1 (London: Penguin, 1989). It has since been published as part of Spiegelman's *Maus II: And Here My Troubles Began* (London: André Deutsch, 1992).

31 In the interview with Graham Smith cited above, for instance, Spiegelman refers to the Nazi propaganda film *The Eternal Jew* in which a montage technique is used to link film clips of Jews in a ghetto with footage of swarming rats.

32 Colin Mercer, 'A poverty of desire: Pleasure and popular politics', in *Formations of Pleasure*, edited by the Formations Editorial Collective (London: Routledge & Kegan Paul, 1983), p.84.

33 Roland Barthes, *The Pleasure of the Text*, translated by Richard Miller (London: Jonathan Cape, 1976), passim.

34 See in particular Fredric Jameson, 'Pleasure: A political issue', the key essay in *Formations of Pleasure*. (Barthes's reference to 'reactionary darkness' is from *The Pleasure of the Text*, p.31.)

35 Jean de Brunhoff, *The Story of Babar the Little Elephant* (London: Magnet, 1985). The book's first British publication was in 1934.

36 Roald Dahl, *Dirty Beasts*, illustrated by Quentin Blake (London: Puffin, 1986), unpaginated.

37 Steve Bell's 'If...' strip appears daily in the *Guardian*. The two incidents quoted here are from 22 March 1989, p.47, and 13 November 1989, p.39.

38 The storyline to be described here ran without interruption in the *Guardian* from 29 June to 8 July 1987.

39 Frank Kermode has discussed at some length the ways in which the unpredictable appearances of the man in the macintosh serve as a 'disturbance of the surface of the narrative'. See his *The Genesis of Secrecy: On the Interpretation of Narrative* (Cambridge, Mass.: Harvard University Press, 1979), pp.49–55.

40 There is now an extensive critical literature on the idea of the look or the gaze as a strategy for the objectification, repression or domination of others. The most influential texts include Jacques Lacan's 'Of the gaze as *Objet Petit a*', in his *The Four Fundamental Concepts of Psycho-Analysis*, translated by Alan Sheridan (Harmondsworth: Penguin, 1979); the 'Panopticism' section in Michel Foucault's *Discipline and Punish: The Birth of the Prison*, translated by Alan Sheridan (London: Allen Lane, 1977); and Laura Mulvey's 1975 essay 'Visual pleasure and narrative cinema', reprinted in an abridged form in *Popular Television and Film*, edited by Tony Bennett et al. (London: BFI Publishing, 1981). My comments here, however, owe rather more to the chapter 'The Other and the eye' in Johannes Fabian's *Time and the Other: How Anthropology Makes its Object* (New York: Columbia University Press, 1983). None of these texts, it should be said, comment directly on the 'othering' of animals through representation.

Part III

Contradiction and change

5

Is it real or is it Disney?: unravelling the animal system

> ... life involves maintaining oneself between contradictions that can't be solved by analysis.
>
> William Empson

In the late 1930s William Empson set out to explore some of humanity's contradictory attitudes to animals in a novel entitled *The Royal Beasts*. It was his only work of prose fiction, and was in fact never completed. Its recent editor has described the chief protagonist of the story, a creature whose status and identity are the subject of dispute, as setting off 'a serio-comic series of reactions which disjoint the cultural presuppositions of Western man'. The story concerns the consequences of an initial encounter between the administrator of a British Crown Colony in Central Africa and a member of a tribe of whose existence he had been unaware. The administrator asks a local messenger where his unexpected visitor is from, and receives the reply: 'The terrible hairy men live up in the mountains, in the wild country; we never go near'. Despite this reference to hairy *men*, the central conceit of the fable is the fact that this obscure tribe defies convenient categorization as *either* human *or* animal. But since (for reasons too complicated to explain fully here) the visitor, named Wuzzoo, has come to see the colonial administrator as a first step towards making contact with the King of England, he becomes enmeshed in a system which insists on classifying him as either one thing or the other.

Much of the story involves teasing out the ironies of this situation; the orderly British mind cannot find an appropriate place for a highly intelligent, upright, talking creature which has a tail and is entirely covered in smooth black hair. As the governor of the Crown Colony is later to put it, 'You can't have a hybrid who's half man and half not, because neither law nor religion nor the state know where to get hold of him.' Wuzzoo is sufficiently conscious of colonial prejudices to resist having his tribe categorized as human if it is going to mean being treated as 'a lot of black men'. As the administrator explains, however, the alternative has serious disadvantages. Having voluntarily introduced itself to Western society, if the tribe now decides that it is animal it will lose (in human eyes) any claim to its land, its property, its gold mines and so on: 'if you are not men nothing belongs to you, nothing is yours'. It will also lack any legal redress when Western hunters come in search of its valuable fur. Wuzzoo is driven to the conclusion that the only safe option may be for the tribe to demand the status of Royal Beasts: to give up their independence in order to belong to the King of England not like his human subjects but 'like his horses and dogs'.[1]

Empson felt no need to spell it out, but the precariousness of this solution becomes all too clear from a very different book, Michele Brown's *The Royal Animals*. This particular contribution to the hagiography of the present British royal family demonstrates that the concept of a royal animal can extend without interruption from heraldic lions and family corgis to those creatures which various royals have hunted or shot. Brown informs her readers, for instance, with neither irony nor distaste, that 'the last royal tiger fell to Prince Philip in 1961'.[2]

Unfortunately only a tantalizing fragment survives of an episode in *The Royal Beasts* in which Wuzzoo visited London Zoo to make a speech to the British public; in it he is warned that 'if you aren't careful you will pull all the strings of popular sentiment the wrong way'. The capriciousness, inconsistency and ambivalence of human responses to animals and animality are very much the point of Empson's fable, but it is only pointing to what is already common knowledge. There is a widespread popular awareness of the ways in which society's contradictory and even hypocritical attitudes to the animal are signalled within the culture, and it would be all too easy to play this up as a major problem. Clearly, for most people, most of the time, it isn't. Empson is quite right to say that everyday life involves working around the contradictions, not resolving them. A theoretical equivalent of this practical perspective is called for: the contradictions embedded in popular attitudes need to be seen not as a matter for complaint but as evidence of how cultural understanding of the animal is structured.

Making sense of contradictions

The evidence of the previous three chapters has shown that animal images, animal symbols and of course animals themselves can evoke a bewildering variety of responses: pride and respect; hatred, contempt and fear; pleasure and affection. The present chapter asks why the apparent incompatibility of these sentiments does not generally seem to trouble the popular imagination.

Some of the most glaringly contradictory representations of the animal are of course to be found in the pages of the popular press. These generally appear to take one of two forms. The first involves the unremarked but telling juxtaposition of two items. A front page of the *Daily Star*, for instance, is given over entirely to two stories. One is a self-congratulatory piece establishing the paper's compassionate attitude to animals: it is entitled '*Star* gets action on cruel fur trappers', and includes a photograph of a 'fox in agony'. Alongside it is a gratuitously exploitative and voyeuristic piece with the headline 'Wolf boy!', about a boy from Bangladesh whose face is covered in hair as the result of a hormone deficiency. The paper claims that his own family 'will not allow him to be treated. They WANT him to look like a monster and make a FORTUNE from his hairy disfigurement'. This, the paper's main news story that day, is dominated by a large and closely framed shot of the boy's anomalous therianthropic features – a modern-day fairground attraction for the reader's delectation.[3]

To give another broadly similar example, an inside page of the *Daily Express* juxtaposes stories headlined 'Sex beast caged' and 'Shake on it, old friend'. The first concerns the return to jail of a man who had been 'freed to prey on little girls'. The second concerns 'Tripper the wonder dog', who had recently saved the life of his 'master'. This item includes a photograph of the happy pair shaking hands, so to speak, and appearing both to be smiling at the camera. In accordance with the conventions of the popular press, the dog's praiseworthy actions are automatically humanized (and its image correspondingly anthropomorphized), whereas the actions of the sex offender can only be comprehended as beastly.[4]

The alternative form is that of the single press story, which can just as easily accommodate inconsistency and contradiction, especially when the conventions of its telling operate largely independently of any boundaries between such categories as the 'real', the representa-

Lionheart James

LITTLE James Branch sits hugging a toy that tells the world of his courage.

The five-year-old is recovering from being mauled by a lion cub during a circus trip.

And yesterday, despite the bites on his back, his shoulder and his neck, he grinned and wrapped his arms forgivingly round his own cub.

His courage showed through as he met the Press and dealt quickly and coolly with their questions.

No, he wasn't frightened. No, it didn't hurt too much. And, no, he wasn't going to bother with circuses in future.

James was mauled by the cub when it broke free from its collar and lead.

His father Richard, from Maidenhead in Berkshire, is taking legal advice about the attack on Wednesday. Safety officials are also investigating the incident which happened when Gandey's Circus made its first visit to the town.

Circus manager Graham Totle was not available for comment yesterday.

29 A lesson in the public display of the animal: the real, the representational and the symbolic stood in a complex relation here as 'Lionheart James' – recently mauled by a circus lion cub – took comfort from his more reliable and photogenic toy lion and decided 'he wasn't going to bother with circuses in future'.

tional and the symbolic. The case of 'Lionheart James' (fig. 29) is typical of this kind of story. A five-year-old boy, 'mauled by a lion cub during a circus trip', is described as having displayed his courage as he 'grinned and wrapped his arms forgivingly round his own cub', a cuddly toy lion, for the benefit of press photographers. The living animal's natural ferocity, the furry toy's docility and the punning symbolism of the headline, far from being in any sense mutually exclusive, are evidently seen as contributing to the thematic coherence of this heartwarming tale. The boy's mother explained to another newspaper that 'James loves animals and he probably thought the cub would be gentle with him'.[5]

In 'Why look at animals?' John Berger quoted an earlier example of a very similar press story and commented on 'the degree of confusion' displayed in the human victim's presuppositions about animals (a lioness in that particular case). The confusion, in both cases, seems to be over *what exactly counts as animal*. Here the views of the analysts (Berger or myself) risk appearing more dictatorial and indeed more anthropocentric than the 'confused' views of those they condescendingly describe. The popular imagination, as reflected in such press stories, allows considerable leeway in such matters. In this respect it calls to mind Freud's comments on dreams and contradictions:

> The way in which dreams treat the category of contraries and contradictories is highly remarkable. It is simply disregarded. 'No' seems not to exist so far as dreams are concerned. They show a particular preference for combining contraries into a unity or for representing them as one and the same thing. [6]

This is certainly rather similar to what the media do with the animal story. It is not that there are no rules; it is rather that they are internal to their own rhetoric and make no reference to an external world, a waking reality, which more strictly regulates what may 'properly' be said or thought about animals.

In fragmentary form, at least, it is quite possible to describe these internal rules. The lion's position here may be clarified by contrasting it with that of the dog. The dogs most often seen on television – the puppy unrolling the Andrex toilet roll, the slow-motion Dulux sheepdog, the Crufts champions fed on Pedigree Chum – are a particular kind of dog. They are never rottweilers or American pit bull terriers or Japanese tosas; they are, in other words, every bit as stereotyped and 'perfect' as the people in advertisements. The image of the bad animal does not exist for advertising. It exists elsewhere in the media and in the popular imagination, of course, and was in large part responsible for the introduction of Britain's Dangerous Dogs Act in 1991. The minister responsible for the act explained the need for it with the astonishing statement 'Many are good dogs, but *there are some evil dogs*'![7]

In the popular press there has come to be a standardized iconography for the 'devil dog' and the 'hellhound'. Typically, it has the photographic image of the offending brute, jaws menacingly open, juxtaposed with (or better still, overlapping) a separate photograph of the wounded child, whose scarred back or face is clinically displayed in its full and open horror. Such explicitness would seem out of place had the wound been inflicted by a lion. Dogs may be 'evil'; lions may not. The lion is in any case more firmly secured in its stereotypical symbolic and iconic identity: in circus or zoo or Channel 4 documentary or heraldic motif, a lion is a lion is a lion. With dangerous and duplicitous dogs, on the other hand, there is no such certainty – last year it was the rottweiler, this year the pit bull terrier: by the time you read these words it could be anything.

All this is entirely familiar; it is as obvious as the fact that Tripper the wonder dog ('Shake on it, old friend') is in a quite different conceptual category to the 'devil dogs'. In the context of their representation, it could even be said that Tripper the wonder dog and Lionheart James's cuddly toy lion and their various pictorial contraries are only intelligible in so far as they conform to and perpetuate stereotypical conceptions of the animal. They are there solely to illustrate a moral, to confirm a cliché – though their relation to the reality of everyday life, of course, is signalled and secured by the 'truth' of their photographic representation.

Common sense, systematicity and the contradictory

As the opening chapter of this book suggested, the sign of the animal typically operates in the unwritten system of common-sense consciousness, of common knowledge, of stereotypes, where meanings are assumed to be self-evident. Much as with a linguistic sign, where a majority of language-users may know nothing of its etymology, its meaning will nevertheless be known to them in the sense of their knowing when and how to use it, and they will do so quite 'naturally' and unthinkingly. Similarly, in the context of its everyday use, there is no need to dwell on the sense of an animal sign – it is part of common sense, part of what everyone already knows, part of everyday reality. The readers of 'Lionheart James' already know how they are supposed to respond.

Here it will be useful to turn to Clifford Geertz's thoughtful essay on 'Common sense as a cultural system'. Commenting on the ways in which the notion of common sense is employed in various societies, he argues in favour of treating it as 'a relatively organized body of considered thought, rather than just what anyone clothed and in his right mind knows'. Like any body of knowledge, it is 'historically constructed':

> It is, in short, a cultural system, though not usually a very tightly integrated one, and it rests on the same basis that any other such system rests; the conviction by those whose possession it is of its value and validity. Here, as elsewhere, things are what you make of them.

That last sentence is perhaps the crucial one. The meanings of common sense are made, not found. They are not pre-existing meanings drawn from or reflecting or referring to a simple material reality: they are locked instead in their own systematicity. And yet this is exactly what common sense will not allow. As Geertz himself notes, 'the unspoken premise from which common sense draws its authority' is that 'it presents reality neat'.[8]

Common sense has, in its own view, something of a monopoly on reality. It is *its* meanings, *its* truths, and *its* particular conception of reality which are undeniably the most convincingly motivated and the most thoroughly naturalized.[9] This alone establishes the common-sensical as the most influential arena of meaning. It may lack the academic credentials and rigour which are popularly attributed to science or philosophy or whatever, but its great advantage over academic knowledge is that it is not constrained to be consistent – its systematicity is not compromised by inconsistencies. Geertz comments specifically on what he engagingly names the 'immethodicalness' of common sense:

> it caters at once to the pleasures of inconsistency which are so very real to any but the most scholastic of men ... and also to the equal pleasures, felt by any but the most obsessional of men, of the intractable diversity of experience ... Common-sense wisdom is shamelessly and unapologeti-

cally ad hoc. It comes in epigrams, proverbs, *obiter dicta*, jokes, anecdotes, *contes morals* – a clatter of gnomic utterances ... Whatever they are, it is not their interconsistency that recommends them but indeed virtually the opposite: 'Look before you leap', but 'He who hesitates is lost'; 'A stitch in time saves nine', but 'Seize the day'.

And so on. This emphasis on a discontinuous, gnomic, formulaic knowledge accords closely with other writers' descriptions of the commonsensical, from Berger and Luckmann's classic account (in *The Social Construction of Reality*) of how the coherence and reality of everyday life is maintained by a 'social stock of knowledge', to Roland Barthes's definition of the *doxa*, the 'reign of the stereotypes imposed by petit bourgeois culture'.[10]

The particular advantage of Geertz's version, however, is that it provides a convincing means of seeing how sense is made of the problematic *visual* examples encountered so far. That phrase 'a clatter of gnomic utterances' could hardly be improved on as a description of the popular press's abrupt juxtapositions of discontinuous and logically inconsistent representations of the animal. But these are by no means restricted to the mass media; they are to be found everywhere.

Given its symbolic complexity, it is perhaps not surprising that such representations figure prominently in the iconography of the butcher's shop, as the next two examples suggest. The first is a passage from an early Julian Barnes novel:

> The butcher wore a blue-striped apron and a straw hat with a blue ribbon round it. For the first time in years, waiting in the queue, Ann thought what a strange contrast the apron and the hat made. The boater implied the idle splash of an oar in a listless, weed-choked river; the blood-stained apron announced a life of crime, of psychopathic killing. Why had she never noticed that before? Looking at this man was like looking at a schizophrenic: civility and brutishness hustled together into a pretence of normality. And people *did* think it was normal; they weren't astonished that this man, just by standing there, could be announcing two incompatible things.[11]

The second manifestation of this perverse normality is evident in the depiction of animals themselves in this context. In some countries – certainly in Britain and France – the customer is frequently invited into the butcher's shop by the smiling image of a painted wooden cartoon pig on the pavement outside. In Britain the pig typically wears the butcher's apron, but the French ones are more varied and less coy.

30 Thankful that for the moment it's horsemeat rather than beef on special offer, but looking well prepared for a swift getaway if its fortunes change at the whim of the butcher, this cut-out cow invites customers into a *boucherie* at Bédarieux in the Midi.

173

They range from the pig as eager victim (smilingly advertising its naked self) to the pig as killer (with chef's *toque* and butcher's cleaver) and the pig as cannibal (with napkin round its neck, and knife and fork held precariously in its trotters).

I have no doubt that this basic taxonomy could be considerably extended; readers may even care to elaborate it for themselves as an instructive holiday pastime. The most extraordinary examples can be found in both countries, and will not necessarily even be pigs. By convention the animal advertizes the butcher's wares on the small blackboard it holds for this purpose (though less frequently, the information may be inscribed directly on to the animal's body). Occasionally, by this means, the symbolic animal eludes its fate by displacing its own identity. Less than a mile from where I live, the butcher's happy pig advertizes steak pies, smiling in evident relief that they are not pork pies. And outside at least one butcher's in southern France (fig. 30), it is a peculiar-looking cow which entreats customers to buy choice cuts of horsemeat. The contradictions are clear enough, but the 'common sense' of such representations needs further comment.

The disnification of the animal

The animal is the sign of all that is taken not-very-seriously in contemporary culture; the sign of that which doesn't really matter. The animal may be other things beside this, but this is certainly one of its most frequent roles in representation. Terms such as stereotyping and trivialization are a little too imprecise to describe quite what is going on here: I propose instead to speak of it as the *disnification* of the animal.

Disnification, it seems to me, is a specifically visual thing. The term may already be in use elsewhere carrying rather different connotations, though I am not aware that it is. With regard to the animal, the basic procedure of disnification is to render it stupid by rendering it visual. This is not a cheap gibe aimed simply or specifically at the image of the animal in Disney productions (at the animal's deliberate 'Disney-fication', in other words). What I have in mind has more to do with the connotations of trivialization and belittlement which are a central and intentional part of the everyday adjectival use of terms like 'Disney' and 'Mickey Mouse' – quite the contrary of what Walt Disney would have wanted.

The term disnification has further connotations: the faint echo of 'signification', for instance, is probably a productive one, since the relation of disnification to meaning is itself rather faint. Disnification is a kind of approximate obverse of signification – it has to do with meaning, but only in a rough-and-ready way (with about as much precision, in fact, as the typographic inversion of the opening letters of the one term would approximate to the other). A cynic might say that it is a process not of making sense of, so much as making-nonsense-of the animal.

The visual priorites of disnification may reflect a more general cultural drift. This is a drift which is evident, for instance, in Barthes's assertion that 'what characterizes the so-called advanced societies is that they today consume images and no longer, like those of the past, beliefs'; and in Alice Walker's lament that 'animals are forced to become for us merely "images" of what they once so beautifully expressed'.[12] Implicit in such observations is a sense that the general shift from textual to visual priorities will be characterized by a drift towards the stupid and the trivial. In very many cases the evidence of animal representation would appear to support this view.

Contradiction has an important place in this process. What I am proposing as disnification is something which in its fullest form positively embraces contradiction. There is a kind of pattern: when the animal is put into visual form, it seems somehow to incline towards the stereotypical and the stupid, to float free from the requirements of consistency or of the greater rigour that might apply in other nonvisual contexts. The image of the animal seems to operate here as a kind of visual shorthand, but a shorthand gone wrong, a shorthand whose meanings intermittently veer from or turn treacherously back upon that of the fuller form of the text.

Consider the *Daily Star*'s front-page 'Wolf boy!' story, which was referred to earlier. The brief text accompanying the headline and photograph of this young Bangladeshi boy gives no clear explanation, but it presumably seemed to many readers that he was described as a wolf boy simply because of his hairy face. Hairiness has long been popularly associated with animality, of course, and the specific tag 'wolf boy' in the present case may perhaps have stirred vague memories that far older tales of wolf children had often come from India and thereabouts. But those older stories – as the wolf-child literature listed in Bruce Chatwin's 'Shamdev: The wolf-boy' and elsewhere attests – have concerned abandoned human children who have been allegedly reared by wolves in the forest. On being returned to or discovered by human society, it has been these children's actions rather than their appearances which have seemed wolf-like.[13] What the *Daily Star* story does, however, is to employ what it presents as common-sensical, self-evident meanings (meanings which are visually self-evident, that is to say) which choose to ignore, or at any rate work quite independently of, a more complex textual or historical order of knowledge. The look is everything: it has no need to call upon a wider frame of reference, nor to assume prior knowledge on the part of the reader. It constructs and maintains its own disnified order of common sense.

This phenomenon is not restricted to the discourse of the press. A rather similar instance of the twisting of meaning in the shift from text to image concerns Freud's famous and detailed case history entitled 'From the history of an infantile neurosis', from 1918. This is the case known popularly as that of 'the Wolf-Man'. In the course of a wide-ranging essay on the historico-cultural role of the wolf, W.M.S. Russell and Claire Russell have remarked on a notable aspect of the popular perception of this case. They note that when Muriel Gardiner's book *The Wolf-Man and Sigmund Freud* (which brought together all the material relating to the case) appeared in paperback in 1973, its jacket illustration lent substance to a popular misconception about the man. What it showed was a montage of a man with a wolf's head. As the Russells explain:

> both his traditional title and the jacket picture of the Penguin edition are oddly . . . inappropriate. For the Wolf-Man was not a lycanthrope, and had no delusions of being a wolf. On the contrary, he had an extreme fear of wolves. When he was a little boy, his elder sister teased him by promising to show him the picture of a pretty little girl. When she took away the piece of paper she had used to cover the picture, the boy saw, 'instead of a pretty little girl, a wolf standing on his hind legs with his jaws wide open, about to swallow Little Red Riding Hood'.

It was the interpretation of this and of later manifestations of that fear of wolves which was the main purpose of Freud's inquiry.[14]

It would be possible, of course, to interpret the book jacket montage of the Wolf-Man quite differently: it need not necessarily be seen as a misleading mistake on the part of the designer. It is clear from Freud's account that at a number of levels the Wolf-Man may have been superimposing his fear of the image of the wolf on to his understanding of various entirely human situations. To mention only the most obvious of the human connections, Freud stresses that 'his fear of the wolf was conditional upon the creature being in an upright posture', and insists that 'the wolf he was afraid of was undoubtedly his father'.[15] From this perspective a jacket design which maps the image of a wolf's head over that of a man has a certain pictorial logic and subtlety. It should be remembered, however, that this is a privileged reading, an insider's reading: it is precisely the kind of interpretation that common-sense consciousness, or popular opinion, is likely to regard as 'too clever by half'. It is not at all in the spirit of disnification.

Disnification is common sense applied to the image of the animal. It is common sense's construction of the visual reality of the animal. And it is the condition under which we ordinarily make sense of animal representations. In suggesting that the gnomic form of the visual image invites a drift into stupidity, I am trying only to describe disnification and not to condemn it. The same applies to contradictions. For a variety of reasons, the sense of an animal image will from time to time end up working against the sense of the text it accompanies or illustrates (as in the 'Wolf boy!' and Wolf-Man examples). That the one contradicts the other is not a problem; it is a characteristic of disnification. There is no single or correct logic here, no 'path to truth' as it were.

A useful parallel might be drawn with a complaint which is sometimes levelled at those Disney films which involve the retelling of traditional fairy tales. In their pre-Disney form such tales have been characterized from a psychoanalytical perspective as open-ended and difficult narratives which are meant to allow the child 'to master developmental conflicts and therefore to grow' towards maturity. Disney, it is said, has failed to appreciate this, the 'true meaning' of these tales, and has settled instead for a trivializing and sanitized cuteness which misses out on (or sometimes even contradicts) their mythological richness and their psychological depth.[16] It is clear that in one respect these psychoanalytical readings have not grasped what the viewing public does with popular imagery. In instances such as these the public isn't aware that it's getting a thinner or a less reliable version of a story – a version that veers from the 'true meaning' of the tale. The public uses whatever versions are currently available to it, and creates its own mythologies and its own sense from these. Disnification cares nothing for 'true meaning', and it is important that its representations of the animal are approached and understood on that basis.

Why representations matter

Tim Ingold's editorial introduction to *What is an Animal?* includes a section entitled 'Culture and the human construction of animality', in which he raises important questions about our access to an imagined truth or reality of the animal through a comparison of the institutions of totemism and conservationism:

> a premise of totemic belief and cult is that it was the animals who made the world for man, who originally laid down the order and design of human social existence, and who are ultimately responsible for its continuation. The Western cult of conservation precisely inverts this premise, proclaiming that from now on it shall be man who determines the conditions of life for animals (even those still technically wild shall be 'managed'), and who shoulders the responsibility for their survival or extinction. Yet from the relativizing perspective of the anthropologist, the animals that occupy the cultic worlds of totemists and conservationists alike are creations of the human imagination. . . . what is the relationship between these 'animals in the mind' and those that actually surround us? . . . Do animals exist for us as meaningful entities only insofar as each may be thought to manifest or exemplify an ideal type constituted within the set of symbolic values making up the 'folk taxonomy' specific to our culture? [17]

This account of a hypothetical shift from a world whose meanings are made by animals (totemism) to a world whose meanings are made by humans (conservation) is enlightening because it presents those institutions as two possible orders of thought, two possible systems of representation, among others. Totemism is not dismissed as superstitious nonsense in comparison to the practical reality of present-day conservation; the two are presented as equivalent ways of making sense of animals and making sense of the world.

Conservation in fact offers a good basis for discussing the inseparability of the 'real' and the representational, for this apparently entirely practical field of endeavour may have a greater investment in the representational than it would be comfortable to admit to itself. Consider the panda (fig. 31), logo of the World Wide Fund for Nature

31 The lovable panda, totem species of the World Wide Fund for Nature, pictured here with the organization's president who some decades earlier drew a less welcome sort of world-wide attention as a result of his own tiger-shooting exploits in India.

(WWF). It has been unkindly suggested that the WWF's donation of over £1 million to the world's largest panda preserve at Wolong in China (which had succeeded in breeding only one panda in captivity in eight years, and even that one died) was motivated in part by a concern to preserve at all costs the species on which it had staked its own visual identity by choosing it to adorn the WWF letterhead – its totem animal, as it were. As W.M.S. and Claire Russell observe elsewhere, 'a totemic clan is obsessed with the need to conserve its totem species'.[18]

The ability to appropriate the living animal for symbolic or representational ends is equally evident in more off-beat varieties of modern-day totemism. Several recent guides to aspects of 'new age' thought include advice on how to locate one's totem animal, whether it be regarded as a clan totem or a personal totem. One such book proposes, for instance, that 'The clan totem is your symbol of belonging and when you work under its aegis you are directly in touch with your ancestors ... If someone has the same token as yourself, this may indicate a deep link between you'. The totemic animal is valued here, certainly, and the reader is implored to 'keep it safe', but the living animal exists here solely to confirm human meanings and identities. This is clear from the example the authors give, apparently in all seriousness, of one of the ways in which a reader might establish the identity of his or her totem animal: '... you may suddenly realize that the neighbourhood dogs have started to take a friendly interest in you and congregate when you appear in the street – could it be that a dog is your clan symbol?'.[19]

Examples like these should not be thought to constitute a perverse misinterpretation of the animal, where by means of an inexplicable inversion the representational has come to be privileged over the real. The animal is only ever knowable in mediated forms. To see animals at all is to see them *as* something – as something we have made meaningful, even if that something is only the display of our own investment in the idea of an authentic nature, a natural order of things, for which the animal is the ideal icon under the order of disnification. As Bob Mullan and Garry Marvin write in *Zoo Culture*:

> Animals quite obviously cannot and do not ... represent themselves to human viewers. It is man who defines and represents them, and he can in no sense claim to achieve a true representation of any particular animal; it merely reflects his own concerns.[20]

The shape of the animal body

That these concerns have little to do with anyone's notion of an objective reality is perhaps clearest in the field of visual representation, especially in its high-street manifestations. Here we find a world constructed in the image of popular culture's preconceptions, a photographic mirroring of a desired reality, a preposterous Athena-print world of cuddly coexistence with even the wildest of animals: 'Boy or girl plus leopard – it's what's called the "aaah" factor'.[21]

As often as not, the 'aaah' factor extends to the preferred *look* of the animal body. The notion of neoteny is now, I think, a fairly familiar one in this context, but it is perhaps worth quoting Elizabeth Lawrence's useful summary of the argument:

Neoteny refers to a condition in which there is retention of youthful characteristics in the adult form. ... No doubt unconsciously, but yet methodically, in order to satisfy our own tastes, human beings have selectively created animals which are neotenous. Shedding light on this process, ethologist Konrad Lorenz has described and diagrammed the innate releasing 'schema' for human parental care responses. He proposes that the physical configuration of a high and slightly bulging forehead, large brain case in proportion to the face, big eyes, rounded cheeks, and short, stubby limbs calls forth an adult nurturing response to such a 'lovable' object, moving people to feelings of tenderness. The same positive reactions are elicited by animals who exhibit these juvenile traits. ... Roundness is the essence of the neotenous configuration – round heads, round cheeks, short rounded limbs, and plump, rounded bodies characterize juvenile forms in both man and animals.

Lawrence notes that doll and toy manufacturers intuitively grasped this 'cuteness' principle long ago, and she also refers to Stephen Jay Gould's famous demonstration of the increasing pictorial neotenization of Mickey Mouse since that character's early appearances in the 1920s.[22]

As these examples suggest, favourable responses to the neotenous image do not distinguish between the living animal and the animal toy. In the case of the giant panda, as Mullan and Marvin neatly express it, 'much of the groundwork for this particular kind of animal shape had been done' even before the first living panda was seen in the West in 1936, because its overall shape so closely corresponded to that of the teddybear. In this sense the panda's immense popularity and its potential for invoking pleasure stems from its chance visual resemblance to a toy – a toy which is so familiar that its own loose derivation from a quite different species of bear is easily overlooked.

All this is highly relevant to the WWF panda logo (fig.31), which may be regarded as a prime example of the graphic neotenizing of an already culturally-neotenized animal. Intended as the symbol of the practical conservation of the living animal, this pleasure-inducing logo may in fact be thought both apt and uncharacteristically (if unwittingly) honest if we choose to go along with Mullan and Marvin's assessment of the essentially selfish project of conservation: 'animals are preserved solely for human benefit, because human beings have decided they want them to exist for human pleasure'.[23]

It is important to keep in mind the extent to which pleasure and 'reality' are entangled here. Access to reality in all its full pleasurable richness is mediated by representations which will guide how and what we think about the world. 'Share something magical with your baby from day one' entreats the advertisement for Disney Babies, the recent brand developed by the Disney Consumer Products Division in New York. That magical something is a Baby Mickey (or Minnie or Goofy), redrawn and remodelled in exaggeratedly infantile form – a product whose design and marketing has been aimed directly at women in their last trimester of pregnancy, and which the advertisement depicts cradled in the mother's arms alongside her new baby.[24] But if it is all too easy to mock the notion that a heightened neoteny smoothes the path to a rewarding reality in the case of Disney Babies, we should be clear that the stylized WWF panda presents us with a near-identical proposition about our relation to the animal world at large.

As I suggested at the outset, there is little point in complaining about this: it is simply how disnification seems currently to operate. Like any other cultural system, it is only answerable to itself, and its representations are fundamentally arbitrary. Once in a while it is useful to throw its representational logic into reverse in order to remind ourselves of this. Francis Masse has done so in a magnificent *bande dessinée* entitled *Les Deux du balcon*.[25] Taking Stephen Jay Gould's ideas on the neotenization of Mickey Mouse as its premise, the book includes a visit to an imaginary museum, a kind of Natural-History-of-Neoteny Museum. The exhibits include a row of trophies: they present the ridiculous spectacle of the progressive ageing and deflating of the cute ideal of

32 A less naive view of neoteny: in a story called 'Le Miquépithêque', Francis Masse presents an imaginary museum of natural history, where the logic of pictorial cuteness is revealed as having less to do with biology than with what Barthes called 'the decorative display of *what-goes-without-saying*', in which history and nature are 'confused at every turn'.

Disney's ageless neotenous mouse (fig. 32). Another room compares the neotenous and non-neotenous forms of various creatures and characters: the neotenized vulture looks more like a budgerigar; *Tintin non-néoténique* is an ugly wrinkled thug whose only remaining connection to Hergé's invention is the wisp of blond hair; and the furrowed features of the non-neotenous pig are contrasted with the idealized form of *porc néoténique* – a sausage. We might well conclude that this must be a museum without walls: it has an uncanny resemblance to the world in which we live.

Notes

1 William Empson, *The Royal Beasts and Other Works*, edited with an introduction by John Haffenden (London: Chatto & Windus, 1986). The epigraph is from p.47; other quotations are from pp.26, 134, 148, 143, and 144–5 respectively.
2 Michele Brown, *The Royal Animals* (London: W.H. Allen, 1981), p.37. Although Brown gives no hint of it, there was in fact 'world-wide outrage' at this particular incident, as John M. MacKenzie describes in his *The Empire of Nature: Hunting, Conservation and British Imperialism* (Manchester: MUP, 1988), p.310.
3 See the *Daily Star*, 11 May 1990, p.1. The press does not offer an unproblematic reflection of public opinion, of course, but neither does it operate independently of it: it must at all times maintain its popular intelligibility, after all. As Stephen Koss has cautiously argued (writing on the question of 'whether the press has ever truly mirrored public opinion' in *History Today*, September 1984, p.5): 'for want of any accessible alternative, the national press may be taken to illuminate, if not necessarily to express directly, movements in British public opinion'. At the very least, the pictorial and textual conventions of the press give an indication of the forms in which that opinion may typically find expression.
4 See the *Daily Express*, 27 May 1983, p.10.
5 See 'Lionheart James', *Today*, 29 May 1987, p.3, and 'Boy, 5, mauled by circus lion', *Star*, 28 May 1987, p.15.
6 Sigmund Freud, *The Interpretation of Dreams* (1900), in *The Standard Edition of the Complete Psychological Works of Sigmund Freud*, edited by James Strachey, vol. IV (London: Hogarth Press, 1955), p.318.
7 Quoted in Judith Williamson, 'The rhetorical forces of evil', *Guardian*, 10 October 1991, p.26.
8 Clifford Geertz, 'Common sense as a cultural system', in *Local Knowledge: Further Essays in Interpretive Anthropology* (New York: Basic Books, 1983), pp.75–6.
9 If this seems too contentious a claim, consider Michael Frayn's tongue-in-cheek demonstration of the self-conceit of the common-sense viewpoint: 'What philosophers have often claimed to be concerned with is truth. But has any philosopher ever managed to say very much that wasn't later meticulously denied by other philosophers? While you and I, going about our ordinary business, manage to speak the truth almost all the time! Or at any rate to say things which are not on the whole systematically denied by our friends and colleagues.' The passage is from Frayn's *Constructions* (London: Wildwood House, 1974), paragraph 190.

10 See Clifford Geertz, 'Common sense as a cultural system', p.90; Peter L. Berger and Thomas Luckmann, The Social Construction of Reality: A Treatise in the Sociology of Knowledge (Harmondsworth: Penguin, 1967), passim; and Roland Barthes, The Pleasure of the Text, translated by Richard Miller (London: Jonathan Cape, 1976), p.38.

11 Julian Barnes, Before She Met Me (London: Jonathan Cape, 1982), p.130.

12 See Roland Barthes, Camera Lucida: Reflections on Photography, translated by Richard Howard (London: Jonathan Cape, 1982), pp.118–19; and Alice Walker, 'Am I Blue?', in Through Other Eyes: Animal Stories by Women, edited by Irene Zahava (Freedom, California: Crossing Press, 1988), p.6.

13 See Bruce Chatwin, 'Shamdev: The wolf-boy', in What Am I Doing Here (London: Jonathan Cape, 1989), pp.233–40; Maximillian E. Novak, 'The Wild Man comes to tea', in The Wild Man Within: An Image in Western Thought from the Renaissance to Romanticism, edited by Edward Dudley and Maximillian E. Novak (Pittsburgh: University of Pittsburgh Press, 1972), pp.183–221; and 'Meeting the Other', chapter 7 of Barbara Noske's Humans and Other Animals: Beyond the Boundaries of Anthropology (London: Pluto Press, 1989). It may be, however, that the Daily Star's use of the term 'wolf boy' followed that of another tabloid paper only weeks earlier. The Sunday Sport's front-page shocker 'Evil dad dumps starving wolf boy' (22 April 1990) purported to concern a hairy-faced Mexican boy suffering from what was described as 'wolf-boy syndrome', 'one of the world's rarest genetic conditions'. While not wishing to doubt the word of such an august publication, a cursory inspection of contemporary medical dictionaries reveals no mention of the condition under that name, so it seems unlikely that this is the sense in which the public is generally familiar with the term.

14 See Sigmund Freud, 'From the history of an infantile neurosis' (1918), in The Standard Edition, vol. XVII, pp.1–122; The Wolf-Man and Sigmund Freud, edited by Muriel Gardiner (Harmondsworth: Penguin, 1973); and W.M.S. Russell and Claire Russell, 'The social biology of werewolves', in Animals in Folklore, edited by J.R. Porter and W.M.S. Russell (Cambridge: D.S. Brewer Ltd and Rowman & Littlefield, 1978), pp.143–82: the quotation is from p.179. Freud reports that the patient later discovered the frightening image to have been an illustration to the fairy tale of 'The Wolf and the Seven Little Goats'.

15 Sigmund Freud, 'From the history of an infantile neurosis', p.40.

16 See David I. Berland, 'Disney and Freud: Walt meets the Id', Journal of Popular Culture, 15, no.4 (1982), pp.93–104. At one point Berland goes so far as to say that 'Disney praises and extols what psychoanalysis would try to cure' (p.102). Robert Darnton has pointed to the extreme historical naivety of some of these psychoanalytical readings in his essay 'Peasants tell tales: The meaning of Mother Goose', in The Great Cat Massacre and Other Episodes in French Cultural History (London: Penguin, 1985).

17 Tim Ingold, 'Introduction', in What is an Animal?, edited by Tim Ingold (London: Unwin Hyman, 1988), p.12.

18 On the WWF, see Simon Long, 'Pan-Pan panders to taste of females in panda love-park', Guardian, 17 June 1991, p.22; and Rowena Webster, 'The Duke's dilemma', Sunday Express, 29 July 1990, pp.10–11. On totemism, see W.M.S. Russell and Claire Russell, 'The social biology of werewolves', p.178.

19 Caitlin and John Matthews, 'Finding your clan totem', in The Western Way: A Practical Guide to the Western Mystery Tradition, Vol. I: The Native Tradition (London: Arkana, 1985), pp.42–4. I am indebted to Ann-Marie Gallagher for bringing this and other such examples to my attention.

20 Bob Mullan and Garry Marvin, *Zoo Culture* (London: Weidenfeld & Nicolson, 1987), pp.3 and 7–8.
21 Spokesperson for Athena describing two recent additions to their range of photographic prints, on *The Art of Pleasing People*, Channel 4 Television, 15 December 1989.
22 The more recent elaboration of Lorenz's ideas on neoteny (which were first published in 1950) can be traced in the following texts: Stephen Jay Gould, 'Mickey Mouse meets Konrad Lorenz', *Natural History*, 88, no.5 (1979), pp.30–6, reprinted as 'A biological homage to Mickey Mouse' in Gould's *The Panda's Thumb: More Reflections in Natural History* (New York: Norton, 1980), pp.95–107; Elizabeth A. Lawrence, 'In the Mick of time: Reflections on Disney's ageless mouse', *Journal of Popular Culture*, 20, no.2 (1986), pp.65–72; and Bob Mullan and Garry Marvin, 'Juvenilization: Mickey Mouse and the giant panda', in *Zoo Culture*, pp.24–8. The quotation is from Lawrence's 'In the Mick of time', pp.67–8.
23 See Bob Mullan and Garry Marvin, *Zoo Culture*, p.28 (on the panda's shape) and p.157 (on conservation).
24 See Karrie Jacobs, 'Mighty Mouse', *International Design*, Special Graphics Issue, March/April 1991, pp.44–9.
25 Francis Masse, *Les Deux du balcon* (Paris: Casterman, 1985).

6

Escaping the ratking:
strategic images for animal rights

'A ratking. Do you know what that is?'

Zen shrugged.

'The king rat, I suppose. The dominant animal in the pack.'

'That's what everyone thinks. But it's not. A ratking is something that happens when too many rats live in too small a space under too much pressure. Their tails become entwined and the more they strain and stretch to free themselves the tighter grows the knot binding them, until at last it becomes a solid mass of embedded tissue. And the creature thus formed, as many as thirty rats tied together by the tail, is called a ratking. You wouldn't expect such a living contradiction to survive, would you? That's the most amazing thing of all. Most of the ratkings they find, in the plaster of old houses or beneath the floorboards of a barn, are healthy and flourishing. Evidently the creatures have evolved some way of coming to terms with their situation.'

Michael Dibdin[1]

In the preceding chapters I have tried to speak as directly as possible from within the space of our contemporary animal *mentalité*, as an active participant in the inconsistencies of its everyday operation rather than as a disinterested outsider. I have tried to adopt what could be described anthropologically as an emic rather than an etic perspective;[2] to speak of what I found around me and to try to make some sense of it as I went along rather than simply imposing the theoretical framework with which I started out. In part, at least, readers will doubtless judge that I have failed in this intention: it's probably difficult for any critical enterprise to do it entirely convincingly. I only raise the matter here because the purpose of this final chapter is somewhat different. Rather than looking at aspects of animal representation and saying 'this is how it appears to be; this is what seems to be going on', I want now to ask whether and how things might be changed – to the advantage of animals – through the constructive use of representations. At the very least, it should be possible to outline the conditions under which we might usefully speak of 'strategic images for animal rights'.

As the previous chapter has indicated, this will certainly not be easy or straightforward. Michael Dibdin's vivid description of the ratking might serve as an analogy: to try simply to tug free of the culture's constraints and stereotypes is to risk getting yet more firmly embedded in this 'living contradiction'. If the cause of animal rights can be thought of as one rat in this larger 'ratking' of our animal *mentalité*, its aim must be to tug the rest of the ratking in its own preferred direction without then being pulled back against its will. At this point the analogy may seem to falter, because unlike the rat which wants simply to escape, animal rights seeks a freedom which will allow it to work *inside* the culture, and to continue to exert its influence, its pull. To be free of the constraints and rules and influence of the ratking but powerless to change them, to be free but irrelevant and excluded, would be to have achieved nothing. But there is in any case no escaping this cultural ratking, no simple opting out of its anthropocentric priorities; any claim to have done so is an effective surrender of power, leaving one 'thereby inhabiting more naively and more strictly than ever the inside one declares one has deserted', as Derrida warns.[3] It is a classic dilemma; and if it can be resolved at all with regard to animal representations it will only be by indirect means.

I should explain that I use the term *animal rights* here in a fairly loose and inclusive sense to refer to the whole range of concerns and disparate opinions of the contemporary animal rights movement. Peter Singer, one of the principal philosophers to have influenced the thinking of that movement, has argued that the term may legitimately be used in this loose sense 'as a concession to popular rhetoric'.[4] This is important, because the legitimacy of the cause of animal rights does not in any sense stand or fall by what is judged to be the philosophical coherence of its case. To disapprove of practices such as vivisection, factory farming, fur trapping and bloodsports is not automatically to grant that ethics and moral philosophy constitute the most effective discourses for persuading others to share that disapproval. The use of the term here certainly implies no rigidly-defined 'moral' stance on my part: I would in any case prefer personally to characterize the support of animal rights as a political rather than a moral undertaking. Representations can claim an important place in that politics precisely because the animal rights movement is concerned, like an advocate, to represent the case for animals as best it can and by whatever means it can.

The chapter takes the form of four loosely-connected commentaries, each of which considers a different aspect of the problem of representation in relation to animal rights. The first sets out a series of objections, both in principle and in practice, to the superficially desirable idea of working towards the creation of a more positive image of animals. The second is a detailed analysis of media coverage of animal rights activism, which pays particular attention to the cultural image of animals which is implicit in that coverage. The third reveals alarming correspondences between the prejudices of the tabloid press and the reasoning of some academic prose on the matter of what it is permitted or not permitted to say about animals: both employ essentially the same means to deny the animal a conceptual visibility. The final commentary discusses three specific representational strategies which may be sufficiently resistant to (or subversive of) stereotyping to provoke some realignments in the cultural representation of animals, and proposes for example that even the products of the Disney industry may have a part to play in maintaining a heightened visibility for the animal.

How animals should be seen

I no longer believe, as I once did, that it is useful or even meaningful to speak of constructing a positive image of animals. A positive image (and I'm thinking here primarily of pictorial images) implies something better or more true or perhaps more beautiful than those which are currently available. It implies too that the beauty or truth of the positive image will be immediately apparent and will, in its dazzling authenticity, cut through the culture's entrenched misconceptions about the animal. It implies political ends achieved by aesthetic means; a stirring idea, perhaps, but not a particularly feasible one.

A little while ago the merchandise catalogue of one of the main British organizations campaigning for animal rights featured a set of greetings cards. The cards showed attractive photographic images of various animals in their natural habitat. They were described as 'featuring animals as they should be seen'. It was perhaps the clearest case I had encountered of something being offered as a positive image, a correct image, and it prompted me to think more carefully about my own reservations and doubts on the matter.

There are three problems with this notion of *animals as they should be seen*, and each concerns the relation of images such as these to all the other animal images already in circulation. The first concerns the question of beauty. Our culture is one in which there are now many thousands of photographic images of animals in their natural habitat, and many of these will be widely regarded as beautiful. To take just one example, there is a popular brand of French chocolate called *Merveilles du Monde*, each bar of which contains a large card printed with just such a photograph. The brand name is entirely appropriate: many of the images strike me as astonishingly beautiful. The fact that the parent company has recently been criticized for funding animal experiments[5] may or may not affect sales of the chocolate, but it does not change what those photographs look like. And if I reproduce here a photograph of this sort (fig. 33), how are most readers to judge whether it is an example of 'animals as they should be seen', or is one of the *merveilles du monde*, or else is from another source entirely? My point is simply that animal rights has no monopoly on what are likely to be regarded as the most beautiful or most positive images of animals.

The second problem is that those images regarded as positive or correct will continue to be outweighed by (or to be seen as no more significant than) the mass of less idyllic representations which are already at work in the culture. Their positivity is no guarantee of their persuasiveness. And the third problem is the word *should* when used in conjunction with animal representations. The difficulty lies not only with its dogmatism but with who happens to be saying it and why. The word itself will do nothing to ensure the well-being of the depicted animal – think only of all the recipe books whose sumptuous photographs carry captions like 'How your turkey *should* turn out: firm and ready for the table'.

Generally speaking, the reality which the positive image purports to depict is nothing more than an aestheticized and romanticized image of nature; it is reality constructed in conformity to our own aesthetic preferences. Those preferences seem most often to be for an image of the wild which evokes a lost origin – an imaginary *edenic* state of nature

33 The undecidability of the image: a beautiful photograph, perhaps, but from the image alone we can make no reliable assessment of its integrity. This particular one may seem to exemplify the idea of 'animals as they should be seen', but what is to distinguish it visually from other such photographs which may serve more cynical ends?

(in which the imagination swiftly passes over the fact that at least one animal emerged from the Eden story with a less than wholly 'positive' cultural image). A particular danger of upholding this myth of the animal in nature as a 'reality' is that the animal – as Keith Tester has controversially but rightly stated – is thus turned into a fetish object. The historical and cultural circumstances which condition our own dealings with the animal are forgotten in the face of this greater visual imperative which tells us *how animals should be seen.*[6]

There is a yet greater problem associated with bringing aesthetics into our thinking about the look of animals. Contrary to what we might expect, aesthetics seems in some way to deflect our attention from the animal and its particular circumstances.

'It shows rather unattractively at the sides'

> A closeup of the central viscera of another specimen ... Here there was only a paper towel under the animal, and it shows rather unattractively at the sides.
>
> *Handbook for Scientific Photography*[7]

The caption to a single photograph in one particular textbook on scientific photography is not in itself any basis from which to generalize, but that aesthetic concentration on a detail which was aside from the central image, the animal's body, seemed more than random. It was borne out in the main text of the book in more general terms:

> Backgrounds, if they show at all in the picture area, should usually be white. Small animals pinned to boards for dissection will present a good appearance if a piece of white card is placed on the board prior to mounting the specimen. Any shadows thrown on this background card will be rendered very light by the reflector fill, and will not be disturbing.

The animal's 'good appearance' depends here wholly on the background. Further, in the aesthetics of this particular discourse, it is not the opened body of the pinned animal which may count as a disturbing image: it is only inappropriate backgound shadows which are thought likely to interrupt the viewer's calm contemplation. The introduction of aesthetic considerations has here served to marginalize the animal. It has achieved this through the excruciating irony that when the animal body is caught in the full glare of the photographic gaze, it is only the margins of the image that are the object of aesthetic attention. The discriminating eye simply overlooks the animal.

There are other quite different circumstances in which the discriminating eye is similarly averted from the animal. Consider, for instance, what has come in our century to be regarded as that most kitsch of all subjects, *animals in art*. The many lavish coffee-table volumes devoted to the subject are viewed with disdain by the professional eye, the discriminating eye, the eye of the typical art historian. The reason is clear: the animal artist is too often concerned with the subject, the animal itself, and not with the proper and serious exercising of aesthetic discrimination. There appears to be an inverse relation between the aesthetic seriousness of the image and the viewer's interest in the animal. Athena prints and greetings cards brimming with cute images of cats exhibit and provoke a greater interest in their subject matter (despite the stereotyped form of their representation) than does the work of the few animal artists who usually escape snobbish disapproval. The general public's fascination with animal images is in this sense the sign of their lack of discrimination. The serious cannot countenance the popular, and only the popular can countenance the animal.

This inverse relation is also found in the mass media. It is the tabloid press which attends with delight to animal stories and, more particularly, to pictures of animals. The mark of the more serious papers' seriousness and discrimination is their restrained use of any images, but above all of animal images. Despite this difference, there is agreement on animals' *unseriousness*. The tabloids can pay them more attention, and even express more concern for their welfare on a day-to-day basis, because by common consent these papers may feature animals even when they're not news. The broadsheets only succumb to the animal either as light relief from serious news or when animals themselves figure in it (usually either as 'bad' animals or as badly mistreated animals). These stories get into the tabloids too, but mainly as a form of sensationalist display – too lurid by far for the discriminating eye – which is broadly equivalent to their enjoyment of animals the rest of the time.

It may be objected, of course, that these examples of the discriminating eye's avoidance of the animal have little direct bearing on the aestheticizing impulse which seeks to specify how animals 'should' be seen. This too, however, is a somewhat ignoble impulse; it seeks to pin the animal down as an image if not as an object, and to fix it under the gaze if not under the knife. But here too, one way or another, the desired truth or reality of the animal seems to elude the viewer, forever slipping out from the edge of the image. A television reviewer writes wistfully: 'Wildlife programmes have grown to become such a televisual industry that . . . you can watch more than a dozen over any seven days. All beautiful, all leaving you frustrated at the brief and distant glimpses you get, at best, of the real thing'. The glimpse is never enough to satisfy the desire for the real. Umberto Eco says much the same thing about the role of the realistic fake wild animal in Disneyland. The crucial thing is 'its obedience to the program': it is there when viewers want to see it, and it stays there. 'A real crocodile can be found in the zoo', he writes, 'and as a rule it is dozing or hiding, but Disneyland tells us that faked nature corresponds much more to our daydream demands'.[8]

Be that as it may, neither Disneyland nor the zoo will satisfy the demand for a morally or politically correct image of animals, an image of *animals as they should be seen*, of animals running free in our imaginary mythical wild. And the problem with the wildlife documentary – in some ways our closest approximation to this image – is that we can hardly know in any very meaningful way what it is that we are seeing (or rather, merely glimpsing). Tim Ingold puts it plainly: 'for the Western television viewer, observing the antics of a strange and exotic animal on his screen, he might as well be watching a work of science fiction as a nature documentary'.[9]

From all this it appears that the notion of a positive image of animals could only ever satisfy a rather selfish urge to capture and to regulate – to bring the slippery meanings of the animal image under control. It implies not only that we have a right to see animals, but that we also have a right to specify how we are to see them. In addition, it risks mistaking its own aesthetic preferences for a visual reality, whereas in visual imagery the reality of the animal can never be more than a proposal, a gesture. In each of these respects the hypothetical 'positive' image of the animal mimics regimes of looking (the vivisector's gaze, the zoo visitor's gaze) which seem to me to be antithetical to the interests of animal rights. It would replace one form of stereotyping with another, very different in intention but little different in its effects. Representation is a subtle enough concept to be used with more imagination than this.

The public image of animal rights activism

One of the ways of investigating what and how people think about animals might be to ask what rhetorics they employ when animals are at issue. Animals are seldom more at issue, as far as the media are concerned, than when the constructed common sense of our everyday ways of thinking about them is challenged by those taking it upon themselves to act *outside the law* in the name of animals. The ways in which our self-styled animal-loving society comes to terms with this challenge deserve fuller consideration than they have so far received, and these are therefore the focus of this second rather longer commentary.

In 1986 the RSPCA issued a most extraordinary and unfortunate press advertisement. Its specific claim was reasonable enough: that the RSPCA works for improvements in animal welfare within the law, and appeals for donations on that basis. But above the headline 'Our supporters prefer to use a pair of scissors' was a staged photographic close-up of a furtive balaclava-clad figure shearing through a fence with a large pair of wire cutters. The only specific allusion in the text of the advertisement to this visual stereotype of an animal rights activist was the assertion that 'cutting the coupon and sending a donation achieves far more in the end than cutting wire fences'. This too was echoed photographically, as a disembodied hand (our own) appeared at the lower edge of the advertisement obediently snipping along the coupon's dotted line. The contrast of the hands was telling. The activist held the powerful wire cutters in a tight grip, the closed hands standing metonymically for the narrow-minded bigotry attributed to the figure. In contrast we were invited to see ourselves as the RSPCA supporter, domestic scissors held in the open hand which represented our reason, our moderation and our open-mindedness.

Whatever the reason, the advertisement thus seemed to display an extraordinary bitterness towards activists who, after all, shared the RSPCA's abhorrence of cruelty to animals but chose to tackle it by different means.[10] It was almost as though these activists, and in particular the Animal Liberation Front, were seen as a greater danger than those perpetrating animal cruelty and abuse. In its imagery if not its words the advertisement's tone was uncomfortably close to one issued by the British Fur Traders Association the same year, which proposed that 'Some of the nicest people are anti-fur ... and some of the nastiest'. The nastiest people, it implied clearly enough, were the activists of the Animal Liberation Front.[11]

I describe the RSPCA image as unfortunate because its appearance in February 1986 coincided with what might almost be described as a growing hysteria in certain circles, including the media, about the dangers of animal rights activism. Only weeks earlier the *Star* had published its classic '21 things you never knew about the animal fanatics', which was set off with the obligatory photograph of a balaclava-clad head. In January the *Mail on Sunday* had devoted a front page to its 'Exclusive: Twin threats by the fanatics', which quite arbitrarily connected separate articles on the ALF and on the IRA with the headline 'Terror alerts'. Fanaticism and terror were key terms used in consolidating a conceptual criminalization of animal rights at this time. Further weight was lent to this notion by the fact that January was also the month in which the intelligence-gathering work of Scotland Yard's special animals rights squad (initially formed about a year earlier) was formalized under the title of the Animal Rights National Index (ARNI). By March Ronnie Lee and other prominent ALF members had been arrested and charged with conspiracy to commit criminal damage; at Lee's trial the following year the judge called him a 'fanatic' and a 'dangerous criminal', and spoke of his 'campaign of terror'.[12] Mid-1986 saw headlines such as 'Animal terror gang threaten Royal Family', and the broadcasting of a programme called 'Animal Warfare' in BBC 2 television's *Brass Tacks* series. When this piece of overt scare-mongering reappeared in paperback format three years later, its cover predictably featured the familiar stooping figure in black balaclava and camouflaged combat jacket, virtually indistinguishable from the figure in the RSPCA advertisement.

As a visual stereotype this ubiquitous image of the activist was a little more complex than it may sound; it demands further attention. It was an image to which, at least in certain respects, the animal rights movement consented. Leafing through publications such as *Liberator* or *Turning Point* in the mid-1980s, the reader would have found considerable photographic evidence of these figures (see fig. 34). Their identities hidden beneath hood, mask or balaclava, they conformed in the context of the animal rights press to something like an heroic Lone Ranger mythology: 'Who *was* that masked man?' It was an image to be proud of; a group of these figures, triumphantly clutching rescued animals, even appeared on a Christmas card published by one respected campaigning organization in 1985.

34 'The face of liberation' was the caption given to this photograph when it appeared on the front page of *Liberator* late in 1985. Within months, however, the national media had decided that with only a little modification such images could serve as the face of terror and fanaticism.

For the media at large, however, this same basic image had come by 1986 to carry entirely different meanings. The man (for the figure was invariably assumed to be a man) was clearly a 'bad guy', a law-breaker who would stop at nothing. When he wasn't cutting through perimeter fences he was doubtless super-gluing butcher's doors or hoaxing the innocent consumers of Mars bars. Worst of all, he was giving decent law-abiding folks like the RSPCA a bad name – it is not hard to see why they wanted to dissociate themselves from this set of meanings.

We can be more specific than this, however. The iconography may have been lifted directly from the pages of the animal rights press, but its *publicly intelligible* meanings came from elsewhere. Lacking at that time any very firmly established visual stereotype for this relatively new breed of outlaw, the media had to draw on and to adapt iconic meanings which were already entrenched in the public consciousness. Consider the following possible source of this image's meanings.

In 1984 an IRA bomb had ripped through the Grand Hotel in Brighton at the time of the Conservative Party annual conference, killing five people and maiming others. The IRA had struck at the symbolic heart of British civilization, at the government itself. The prime minister only narrowly escaped injury. In the days following, the media struggled for words which could adequately express their horror and disbelief. It was no real surprise to see the IRA described as 'rats' and as 'animals of evil'. But visually matters were handled differently. The present conventions of political caricature allow vicious therianthropic images to be applied to those one happens to oppose within the democratic framework of the society; something far more extreme was called for to depict those who had set out to destroy that democracy. No national press cartoonist depicted the bombers as animals at that time; of the four cartoons which did show the IRA in animate form, one had it as a cloaked and hooded skeleton and the other three – as readers will by now have anticipated – showed a hunched and masked figure closely resembling the subsequent photographic stereotype of the animal rights activist.[13]

In retrospect it may seem somewhat drastic to have appropriated the most extreme image of hate and fear that the press had been able to devise in recent times in order to characterize the cause of animal rights and to turn the public against it. At the time, however, the image must have seemed an ideal metonymic expression of those connotations of fanaticism and terror which large parts of the media seemed keen to pursue.

By the end of the 1980s, it must be said, things seemed to have moved on. The cover of the *Animal Warfare* paperback looked like a last gasp of that particular stereotype. The ALF was still in the news from time to time, for instance over the firebombing of various department stores in 1988, but other quite different things were gaining publicity. The anti-fur organization Lynx had been formed in 1985, for example, and quite quickly established a high level of public awareness and support. It did so not least through its sometimes controversial poster campaigns (the first of these, with the caption 'It takes up to 40 dumb animals to make a fur coat. But only one to wear it' is the one which has lodged in the public memory), through its uncompromising cinema commercials, and through its effective marketing of a range of fashionable merchandise (such as the 'Roar of disapproval' designer T-shirts which first appeared in 1986). By January 1989 Lynx had its own shop in Covent Garden.

The later 1980s was a period in which these kinds of activities became more important to a number of the established British animal rights organizations, as indeed they did for People for the Ethical Treatment of Animals (PETA) in the United States. Animal welfare groups were also making active use of the media: the RSPCA launched an extensive and highly effective media campaign for dog registration (see fig. 35), which persuaded a majority of the public if not of the politicians. Hooded liberators could still be found in the iconography of *Arkangel*, the magazine launched in 1989 by Ronnie Lee (from prison) and Vivien Smith, but they were much less in evidence elsewhere in the newly image-conscious animal rights magazines.

Attitudes in the British national press were also shifting, or so it seemed. Some of the causes of animal rights were taken on board with enthusiasm, whether as part of a fashionably 'green' consciousness or – as an earlier chapter mentioned – as another outlet for the thinly-veiled xenophobia of some of the tabloids. The audacity of the volte-face was sometimes astonishing. The paper which in 1986 had trumpeted the '21 things you never knew about the animal fanatics' was by 1990 giving over a double-page spread to congratulate itself on the 'Top Tory backing for *Star*'s animal crusades'![14] Actions such as the poisoned Mars bars hoax or the Hunt Retribution Squad's attempt to disinter the coffin of the fox-hunting Duke of Beaufort (both in 1984),

This doggy bag contains a dead doggy.

Thousands of them go to the incinerator every week.

The dogs are healthy but unwanted.

If they can't be placed, local vets, the RSPCA and other animal charities are forced to put them down.

When the Government killed the dog licence they left us to kill the dogs.

Urge your MP to press for a dog registration scheme.

For it is a sick nation that kills healthy dogs. **RSPCA**

Registration, not extermination.

35 First used in February 1989, this was one of the advertisements in the RSPCA's sustained campaign for a national dog registration scheme. The understated power of the image owes much to the fact that the body of the dog, like its unnecessary death and its imminent incineration, can only be pictured in the viewer's imagination.

which had once so excited the sensation-hungry imagination of the British public, now seemed very distant memories indeed.

The June 1990 bombings: Identity and representation

In his 1989 book *Animal Revolution* the respected and eminently respectable campaigner Richard Ryder writes of the ALF that 'public sympathy for the Front continues to be widespread in Britain'.[15] He offers no specific evidence for this, but the statement is a striking one because it is so utterly at odds with the impression given throughout the media – and here it must be remembered that ALF activity is something which much of the public knows of *only* through media coverage. The media had become keen enough to reflect back to the public the merits of saving elephants and whales, of buying cruelty-free products, and even of returning performing dolphins to the wild,[16] but the ALF was a different matter altogether.

This became clearer than ever in the reporting of the two bombings in June 1990 which were attributed to the ALF, in one of which a very young child was badly injured. This was almost certainly the first occasion on which anyone had been seriously injured in Britain or elsewhere as a result of an action taken (or at least apparently taken) in the name of animal rights.[17] It understandably provoked an unwaveringly hostile reaction. In reviewing the reporting of this highly contentious subject, I have chosen to focus solely on its coverage in the national press rather than the broadcast media for the simple reason that the newspapers are more readily available to other researchers who might wish to interpret the same material differently. My purpose is not to comment on the bombings themselves, let alone on their 'morality' or lack of it, but rather to concentrate on *what was made of them*. What happened in the process of the reporting revealed a great deal about how we are invited to think about animals, and also about the obstacles faced in any attempt to shift those patterns of thought.

It is not really possible to separate description from interpretation, but I will try to offer a brief and relatively uncontentious summary of the reporting before considering some of its themes more critically.

Saturday 9 June. Several papers carried the story of Margaret Baskerville, a vet working at the Porton Down Chemical Defence Establishment on Salisbury Plain, whose job was to oversee the welfare of animals used there in laboratory tests. (In the animal rights press this work was said to involve giving clinical advice on the diseases contracted by animals used in germ warfare experiments.) On Wednesday 6 June a bomb utilizing a mercury tilt device, which had been positioned next to the fuel tank of her mini-jeep, exploded as she set off for work. She escaped, without serious injury, through one of the jeep's blownout windows as the vehicle went up in flames. It was said that Mrs Baskerville had previously received death threats as a result of a research paper she had published in a scientific journal, and that after the explosion a man claiming to represent an animal rights group had phoned a BBC journalist to say that anyone working at the Porton Down base was now a target. The police had imposed a news blackout on the incident until the Friday, and were quoted as saying that no group had claimed responsibility. The *Daily Mirror* gave over its front page to the story; other papers gave it rather less prominence.

Sunday 10 June. The *Observer* carried a very brief news item summarizing the same story; it was not even mentioned in the other national Sundays.

Monday 11 June. A second story made front-page headlines in three of the papers and was reported in most of the others. On Sunday morning a bomb had exploded under a car belonging to Dr Patrick Max Headley, a psychologist at Bristol University who was engaged in research on the conscious reactions of sheep. John Cupper, a thirteen-month-old child whose father was wheeling him along the nearby pavement in a pushchair, was badly injured in the explosion. He was reported to have flash burns, a partially severed finger, and shrapnel wounds in his back. The police were quoted as saying that 'a connection with animal activists cannot be ruled out', and they were investigating 'possible links' with the previous bombing.

In the reports of the incident and in supporting stories, much reference was made to the ALF; several papers drew comparisons with IRA tactics and more than one suggested that the ALF may have links with the IRA. The story prompted five editorials, and a cartoon by Dave Gaskill in *Today* (fig. 36). I will return to the cartoon later.

Tuesday 12 June. The story of the second bombing attracted further attention in all of the papers. The main development, to which most papers gave front-page coverage, was the revelation that the day before the explosion a neighbour had notified the police of a suspicious-looking box attached to the underside of Dr Headley's car, but the police had failed to act on this information. They now admitted that the explosion could have been avoided had they done so. It was also widely reported that John Cupper's condition in hospital was stable, that the police had apologized to his family, and that the pro-vivisection Research Defence Society was offering a £10,000 reward for information leading to the conviction of the bombers. The *Daily Mirror* was offering its own £5,000 reward. Police were said to be treating seriously a call saying that the ALF was behind the attack. Several papers quoted remarks made by Dr Headley noting the 'irony' of the fact that his work included research into the drugs likely to have been used to treat John Cupper in hospital.

There were four further editorials relating to the story, and a number of supporting features on related topics, including animal experimentation, bomb-making techniques, and Scotland Yard's ARNI unit. The animal rights movement was widely discussed, and some of its representatives commented on the bombings.

Wednesday 13 June. One tabloid struggled to keep the issue in the headlines by embroidering an older story ('Animal mob hit cancer docs'), but the only real developments were that the ALF was now said to have claimed responsibility for both bombings, and that on Tuesday eight of the principal animal rights and animal welfare organizations had jointly condemned the bombings.

Sunday 17 June. Having missed out on the story the previous week, several of the Sundays seemed eager to wring the last drops of sensationalism from the issue. Particular interest was therefore taken in anyone still prepared to express any degree of support for the bombers. There were also further features on animal experimentation, on the ALF, and on the animal rights movement as a whole.

Some time later. The story was soon enough forgotten by the press, though the search for the bombers continued. At the end of the year, in *Arkangel* no.4, Ronnie Lee wrote that 'seemingly even the police now believe that the ALF was not responsible' for the bombings. Lee had himself maintained from the outset that they were not the work of the ALF.

There are two principal themes which I now wish to pursue in more detail; both concern identities and representations (visual or otherwise), and both are evident across the political spectrum of the papers.

The first theme concerns the surprising difficulty which the papers found in fixing on a satisfactory stereotype of the culprits, and the anxiety which the absence of such a stereotype evidently caused them. The second concerns the way they worked towards a consensus without seeming to be aware of what (rather than who) it was that their consensus excluded.

The identity of the bombers naturally excited curiosity. Uncertainty was heightened, if anything, by contradictory claims. When the Porton Down incident was reported on the Saturday, the *Express* followed its own claim that 'it is believed the Animal Liberation Front was responsible' with the police statement that 'no group has claimed responsibility'. On the Monday the *Guardian*'s report of the second incident, in which John Cupper was injured, noted that 'no group has claimed responsibility', and quoted a police spokesman's cautious statement that 'a connection with animal activists cannot be ruled out'. This did not inhibit the *Express* from speaking of the child's 'shrapnel injuries from an Animal Liberation Front bomb'. No other paper went this far, but it was widely taken for granted that some sort of animal rights activists had been responsible. The question then became, as a *Sun* headline put it, 'Who are animal lib loonies?'.[18]

Most papers posed this question in one form or another in the course of the week. The answers seemed to mix in about equal proportions an anxiety over the fact that the supporters of activism were now acknowledged not to fit any single easy stereotype, and a description of them which nevertheless often approximated to whichever social groups the newspaper in question already took a dim view of. The *Sun* consoled itself with the thought that though they ranged 'from thugs to little old ladies who dote on their cats', the factors common to most of the 'fanatics' were 'having a university degree and being unemployed'; they were in other words 'brainy loafers'. The *Guardian* suggested that 'activists ... include clergymen, National Front members and anarchists'. An *Express* editorial characterized them as 'nihilistic inadequates' and 'vicious dropouts', many of whom 'were at the anti-poll tax demo that brought terror to the West End of London in May'. *The Times* spoke with contempt of 'young people worked into righteous indignation by ecologically-minded teachers'.[19]

Part of the problem was that these people were often, one might almost say, wolves in sheep's clothing. *Today* spoke of 'Terror tactics over gin and tonic', and quoted the outspoken views of 'convent-educated' Vivien Smith. The *People* interviewed a 'well-heeled' couple whom it described as 'unlikely middle-aged revolutionaries' – they owned 'two luxurious homes' and had 'his-and-hers Mercedes cars and a valuable antique collection', but they believed that vivisectors 'should die the way animals die'. Most papers featured warnings similar to this one from the *Sunday Correspondent*: 'Police say there is no typical profile of the person who takes "direct action" ... it is dangerous to conceive of them all as stereotypical anarchists'. It was all so very unfair, they seemed to be saying.[20]

The *Telegraph*'s 'Fanatics behind the Front' followed similar lines, pausing only to ensure for the benefit of its readers that its own list of suspect individuals included – horror of horrors – 'disaffected academics'. But this piece inadvertently revealed that what the press was really lacking, and was desperate for, was a *visual* stereotype. The hooded liberator would no longer do, for the greater danger now lay in the fact that 'these days you might not recognize an animal liberation activist'. The piece did what it could to compensate for this lack, by opening with a photographic close-up of Ronnie Lee's face and an astonishing expression of faith in the truth of physiognomy:

> Take a look at the picture of Ronnie 'The General' Lee, the Animal Liberation Front activist who was jailed for ten years in 1987 ... and you see a face that might have come from Central Casting's Revolutionaries file. Close-bearded, round wire-frame glasses, Lenin-style cap set back on the head, Lee was convicted ... [21]

Guilty by appearance; no wonder he was convicted. The writer seemed grateful that the meanings of some images, at least, could still be relied on in this world of shifting identities.

There were other ways of working towards certainty and consensus, of course. The press unfalteringly established the correctness of its own position by ensuring that it was seen to be *everyone*'s position. At the start this was simply a matter of terminological solidarity: from the outset the tabloids' preferred name for the perpetrators was 'animal rights fanatics'. Readers might have had some sympathy for the cause of animal activists or even 'animal libbers', but fanatics were safely beyond sympathy. Their motivation was incomprehensible; the *Mirror* headline 'How could they?' caught the tone perfectly. They could only be compared (and they were indeed widely compared) to the IRA, or to the 'Muslim fundamentalists who are trying to assassinate Salman

Rushdie'. The papers were in better control of their meanings here, and in patrolling the boundaries of decency and common sense it was clear that words counted for more than images. The *Sun* for instance felt able to use a photograph of two laboratory beagles, their bodies held firm in stocks and their heads clamped into smoking masks, confident that it would be the caption which carried the weight of consensus, effectively erasing the impact of this horrific image. The caption read 'Tobacco tests on beagles enrage thugs'![22]

On the one side thugs and fanatics; on the other side everyone else. That 'everyone' had to be seen to reflect the whole spectrum of the lawful, from vivisectors to their opponents. Most of the broadsheets carried reports on the need for animal experimentation to continue, but editorials also appealed to law-abiding animal rights groups 'to dissociate themselves' from the bombers and to speak out against them. This they duly did. A representative of the League Against Cruel Sports said 'there is such a gulf between those prepared to do this kind of thing and ourselves that I can't begin to describe it'. Speaking for the British Union for the Abolition of Vivisection, Steve McIvor called on all those opposed to animal experiments 'to help the police seek out and put away the lunatics responsible'. The press needed the support of more extreme voices than these, however. A piece in the *Express* proposed that at the core of animal rights extremism was 'a bunch of inadequates' whose 'bible' was a book by John Bryant expounding such bizarre theories as 'the closer to a slaughterhouse you live, the more violent crime you are likely to find', but that *even Bryant* was appalled by these bombings. By the end of the week the ALF activist Roger Yates had also spoken out against the bombings from his prison cell.[23]

The bombers, as an editorial in *The Times* put it, 'represent virtually nobody in their extremism'. Everyone was opposed to them, and – a stroke of brilliance on the part of the press, and final proof of consensus – *this 'everyone' included the animals*. The symbolic incorporation of animals in the consensus was achieved by a variety of means. The bombers' claim to be acting on behalf of animals was disputed: their acts 'proclaim that they hate people more than they love animals'; 'what motivates them is not love of animals but hatred of humans'. In stark contrast (but in common with the British at large) their victim Margaret Baskerville proclaimed herself 'an animal lover'. So too of course were the police, as they demonstrated by giving the injured

John Cupper a teddybear when they visited him in hospital.[24] And as Dave Gaskill's cartoon (fig. 36) proposed, the animals themselves disowned the vile action purportedly taken in their name, and instead stood shoulder to shoulder with the public. (It is significant, indeed essential, that the animal shedding tears for the injured baby in this cartoon is visually similar to the already-anthropomorphized Dulux sheepdog; a rottweiler or some other variety of 'devil dog' just wouldn't do here.)

More important than any of these, however, was the fact that throughout the week the papers' stock-in-trade of cuddly animal stories and abusive animal rhetoric had continued without interruption. Normality had been maintained, and the animal had maintained its

"And they call *us* animals"

36 An apt comment on the bomb which injured a young child instead of the scientist it was intended for? Or a clever manipulation of our sentimental liking for big soft dogs, persuading us to share its view of the culprits' character and identity even before any group had claimed responsibility for the bomb?

familiar if contradictory roles in the construction of that normality. Only the *Sunday Sport* dared to propose the incongruity of all this, and to consider how the one discourse might impact upon the other, by deliberately contriving to position its report 'Sicko animal rights fanatic's death sentence' opposite an example of its more usual fare, 'Mad animal sex beast savages blonde'.

One by one, then, the counters had all been moved across to the same side of the board – the side of common sense, reason, reasonableness; of all that conforms to the constructed normality of the everyday, the known, the approved and the safe. Left on the other side were only the bombers themselves and whatever unimaginable remnants of support they could still muster. Deserted and disowned by the whole population, they were now (in the words of the *Independent*'s editorial) 'beyond the reach of morality and rationality. They have passed into a kind of evil madness'. And how were these evil exiles to be characterized? Other editorial writers were in no doubt. They were to be characterized as *animal*; they were 'Animals who turn to terror'. More than this, in their evil madness they were the very essence of animality: it was they who were 'The real animals', 'The *REAL* beasts'.[25] While the cuddly animal (teddybear, Dulux dog) had been incorporated in the consensus, the 'real' animal was precisely what that consensus excluded. Where stood the famous British love of animals now?

One might of course say that none of this is surprising: it's part and parcel of the popular rhetoric which is (and has long been) available to the press, so why make a fuss about it? There is one clear reason for maintaining that it did matter, and that it was a problem: the law-abiding mainstream of the animal rights movement had accepted the invitation to go along with it all, and to lend it support. The *Daily Mirror* reported with satisfaction that 'Mark Gold, of the non-radical Animal Aid group, said: "The way the *Mirror* has crusaded for animal rights is the way to change the face of public opinion, not by bombing innocent people"'. And in *Today* the BUAV's Steve McIvor wrote 'I should remind you of the huge successes that my own organization, backed by newspapers like *Today*, have chalked up in recent years and months'.[26] Both endorsements appeared on the Tuesday, the day after the Bristol bomb, but what exactly would these papers' readers believe had been endorsed here?

The previous day's editorials provided the answer. 'Like millions of our readers, the *Daily Mirror* opposes all cruelty to animals. We condemn unnecessary tests – including of cosmetics – on animals. But we must accept the need for those experiments which help to defeat cancer and other disease.' '*Today* is totally against unnecessary product testing on animals and we detest cruelty in labs or farms. But we detest far more bringing political terror tactics into any campaign in our democracy.' It takes little imagination to see that this half-hearted editorial stance – we don't mind condemning unnecessary cruelty, but we'll be the ones to define 'unnecessary' – does not sit too comfortably alongside the BUAV's commitment to the *abolition* of vivisection, for example. But it was not only these mealy-mouthed editorial positions which appeared to be endorsed by the animal rights representatives: it was also the offensive rhetoric of these particular papers. For the *Daily Mirror* editorial was the one whose headline cast the bombers as 'The REAL beasts', and it was *Today* which that same morning published Gaskill's 'And they call *us* animals' cartoon. It looked disturbingly as though the lawful face of animal rights was quite prepared to see the concept of 'the animal' continue to be used as the rhetorical embodiment of evil.

One thing must be made quite clear: I am not trying to use the benefit of hindsight to criticize animal rights groups for distancing themselves from the bombers. They were absolutely right to do so, and they could hardly have done otherwise. But what is evident in retrospect is that being seen to belong to the consensus was something that only came at a price. In the *Mirror* Mark Gold spoke of such consensus as 'the way to change the face of public opinion' on the matter of animal rights, but there is scant evidence from the media that this is the case. If anything the cause is now presented less sympathetically, or at least more cynically. In the early 1980s the tabloids more than once used supportive headlines such as 'Rescued!' in their reporting of unlawful laboratory raids,[27] and the image which accompanied that particular headline is in fact still used in the Animal Liberation Front's own publicity (fig. 37). A decade later, it often seems as though those same tabloids only speak out against cruelty abroad because of their own xenophobia, and against cruelty at home because the cause of animal welfare (which they always supported anyway) is a relatively uncontroversial one which gives them a warm glow inside. On the rare occasions when they are prepared to go further, and to venture into the territory of animal rights, it is only ever on their own terms. The June 1990 coverage left no room for doubt about that.

THIS YOUNG MAN HELPED RESCUE BEAGLES FROM A TORTURE LAB....

....HIS REWARD WAS PRISON

37 Animal Liberation Front Supporters Group leaflet, still in use in the 1990s. The image itself is from the early 1980s, and was featured in almost identical format in the *Daily Star*'s 1982 front-page report of a laboratory raid under the headline 'Rescued!'.

The papers that week demonstrated something else, which was that they were still very much in control of the symbolic meanings of the animal. Some of the major campaigning organizations had seemingly shifted towards the middle ground in order to gain a higher media profile, but in doing so they did not think to address the media's own representations of the animal. And since they had not wrested control of any of those meanings, they were in no position to modify the ways in which animals figured in the discourses of the popular – in the 'space of representation', as my opening chapter called it. I believe that this is a considerable problem to which animal rights has yet to face up. It is not clear to me that the animal rights movement will be able to bring about any fundamental change in popular attitudes until it is prepared to acknowledge and to take more seriously the symbolic and representational functions of the animal in the culture at large.

Refusing the denial of the animal

The problem is not only to modify the ways in which animals may be represented pictorially or rhetorically in the culture. It is just as important to open up ways of thinking about animals which are currently discouraged or closed off, and to work out whose interests are served by their present closure. A prime example is the denial of the animal, a theme already touched on in my chapter on animal narratives. There it was seen that in Bruno Bettelheim's work on fairy tales and in Dorfman and Mattelart's account of the Disney comics there was a common tendency to deny the animal, by proposing that the stories must be properly understood not to be about animals but about something else entirely.

This third commentary will show that there is another circumstance in which the denial of the animal is encountered. It appears as a common ploy to discredit those involved in animal rights activism. In June 1990 it was glimpsed in editorial comments, as we have seen. The bombers could not really have been acting on behalf of animals because their acts 'proclaim that they hate people more than they love animals'; 'what motivates them is not love of animals but hatred of humans'.

It crops up too in *Animal Warfare*, David Henshaw's highly unsympathetic account of the contemporary animal rights movement, where it is expressed through unsubstantiated allegations that prominent individual campaigners in certain law-abiding organizations actually disliked animals rather a lot.[28] The truth or otherwise of such stories is strictly irrelevant; what must be understood is their function in Henshaw's text. They are calculated to shock the great British animal-loving public, and to make that public question how anyone could possibly be speaking and acting on behalf of animals if they didn't even like them.

It is a clever move on Henshaw's part, it must be said, because this supporting-without-liking stance would rightly attract scepticism in other fields. We would have little enough respect for someone who proclaimed 'I'm thoroughly opposed to racism, though personally I don't like foreigners', or 'I can't stand women myself, but I can see that sexism's a bad thing'.

At any rate, precisely because of this guaranteed public reaction, attributing a dislike of animals to an animal rights activist is a most effective means not only of setting them adrift from public sympathy and understanding, but also of denying that it is the cause of animals which actually motivates their actions. The imagination is immediately stirred – what might their shadowy motivation *really* be? In journalism this is all par for the propagandistic course, but it is perhaps more surprising to find these same themes apparently emerging in a serious academic study. The work in question is Keith Tester's *Animals and Society*.

Tester states emphatically that 'animal rights is not about animals'. I regard this statement as utterly misconceived, but it will be instructive to consider how he comes to make it and, more importantly, what its consequences appear to be for the cultural representation of animals. As I argued in my opening chapter, Tester's characterization of the historical development of what is now called animal rights is frequently subtle, persuasive and well-documented; this is especially true of his treatment of the heterogeneous strands of nineteenth-century thinking on animals. In marked contrast, however, his description of the contemporary animal rights movement (which he dates roughly from the 1976 publication of Peter Singer's *Animal Liberation*) is altogether cruder. He presents it, for the most part, as a monolithic whole, and it is this which allows him to make a series of highly questionable generalizations.

Those who support the cause of animal rights, he suggests, will invariably refrain from doing certain things; they will not eat meat, and they will not condone hunting, vivisection and other kinds of cruelty, for example. The problem lies in how he chooses to interpret what he quite reasonably terms these 'avoidance strategies'. He will not allow, it seems, that they may be an attempt to avoid complicity in the worst excesses of the society's abusive or contemptuous or cruel treatment of animals. He prefers to characterize them as strategies for *the avoidance of animals themselves.*

The motive for this avoidance is, Tester proposes, an obsessive need for the maintenance of a clearly-defined and secure identity which finds both public and private expression through a regime of bodily purity. Animal rights thus stands as a metonymic if extreme expression of the entire society's need for an intelligible identity. Its supporters 'distance themselves from any relationship with animals and thereby begin to know themselves all the better'. They oppose cruelty to animals primarily because it constitutes 'an illicit touching which corrupts humanity; an aggression which does violence to our human being'. 'Animal rights can be reduced to a ritual avoidance of touching animals; it helps society firmly delimit itself.' 'Animal rights may well be one way society entrenches its own taxonomic centrality in contradistinction to the animal (by treating animals as things to be avoided if human-ness is to remain undiluted).' Against all appearances, the cause of animal rights stands revealed (or so Tester believes) as an appalling self-deluding sham: an extreme form of anthropocentrism.[29]

This is not all. What animal rights supporters are really doing in avoiding animals, he maintains, is attempting to expunge or exteriorize their own animality, which they see as a contamination, an abomination, lurking at the heart of their identity and constantly compromising the integrity of that identity: 'animal rights, and kindness to animals, are a product of . . . human embarrassment at our own animality'. He links this embarrassment and fear of animality to a distaste for and dislike of animals. He does not doubt that some people may love animals; he alleges only that animal rights supporters do not do so:

> There is a world of difference between animal love and animal rights. As a leading antivivisectionist once said of herself and her animal rights colleagues: 'We strongly dislike the term "animal lover" . . . It is a derogatory term like nigger lover'. . . . Animal love, indeed even liking animals, is repudiated as an inclination and a sentiment. It is quite possible actually to dislike animals but still believe that they possess inalienable rights. To repeat: animal rights is not about animals . . .

Much of Tester's case against contemporary animal rights rests on this alleged concern to avoid physical contact with animals, but his evidence is highly selective. One example will suffice: he draws the unpleasant quotation about the term 'animal lover' from a *New Society* feature on animal rights which nevertheless recorded, in the sentence immediately following that quotation, that 'most radicals will admit to keeping pets'.[30] Keeping pets – even when they're likely to have come from animal shelters rather than from breeders or high-street pet shops – is difficult if you're not prepared to touch animals, and largely pointless if you also dislike them.

The fascinating thing about Tester's distinctive and contentious analyses is the extent to which they actually conform to certain entrenched ways of thinking about animals – ways of thinking which have no strict correspondence either to the politics or to the seriousness of those who hold them. Thus his distinction between animal love and animal rights would need little modification to be at home in a tabloid editorial, where it would be couched in terms of the patriotic animal-loving public versus a bunch of loonies who represent no one and don't even really care about the animals they claim to represent. The common theme is the insistence that the outlawed or outcast group – to the *Daily Express* they are 'a bunch of inadequates', to Tester they are 'interstitial individuals' – may not be allowed to control its own meanings. The animal is denied to it; the meanings of the animal lie with the consensus, with common sense, or with whatever the privileged mode of interpretation may be in a particular discourse.

Psychoanalysis provides a convenient example. In 1917 Jelliffe and Brink published a closely-argued paper entitled 'The role of animals in the unconscious, with some remarks on theriomorphic symbolism as seen in Ovid'. What interests me in this piece is the structural relation it implicitly proposes between three groups: animals, those humans who express a particular concern for animals, and those others (including the analysts) who assume the neutrality or normality or well-adjustedness of their own views on the subject. Despite its age and the outmodedness of some of its sentiments, it manages to deny or displace the animal in ways which often correspond strikingly to those we have already seen. Consider first how Jelliffe and Brink manage to position those who express a particular concern for animals outside the norm:

> It seems ... the typical neurotic attitude, like that of the savage, to accord to animals a consideration and reverence, even a fondness, which their egoistic impulses deny to their own fellows. ... Too often psychoneurotics ... view the world of men with suspicion and hatred ... and centre all

their kindly affection and interest upon animals, so that ... they are utterly blind or indifferent to the advancement of human welfare, for example through vivisection, but resent rather that science should take any liberty with the animal world.

In short, such people are unbalanced, they are uncivilized, they are childishly selfish, and they lack the common sense to see that humans are worth more than animals. The cause of these people's being so out of kilter with proper social values, Jelliffe and Brink continue, is in fact an 'unsatisfied eroticism':

> At the same time these tendencies so cleverly disguise themselves under the virtues of sympathy, kindliness, tenderness of heart, for all of which the neurotic longs as corrective of the crueler egoistic tendencies, that the erotic character of the transference to animals is successfully obscured.

In other words such people cannot allow themselves to understand what really motivates their concern for animals, but the authors can reveal it to be the 'unconscious expression' of repressed sexuality – and more specifically, as they contend with their examples from Ovid's *Metamorphoses*, of 'strongly repressed incest feelings toward the parents'. It is most interesting to see, in contrast to these disorders, what Jelliffe and Brink propose as the proper and well-adjusted view of the place of animals:

> They must be, for logical, effective use, the tools of man's advance. Science in making them such certainly does not lose sight of ... the psychical service as well as physical service the animal kingdom has rendered throughout the past.... Every advance then in scientific control of the animal kingdom, every increase in efficiency through their service, means freedom from the ancient bondage and symbolizes increasing control over man's own animal nature.[31]

Thinking back to the June 1990 press coverage, it is now possible to see that (exactly as with Tester and with Jelliffe and Brink) the crucial distinction is not between the law-breaking extremists and the rest. The offending group consists of all of those whose particular concern for animals can be represented as a deviation from the norm. This whole group's meanings and intentions will be disallowed. They do not 'really' speak for the animal. Whether they know it or not, their concern is the sign of something else (*anything* else): political subversion, self-centredness, repressed sexuality, madness, a hatred of humanity – take your pick.

This cultural denial of the animal is maintained by means of a rather effective two-pronged attack: it comes from common sense (in the form of the discourse of the press) on the one hand, and from theory (psychoanalysis, historical sociology, and a good deal more besides) on the other. Any attempt to refuse or deny this systematic denial of the animal, of course, must then be taken as an expression of precisely what it sought to deny! It is Catch 22. The possibility of addressing the issue of animals has been closed off.

Let us turn the denial back upon itself. What does the refusal to allow sympathy for animals to be itself (rather than a sign of something more deeply repressed) say, psychically or otherwise, of *those who refuse?* The refusal itself signifies, after all, and the complacent acceptance (by Jelliffe and Brink and by the June 1990 press) of the benefits of vivisection may give a clue to what it signifies. The thing which the culture finds too hard to accept is that anyone might consider animal abuse sufficiently objectionable to be prepared to break the law to do something about it. This is not to say that those speaking from within the consensus expressly condone particular forms of abuse: they may want to see such practices ended, but by legal means. But their denial of the animal constitutes a failure of imagination, because they don't (and they can't believe that others do) take the issue that *seriously*. This is no great revelation; it is one more mundane instance of the trivialization of the animal.

In attempting to shape a discourse or certain forms of representation which would insistently refuse that denial and that trivialization, the difficulty lies in working out how to counter the extraordinary weight of cultural opinion. It will be clear by now that the familiar prejudices of the popular press are only the tip of the iceberg. The idea of the animal's comparative worthlessness has been (and is still) enmeshed in most notions of what it means to be civilized, as Elaine Scarry distressingly confirms in *The Body in Pain*:

> a dividing line can be drawn between human hurt and animal hurt; for the displacement of human sacrifice with animal sacrifice (and its implicit designation of the human body as a privileged space that cannot be used in the important process of substantiation) has always been recognized as a special moment in the infancy of civilization.[32]

The idea that civilization is founded on a disregard for animals – a denial of their pain, a refusal to countenance it – comes as no surprise.

The challenge is to devise those ways of looking (and indeed of speaking) which will most effectively bring the animal into the visibility it is currently denied.

Representation and change

We've had a very arrogant assumption of human superiority and I think that's what we've got to change.

Jane Goodall[33]

This final commentary turns more directly to the question of strategies for change. In a rather obvious way, stereotypes are the enemy of change. While it is therefore vital to contest existing stereotypical conceptions of the animal, it is just as important not to replace them with new stereotypes, new forms of conceptual closure. There will be no single ideal way of representing animals, and the favoured forms of any particular moment should never be mistaken for a simple pictorial reality. This consideration will necessarily effect the kind of visibility into which the animal may be brought. The problem with the idea of the 'positive' image, as noted earlier, is that it insists on a particular form of visibility. This would inevitably be just as rigid as the culture's existing regulatory forms of what may or may not be made visible with regard to animals – and once the culture at large had got its measure, its idealistic meanings would be left behind as the hollow shell of the imagery was appropriated for quite different purposes. A more productive way forward may be to think in terms of engendering an unpredictable play of the visible and the invisible, where meanings would be less susceptible to this kind of cultural recuperation.

All three of the strategies I describe below engage in this 'game' of looking and not looking, of being permitted or not permitted to see, and of casting doubt on what it is that is being seen. They do not prescribe how the animal should be seen; instead they serve in their different ways to get the animal into visibility without tying it to a fixed iconography, familiarity with which would soon return it to a conceptual invisibility. These are not strategies of my own devising: each of them is already in use; but each deserves greater acknowledgement. In my view they offer a valuable opportunity for some productive realignments in 'the politics of animal picturing'.[34]

Picturing the unpictured

The location should be quiet, undisturbed by traffic, vehicular and human; there should be no clue given that animal experiments are carried out. If the building is overlooked, the window panes should be opaque (no dependence should be put on blinds for this purpose). The unit should have its own private entrance doors which should be locked. ('No Admission' notices are no deterrent.) The aim is a closed community to which the general public has no right of entry.

Home Office guidelines[35]

They came, they saw, they 'stole' "your" animals.

ALF graffito, 1991

A politics of animal picturing must necessarily concern itself with seeing that which it is not permitted to see, and with getting others to see it. It is not enough to consider the ways in which animals are pictured (as most of this book has done), for that is to overlook, literally, those areas in which they are kept deliberately out of sight (fig. 38). In what is at present, to the best of my knowledge, the only substantial discussion of animal rights photography, Tim Phillips has noted that most of the images 'stolen' from this realm of the unpictured are in fact obtained legally. The obvious advantage of any such photographic or filmic evidence of animal abuse, 'be it on the hunting field, in the laboratory or on the factory farm', is that it is 'usually less easy to refute than the written word'.[36]

As it happens, a clear demonstration of the effectiveness of such imagery was in the news in the very week I was writing this. The senior and second Masters of the Quorn hunt (well known as the favourite of Prince Charles) had been suspended as a result of the incriminating evidence against them in a video shot secretly by the League Against Cruel Sports. Within days, as a result of the Quorn's admission that the video did indeed show the Masters breaking the rules of their own Association code of practice with regard to the 'humane' treatment of foxes, the chairman and all four joint Masters of the Quorn resigned from their posts. This embarrassed response was without precedent in the hunt's long history. Perhaps more significantly, and again as a direct result of the video, the Quorn was banned from hunting on the 280 acres of National Trust land in Derbyshire and Leicestershire.[37]

Much of Tim Phillips's article, written over a year earlier, is devoted to technical and practical advice for the animal rights photographer. His more general comments on the use of the image as evidence, how-

38 The power of the image: the conditions shown in the secretly-made videotape from which this image is taken led to the first American criminal conviction of an experimenter on charges of cruelty to animals (the monkeys had been deliberately crippled), and to the closing of his behavioural research laboratory.

LIVERPOOL
TEL. 051 231 3701/3634

ever, provide an interesting counterpoint to the conventional ideas of a positive image of animals. The common factor in many of the most effective animal rights photographs, after all, is that 'they are not pleasant to look at'. Additionally, the examples he discusses are not usually the work of 'professionals', and they are frequently taken at speed, under pressure, in difficult circumstances and in poor light – the aesthetics of the image is therefore not a high priority. The technical advice he offers is less concerned with producing aesthetically satisfying images than with, for instance, using flash in a way that will not further distress the photographed animal. The practical advice is again strategic rather than aesthetic: if a greater proportion of hunt saboteurs carried cameras, for instance, it would be harder for the hunt's supporters to single out the lone photographer for attack as they currently often do. These sorts of considerations could hardly be further from irrelevant aesthetic notions of how animals 'should' be seen.

It may sound as though this propagandistic use of imagery presupposes a simple reality which the camera can record directly. Phillips makes two points which acknowledge that photographic evidence of the animal is not necessarily so straightforward, and that neither is it always so resolutely unconcerned with the pleasures of looking. His first point concerns a photograph taken by the Central Animal Liberation League in 1985 (fig. 34); it was widely reproduced at the time and became something of an icon of animal liberation. In fact, however, it was taken during a reconnaissance of the centre in which this dog and others were held, some time prior to the raid in which the dogs were actually rescued. The video footage of the raid itself produced less satisfyingly composed images; the earlier image is the pictorial encapsulation of the idea of rescue – its effectiveness as propaganda was in no way diminished by the fact that it did not in fact depict the moment of rescue.

The second point concerns the difficult question of the acceptability of the imagery. As editor of *Turning Point*, Phillips explains that he is constantly obliged to strike a balance between the responsibility to reproduce the often gruesome pictorial evidence of animal abuse, and the awareness that it would be counterproductive to sicken readers to the point where they would no longer be prepared to look at it and read about it. The 'reality' of the image will count for nothing if that reality seems too horrific to be countenanced. This is a familiar problem, though one more often encountered in discussions of war. Writing on the subject of 'the hell of images', Paul Virilio has acknowledged the 'age-old military technique based on the simple idea that "man can only take a certain amount of terror"', and has proposed that in this sense 'one might say that the concept of reality is always the first victim of war'.[38]

This is most important; 'reality' does not have a privileged pictorial status, and even within this narrow band of the evidential image there is something more complex going on. In most animal rights publicity the balance of seeing and not-seeing has in fact to be played out entirely through the images of the animal which *are* seen. The viewer's response is something like: 'if this scrap of documentary evidence has been brought to light, "stolen" from the realm of what we are not permitted to see, how much more remains unseen?' It is this vast imaginary unseen which carries the greater symbolic weight or force in such explicit images.[39]

The complex play of the seen and unseen is used across the range of photographic evidence of animal abuse, whether it is presented by groups like the ALF or by milder-mannered animal welfare organizations. Surprisingly, perhaps, it is exploited in a far more calculating and overtly propagandistic way in the advertising of these more 'moderate' groups. When the RSPCA launched its poster and press advertising campaign for dog registration early in 1989, the first advertisement used a photograph of a huge pile of dead dogs to illustrate its claim that governmental irresponsibility was leaving it with the job of putting down a thousand unwanted or stray dogs every day. Iconographically the photograph closely (and I assume deliberately) echoed those familiar but awful images of piles of bodies in Nazi concentration camps; it understandably caused controversy and offence. The second advertisement was, superficially, more restrained: it showed only the 'doggy bag', not the 'dead doggy' inside it (fig. 35). But by the very act of leaving it to viewers' imaginations to picture the animal body which the bag concealed, thus denying them the catharsis of responding to its literal depiction, the image arguably remains more potent and more horrific than the pile of dogs.

Animal welfare organizations (or at least their advertising agencies) have become adept at this practice, and now play on the delicate sensibilities of the British public as imaginatively as Mickey Mouse played the bodies of his improvised animal band in *Steamboat Willie*. In 1990 the RSPCA found itself requested by the Advertising Standards Authority to withdraw a press advertisement featuring a photograph of a dead horse suspended from a meat hook in an abattoir, as the ASA thought it likely to cause 'distress and revulsion' to the public. The society continued to run the advertisement, but with an entirely blank page where the photograph had been – the unimaginable horror of the unpictured more than matching the anticipated 'distress' at the original image.

In 1991, playing on exactly this ambivalence, the International League for the Protection of Horses issued an advertisement which included an even more shocking photograph. It showed a horse suspended by its hind legs as it was winched up through the decks of the ship transporting it from Argentina to Italy, moments before it died from the wounds it had sustained in transit. The headline openly acknowledges the reader's desire to avert the eyes from this too-horrific reality: 'If you can't look at the picture, please help us face the problem'. Here it is realized that nothing will be gained by insisting that readers 'should' be able to face up to such realities; the exploitation of their delicate sensibilities can achieve far more. The documentary image is openly put to work as propaganda (in an entirely worthwhile way, I should add), in the knowledge that the 'reality' of the event to which it attests is the least persuasive of its pictorial attributes. The literal, the real, is an altogether *thinner* thing than its symbolic elaboration, either in or out of the picture.[40]

The open body

> The left weakens itself politically by failing to take images seriously, leaving the important field of these symbolic identifications to the right.
>
> Jacqueline Rose[41]

The cause of animal rights is one which has not, in its recent history, been exclusively associated with the political left. Like the left, however, its preference for notions of hard-headed practicality or scientifically-verifiable reality has often led to its neglecting or failing to comprehend the rich attractions of the visual and the symbolic. In the case of animals the general public is well aware of those attractions, and it will not give them up lightly.

Zoos offer a clear case in point. In *Zoo Culture* Mullan and Marvin note that 'most zoos which are concerned to educate the public promote a detached, objective, scientific understanding of animals and how they live in their natural habitat', but that despite this 'most visitors to zoos simply do not seem to be interested in thinking zoologi-cally, ecologically or ethologically'. It is the animal 'draped with un-suitable symbolic values' (Mary Midgley's words) which continues to provoke public fascination and to draw visitors to its ritualized display in the zoo. This is not to condone these institutions, but simply to acknowledge the public's preference for a rich (if exploitative) symbo-lism over a mundane scientific 'reality'. Mullan and Marvin's point about zoo educationalists could equally be applied to the animal rights movement's general endorsement of a rhetoric of the real: it risks fail-ing even to address popular cultural conceptions of the animal when it denies that its preferred scientific form 'of seeing and understanding is itself cultural and in a sense is no more a true picture of the animal than any other'.[42]

It is one thing to propose that greater attention be paid to the popu-lar symbolic investment in the animal, but the more important ques-tion is how this may lead to strategies for modifying existing cultural representations of the animal. It is the body of the animal which may offer the best way forward here. In one of the comparatively few writ-ings directly to address the question of how cultural representations can be changed, Laura Mulvey has observed that in most forms of human power relations where one group dominates another, there is a common representational pattern: 'the oppressed are linked to nature (the body) and the dominant to culture (and the mind)'. The point is very similar to Elaine Scarry's observation that power is 'always based on distance from the body'.[43] The visual stereotyping of the animal necessarily focuses on its body, and my concerns over notions of 'how animals should be seen' are that they too seek to fix the image of that body in an image of nature, taking both to be an unproblematic reflec-tion of reality. It is therefore the image of the animal body, I suggest, which needs to be taken out of nature and rendered unstable as a sign.

Only when the animal body is taken 'out' of this myth of nature does it become clearer what culture has invested in the animal. Once the body is regarded as abstract, conceptual, arbitrary, unstable, and not as the site of a fixed 'real', it is more easily recognized as a prime symbolic site: the very site of identity. For the relation of oppression to work successfully, of course, images of the animal body and the human body must be held firmly apart: the self-serving illusion of human superiority demands this. For exactly this reason it is worth reconsidering the two classes of imagery which deliberately blur this vital distinction and render it less visible. They are those of therianthropism and anthropomorphism.

Therianthropism, as described in my chapter on the rhetoric of animality, appears only to operate successfully when used as a means of discrediting or demeaning other people. In showing them partly in animal form (or with animal characteristics or attributes), therianthropism does pictorial violence – symbolic violence – to the image of one's rivals or opponents. It deprives them of their bodily identity and integrity and propriety by depicting them not only as other than wholly human, but as *less than* wholly human. It can achieve this effect only through the common agreement of victim and victimizer that the introduction of animal elements into the image of the body will be understood and acknowledged as a pollution of the purely human. In contemporary cultural practice, the cartoonist's or propagandist's use of the technique is invariably intended to unsettle its object, its victim.

What might happen if the technique could be put to the use of subverting its own anthropocentric meanings? The question is prompted partly by a poster issued in 1990 by the World Society for the Protection of Animals; the caption 'Bullfights would stop if tourists weren't led there' is graphically and painfully illustrated by a young tourist's face rendered therianthropic by the large metal ring through his nose (fig. 39). The poster had been intended partly for use in British airports, but six of those with regular holiday charter flights to Spain had banned it from their advertising sites. The director of one of these airports said he would only allow the use of anti-bullfighting posters that were 'not disturbing'.[44]

Without wanting to restrict the meanings of this multivalent image by insisting on my own reading of it, I suspect that its power to disturb comes from the fact that (in contrast to the purpose of a more conventional therianthropic image) we are not meant to hold the depicted individual in simple contempt. The distortion of the body here is 'felt' so acutely – and so is easier to identify with – precisely because it is that of a human. We are not shown the animal suffering; we are shown a human treated *like an animal*. If we describe this anomalous image as grotesque the word implies no distaste for the animal but rather an acknowledgement of the preposterousness of this human imposition on its features (an imposition reversed here for rhetorical purposes). It matters little that there may be a good deal of sentimentality or of

Bullfights would stop if tourists weren't led there.

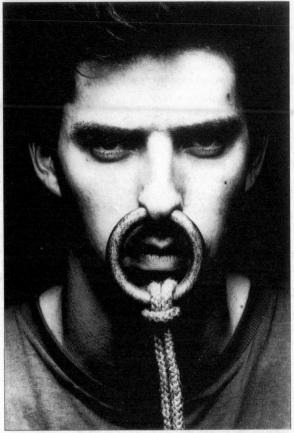

DON'T LET TOUR GUIDES TELL YOU BULLFIGHTING ISN'T BRUTAL. BULLS ARE DRUGGED, TORTURED AND STABBED TO DEATH. *World Society for the Protection of Animals*

39 The disturbing photographic collision of the human and the animal. The director of one of the airports which banned this poster said: 'I'm not in the business of making moral judgements, and I'm certainly not in the business of offending our customers and operators'.

selfishness in such a response. The symbolic wound on this human face opens our own eyes to the reality of an *unpictured* animal suffering. As Elaine Scarry observes in a different context, 'wounding is able to open up a source of reality that can give the issue force and holding power ... the open body has lent it its truth'.[45]

My comments on this poster are also informed by Bakhtin's notion of 'the grotesque body' – a term he used approvingly to describe a liberating and profoundly anti-reactionary experience whereby 'the borders between one's own and other bodies and between the body and the world are breached'. For him the importance of the grotesque image of the body lay in its refusal to conform to its own proper or self-defining limits: 'the grotesque image ignores the closed, smooth, and impenetrable surface of the body'.[46] It operated as a constant (but constantly shifting) challenge to those who sought to maintain more orderly regimes of the body's symbolic meanings. It refused to submit to the closure of the stereotype.

Appropriating Disney

> If, before a cartoon sequence by Disney, one read and believed the caption, *There is nothing else*, the film would strike us as horrifically as a painting by Bacon.
>
> John Berger[47]

It would be quite wrong to give the impression that only horrific or distressing representations can serve to promote change, but Berger's observation is a useful reminder that the meanings of images – I'm tempted to say *of even the most unpromising images* – are constantly open to negotiation. The ubiquity of the cute image makes it all the more important to have a go at unsettling its meanings, though the results may still look just the same. Disney material offers a potentially fascinating example because it exploits both the anthropomorphic (in the animal characters themselves) and the therianthropic (in filling theme parks with people dressed up as those characters). Additionally, it appears to care very little about the distinction between these two classes of representation.

A word of caution is called for before this distiction is discussed. It may be that the closure which we typically attribute to Disney productions has more than a little to do with intellectual fashion. I speak here entirely subjectively, but my impression is that in Britain in the early 1990s – and not only in the field of cultural criticism – there is an almost unbroken intellectual contempt for the whole Disney industry. There is admittedly a choice of two positions: one emphasizes aesthetics, the other ideology. The aesthetic position permits one to express a nostalgic admiration for the very earliest Mickey Mouse cartoons, for instance, but only to heighten their stark contrast to 'the permanent simpering smile of Citizen Disney's living colour luridly lit monster money-making Mickey' of the present-day theme parks. The ideological position appears hardly to have shifted at all since the 1975 publication of Dorfman and Mattelart's *How to Read Donald Duck*, where the specious wholesomeness or innocence of the material was shown to mask a rampant cultural imperialism. David Kunzle's introduction to that book spoke of wanting 'to locate Disney correctly in the capitalist system', and this classic study is still widely regarded as if not the last word then at least the 'correct' line to take on Disney.[48]

Whatever its merits, it is manifestly not the only line. Kunzle wrote in evident disgust that 'important sectors of the intelligentsia in the US have been lulled into silent conspiracy with Disney', and it is still certainly true that much of the fairly serious American writing on Disney – in the *Journal of Popular Culture*, for example – seems less overtly hostile than contemporary British attitudes. Any useful attempt 'to locate Disney' will need to address its own position in a shifting play of historical and geographical factors, let alone intellectual trends. It will be interesting for example to see whether European readings of Disney, of the sort found in Eco's 'Travels in hyperreality' or Marin's 'Disneyland: A degenerate utopia', shift in any significant ways over the next few years with the arrival of Euro Disneyland.[49]

All this is by way of introduction to my main point: the majority of these varied writings pass over the animal content of the Disney material with little comment and with less concern. In an earlier chapter I explained Dorfman and Mattelart's position on this matter; it is summed up well enough in their rhetorical challenge 'Mr Disney, we are returning your Duck. Feathers plucked and well-roasted'. This last sentiment in particular prompts the question of how the animal rights movement might choose to respond to Disney's animals, and how it might understand its own responses.

I had not realized the extent of my own unquestioning (and probably very British) contempt for these representations until I read with surprise some remarks made by Kim Stallwood about his own reactions to the Disney parks. Stallwood had moved from Britain in 1987 to work with People for the Ethical Treatment of Animals (PETA) in the United States. In 1990 he wrote:

> When you visit Disneyland and Disney World you enter a completely different universe where cartoon characters become an everyday reality. It is difficult to comprehend this without ever going to one of these parks. I never understood it before. ... There is real animal exploitation at the Disney parks, and charges have even been filed against them for cruelty to wildlife, but there is a fundamental message that is hidden about being kind to animals through the characters in all the Disney stuff. [50]

It is quite irrelevant whether or not this was what Disney had intended, or whether cultural critics take the view that this is to miss the 'real' point of Disney's manipulative industry. If an underlying notion of kindness to animals is indeed one of the messages that the public at large is taking from its experience of the parks (as a result of shaking hands and posing for photographs with human-sized Minnies and Mickeys, buying their own 'Mouseketeer' hats, and so on), then an interesting space is opened for negotiating the meanings of these representations. There are two points to be made here, which can be considered under the respective headings of therianthropism and anthropomorphism.

Souvenir Mickey Mouse ear sets, whether bought in the parks or outside on the international market, are one of the most popular items of Disney merchandise. What has been called 'the power of Mickey's symbolic ear imagery' has generally been discussed either in terms of an ironic/iconic confirmation of imperialistic ambition (the Walt Disney World logo echoes the shape of Mickey's head by showing these ears surmounting the globe) or in terms of its standing metonymically 'for the process of becoming juvenile'.[51] But these ear sets are also the sign of a willing engagement with the therianthropic. In buying them people are taking a bit of that 'different universe' of the parks – a sign of how that universe conceives of the animal – back into their everyday lives, for whatever reason.

A clear indication that at least in the United States this schematic imagery can serve as a sufficient sign of 'the animal' is seen in figure 40. Protesting against 'tests in which Cosmair burned live mice to death in a crude sunscreen experiment',[52] human volunteers wrapped themselves in tinfoil and established their temporary animal status by wearing Mickey Mouse ears. To me, here in Britain, the image seemed faintly ridiculous (for the reasons already given, I presume), but that response in itself might serve as a warning against taking a prescriptive attitude to animal representations. It is not only that we are frequently uncomfortable with the therianthropic image – that, after all, is its general purpose and its particular advantage if it can be turned back upon its own stereotypical meanings. Just as important here is the

40 The fact that these animal rights protestors denote their temporary animal status by wearing Mickey Mouse ears attests both to the complex meanings already carried by Disney imagery in the United States, and to this imagery's surprising potential for manipulating and undermining stereotypical conceptions of the animal.

point made earlier in the chapter: notions of how animals 'should' be represented have more to do with personal taste (the social construction of which is often hard to keep in mind) than with any loftier motives.

Much the same can be said of anthropomorphism. The merchandise currently offered by British organizations campaigning for animal rights include such items as neotenized and beribboned cuddly toy bunnies. These strike me as embarrassingly kitsch, but they do at least acknowledge the need to participate in a world of representations which extends beyond my finicky tastes. I am also less than clear how they are to be meaningfully distinguished *as representations* from their ideological opposites such as the real mink teddy bears on sale at the Jindo Fur Salon in Bond Street; however, this kind of complicity in the space of the popular is itself a prerequisite for any effective loosening of fixed meanings.[53]

Anthropomorphism is always an uncertain undertaking. Much of the difficulty lies with assigning any clear status to what it is that is being seen anthropomorphically. As Richard Schickel notes in his famous book on Disney, the authentic footage of wild animals in Disney's series of True-Life Adventure films which began with *Seal Island* in the late 1940s was already marred by a patronizing anthropomorphism achieved through a combination of editing, musical effects and running commentary. This, of course, was as nothing compared to the manipulative dishonesty of later films such as *The Legend of Lobo*, 'in which a seemingly wild animal was trained by handlers to do tricks that he could not and would not normally do in his wild state but that, of course, the audience did not know were unnatural to him'.[54] Clearly, any appropriation of Disney for the cause of animal rights will need to be equally manipulative and opportunistic, playing on the popular notion of the 'innocence' of Disney material in exactly the way *The Legend of Lobo* played on the True-Life Adventure series' reputation for authentic footage. It will be a matter of creatively re-reading the material in complete disregard of Disney's own intentions, and of turning it to strategic effect.

A fascinating example of this kind of appropriation was seen in the summer of 1991. It was prompted by television commercials in the United States advertising the re-release (on its thirtieth anniversary) of the Disney animated classic *One Hundred and One Dalmations*. An editorial in the trade paper *Fur Age Weekly* had expressed 'outrage over an injustice' – the injustice being that the commercials had tried to lend the film a particular topicality by stressing its implicit anti-fur message. They had used clips from the film showing the puppies running for their lives from Cruella De Vil ('I live for fur!') who wants to turn them into a unique Dalmatian fur coat. The editorial feared that children who saw the film would shriek in horror the next time their own mothers put on a fur coat, believing it had come from killing someone's pet. The *New York Post* and Fox television news pounced with glee on this ludicrous item, and the 'innocence' theme loomed large: it was said in mock horror that the offending editorial 'blasts the movie giant for making the cuddly kiddie tale seem like a social diatribe'. The Fur Information Council of America rushed to distance itself from any public criticism of 'a top movie giant like Disney studios'.

A subsequent editorial in *Fur Age Weekly* acknowledged the damage done to the industry by the way the television report had played up the animal rights angle of the story, lamenting that 'That shows what strategic editing can do'. Far from leaving well alone after its mauling in the media, the paper then ran a yet more outspoken piece by Kathleen Marquardt entitled 'Brainwashing America's children', which complained that 'Walt Disney was an animal rightist before there was a name for it. Disney perfected anthropomorphism, using his brilliant cartoons to insidiously inject that myth into several generations of America's children'. The media were keen to report this further rubbishing of a national folk hero to a wider audience, and the animal rights movement was able to sit back and watch its work being done for it. A spokeswoman for PETA said 'We're just thrilled that they keep digging themselves deeper and deeper . . . you can't slap Walt Disney in the face in this country and get away with it'. While distancing itself in principle from Disney's use of animals for entertainment, PETA nevertheless felt able in these particular circumstances to exhort the public to see the film for its 'playful yet solid anti-fur message'.

It was Disney studios which benefited financially from all this manoeuvring, of course, but in some ways the film was no more than a pawn in a quite different game. The look of its cute anthropomorphic characters had not been changed, and Disney himself had arguably been lent a spurious 'animal rights' credibility, but the animal rights movement had gained a month or so of invaluable publicity in the national media, and *One Hundred and One Dalmations* – at least for a while – now carried signifiantly different connotations.[55]

In conclusion

Some readers may strongly oppose the representational strategies of which I have written in favour here: the use of the conventions of photographic display to 'picture' animal abuse (regardless of whether it may actually be shown); the willing adoption of therianthropic attributes in order to exploit their troubling connotations; and the provisional appropriation of cute anthropomorphic imagery in an attempt to destabilize its traditional meanings. I certainly make no claim that these represent the only valid way forward. Each of them, however, seems to me to have a similar advantage. Each does its best to avoid centring the human subject, and each avoids objectifying the image of the animal. Each discourages complacency by remaining awkward, problematic, and provisional. They therefore have at least some small chance of keeping open the options for 'picturing the beast', refusing it a fixed iconic form, keeping an open mind about the meanings it might carry, the better to contest those meanings which seem manifestly to work against what we take to be its interests.

It is often objected that there is a contradiction at the root of claims for animal rights or animals' interests: that in speaking out against a culture which treats animals as so much inanimate 'property', the animal rights movement itself claims a proprietary interest in the animal. The contradiction is certainly there. It may be (as Derrida observes in relation to the politics of representation) that only through a rhetorical *imposition* can one group ever claim to represent another. The contradiction and the imposition are not matters for shame or signs of hypocrisy, however; they will only discredit animal rights in the minds of critics who consider that a rather narrow sense of philosophical consistency matters more than the sense of social justice which motivates supporters of that cause. Laura Mulvey's essay on change quotes the historian Emmanuel Le Roy Ladurie's words on how representational strategies have in the past been used in 'modifying the society as a whole in the direction of social justice and political progress'. Those may seem pompous sentiments to introduce in these closing remarks, but if the ongoing project of modifying cultural representations of the animal can in any way help to work against the contemptuous attitudes and painful practices to which animals are still too often subjected, then admitting to a proprietary interest will be a small price to pay.

Notes

1   Michael Dibdin, *Ratking* (London: Faber & Faber, 1988), p.80.
2   These terms were coined by Kenneth L. Pike and are explained in his *Language in Relation to a Unified Theory of the Structure of Human Behavior*, second, revised edition (The Hague: Mouton, 1967). The etic approach is described as comparative or cross-cultural, and is based on criteria and classifications which have necessarily been determined in advance of the analysis. In contrast, the emic approach can only be applied to one cultural system at a time, and its criteria are developed 'relative to the internal characteristics of the system'. The value of the emic approach is that 'it leads to an understanding of the way in which a language or culture is constructed, not as a series of miscellaneous parts, but as a working whole' (see pp.37–8 and 40–1).
3   Jacques Derrida, *Margins of Philosophy*, translated by Alan Bass (Brighton: Harvester, 1982), p.135.
4   Peter Singer, quoted in Keith Tester, *Animals and Society: The Humanity of Animal Rights* (London: Routledge, 1991), p.5.
5   See the BUAV *Campaign Report*, autumn 1991, unpaginated.
6   On the question of animals' place in an aestheticized image of nature (albeit in an earlier period), see Alex Potts's marvellous essay 'Natural order and the call of the wild: The politics of animal picturing', *Oxford Art Journal*, 13, no.1 (1990), pp.12–33. For Tester's remarks on fetishism, see his *Animals and Society*, p.172. I concur with his specific warning that the animal viewed in isolation risks becoming a fetish object, but his further claim that 'animal rights is a fetish' is both more mischievous and less well-founded. For my general objections to his account of the contemporary animal rights movement, see below.
7   Photograph caption, from Alfred A. Blaker, *Handbook for Scientific Photography* (San Francisco: W.H. Freeman and Company, 1977), p.262. The subsequent quotation is from p.260.
8   Umberto Eco, *Travels in Hyperreality*, translated by William Weaver (London: Picador, 1987), p.44.
9   Tim Ingold, 'Introduction', in *What is an Animal?*, edited by Tim Ingold (London: Unwin Hyman, 1988), p.12.
10 The advertisement appeared in February 1986: see for instance the *Observer*, 23 February, p.10. Its tone may have reflected the RSPCA's concern to maintain its 'moderate' public image at a time when this was being challenged from within, notably by the RSPCA Action Group. This group had been formed in 1985 in a continuing attempt to radicalize the society's largely traditionalist ruling council, following the dismissal of an elected member of that council for drawing attention to the fact that the society was allowing members of the pro-vivisection Research Defence Society to sit on some of its committees.
11 The British Fur Traders Association advertisement is described and reproduced in Tim Phillips's 'What do we want?: A look at a decade of animal rights campaigning', *Turning Point*, no.16 (1990), pp.19–26.
12 The judge's comments are reported in Richard D. Ryder's *Animal Revolution: Changing Attitudes Towards Speciesism* (Oxford: Basil Blackwell, 1989), p.276.
13 The four cartoons are those from the *Sun*, 13 October 1984, p.6; *Sunday Express*, 14 October, p.16; *News of the World*, 14 October, p.8; and the *People*, 14 October, p.6.
14 See the *Star*, 5 February 1986, p.22, and the (retitled) *Daily Star*, 8 February 1990, pp.4–5.

15 Richard Ryder, *Animal Revolution*, p.275.

16 The organization Zoo Check had worked in conjunction with the *Mail on Sunday* to raise funds for the release of dolphins from British dolphinaria. This, and the continuing campaign to close Britain's last two dolphin shows, was reported in the programme 'Must the show go on?' in BBC2's *Nature* series, 21 October 1991. See also the 'Zoo Check' entry in *Arkangel* no.5 (1991), p.10.

17 See the sections 'Violence inflicted' and 'Violence suffered' in Ryder's *Animal Revolution*, pp.280–7.

18 'Vet escapes as animal libbers bomb her jeep', *Daily Express*, 9 June 1990, p.13; 'Baby hurt in Bristol car bomb', *Guardian*, 11 June, p.1; 'Fears for baby in ALF blast', *Daily Express*, 11 June, p.1; 'Who are animal lib loonies?', *Sun*, 11 June, pp.8–9.

19 'Who are animal lib loonies?', *Sun*, 11 June, pp.8–9; 'Animal crusaders who risk murder', *Guardian*, 11 June, p.3; 'Animals who turn to terror', *Daily Express*, 11 June, p.8; 'Green fascism', *The Times*, 12 June, p.17.

20 'Terror tactics over gin and tonic', *Today*, 12 June, p.2; 'We back bombers', *People*, 17 June, p.17; 'Bombers must be treated like terrorists', *Sunday Correspondent*, 17 June, p.6.

21 Eric Bailey, 'Fanatics behind the Front', *Daily Telegraph*, 12 June, p.21.

22 *Daily Mirror*, 11 June, pp.1–2; *Sun*, 11 June, p.8.

23 The LACS and BUAV spokespersons were quoted in 'Bombs intensify split in animal lobby', *Independent*, 12 June, p.2; the references to Bryant are from Alun Rees's 'Evil hand of the IRA lies behind animal terrorists', *Daily Express*, 12 June, p.8; Yates made his statement in a letter in the *Guardian*, 16 June, p.22.

24 See the *Daily Telegraph*, 12 June, p.20; *Daily Express*, 11 June, p.8; *Daily Mail*, 12 June, p.2; *Daily Mirror*, 12 June, p.5.

25 *Independent*, 12 June, p.16; *Daily Express*, 11 June, p.8; *Daily Star*, 12 June, p.8; *Daily Mirror*, 11 June, p.2.

26 'Get the bombers!', *Daily Mirror*, 12 June, p.5; Steve McIvor, 'I'll fight for animals but never join these barbarians', *Today*, 12 June, p.6.

27 See Steve McIvor, 'The media experience', *Liberator*, July/August 1988, pp.23–4.

28 David Henshaw, *Animal Warfare: The Story of the Animal Liberation Front* (London: Fontana, 1989), passim.

29 Keith Tester, *Animals and Society*, pp.178, 188, 44–5 and 49.

30 See Keith Tester, *Animals and Society*, pp.60 and 177; and Martyn Harris, 'The animal rights brigade', *New Society*, 31 January 1985, p.170.

31 Smith Ely Jelliffe and Louise Brink, 'The role of animals in the unconscious, with some remarks on theriomorphic symbolism as seen in Ovid', *Psychoanalytical Review*, 4, no.3 (1917), pp.258–63 and 271.

32 Elaine Scarry, *The Body in Pain: The Making and Unmaking of the World* (Oxford: OUP, 1985), p.148. Scarry's apparent belief that animal suffering actually does count for less than human suffering should not discourage readers from using this book, which in all other respects I regard as a most important one.

33 Jane Goodall, speaking on the programme 'Jane Goodall on Chimp Beach' in the *Nature Watch* series, Central Independent Television, 29 May 1990.

34 The phrase is Alex Potts's. See note 6, above.

35 Home Office guidelines for the siting of vivisection laboratories, quoted from the *Peace and Animal Welfare* newsletter, June 1987, p.4.

36 Tim Phillips, 'In focus: A look at animal rights photography', *Turning Point*, no.17 (1990), pp.26–30.

37 A concise summary of the week's events is given in the report 'Masters quit Royal

hunt in row over fox cub death video', *Sunday Telegraph*, 3 November 1991, p.1. Even more recently, the BBC Radio 4 programme *File on 4* (28 January 1992) has quoted the animal rights campaigner Mike Huskisson's comments on the importance of videotaped imagery as evidence: 'What I felt was that the movement is strong in terms of major groups that can campaign in parliament and produce all the leaflets and all this sort of stuff. If you like, they're the generals and they've got a good bunch of troops fighting for them. But where does the ammunition come from? The hard ammunition is the *images* of the suffering that occurs, the factual record of the suffering that occurs, whether it's the videotape, or the still pictures, or the documentary evidence that we can acquire: that is the thing that's going to allow us to win.' Asked by the interviewer 'How important do you think the video is in this field?', Huskisson replied: 'It's devastating. It is the only effective weapon.'

38 Paul Virilio, 'Abandon·all hope, ye who enter the hell of images', chapter 3 of *War and Cinema: The Logistics of Perception*, translated by Patrick Camiller (London: Verso, 1989), p.33.

39 The words *real*, *imaginary* and *symbolic* are used here in their popular sense; they are not intended to allude to Lacan's psychoanalytical use of the same terms. It is admittedly tempting to suggest that the delicate balance of seeing and not-seeing might be thought of as a variation on, or an inversion of, the child's game of *fort/da* to which both Freud and Lacan refer (a game of reassuring presence and distressing absence), but the comparison may raise more problems than it solves. On *fort/da* in relation to photography, see Victor Burgin, 'Re-reading *Camera Lucida*', *Creative Camera*, November 1982, pp.730–44.

40 The two RSPCA dog registration advertisements referred to in this section were both in use in February 1989; the RSPCA advertisement opposing a return to the exporting of live horses to Europe for slaughter (under EC regulations from 1992 onwards) is from November 1990; the ILPH advertisement on the same subject is from July 1991.

41 Jacqueline Rose, 'Margaret Thatcher and Ruth Ellis', *New Formations*, no.6 (1988), p.5. Roland Barthes and Stuart Hall have made the same point in their own writings.

42 See Bob Mullan and Garry Marvin, *Zoo Culture* (London: Weidenfeld & Nicolson, 1987), pp.6–8.

43 See Laura Mulvey, 'Changes: Thoughts on myth, narrative and historical experience', *History Workshop*, no.23 (1987), p.11; and Elaine Scarry, *The Body in Pain*, p.46.

44 Quoted in Greg Neale, 'Airport row over anti-bullfighting poster', *Sunday Telegraph*, 8 July 1990, p.3.

45 Elaine Scarry, *The Body in Pain*, pp.124–5. 'Reality' is here (as elsewhere in Scarry's book) defined as, or in terms of, terror.

46 Mikhail Bakhtin, quoted in Katerina Clark and Michael Holquist, *Mikhail Bakhtin* (Cambridge, Massachusetts: Harvard University Press, 1984), p.303.

47 John Berger, 'Francis Bacon and Walt Disney', in *About Looking* (London: Writers & Readers, 1980), p.117.

48 Ariel Dorfman and Armand Mattelart, *How to Read Donald Duck: Imperialist Ideology in the Disney Comic*, translated by David Kunzle (New York: International General, 1975). The earlier 'simpering smile' quotation is from Michael McNay's 'Le Kingdom come', *Weekend Guardian*, 19–20 October 1991, p.23.

49 Umberto Eco, 'Travels in hyperreality' (1975), reprinted in his *Travels in Hyperreality*, pp.1–58; Louis Marin, 'Disneyland: A degenerate utopia', *Glyph*, no.1

(1977), pp.50–66.

50 Personal correspondence, September 1990. From 1987 to 1992 Stallwood was the Executive Director of PETA, which is based in Washington, DC. On the charges he refers to, see for instance the report 'Walt Disney World fined for violating bird law', *Wall Street Journal*, 8 January 1990. Thirteen state and federal animal-cruelty charges which were filed (in September 1989) over the same incident were finally dropped in January 1991.

51 Elizabeth A. Lawrence, 'In the Mick of time: Reflections on Disney's ageless mouse', *Journal of Popular Culture*, 20, no.2 (1986), p.69.

52 The description is from *PETA News*, 4, no.6 (1989), p.9, as is the photograph.

53 There is another obvious sense in which the aesthetic can be said to matter here less than the strategic: the merchandising of popular items is now one of the most effective means of income generation for some animal rights organizations.

54 See Richard Schickel, *The Disney Version: The Life, Times, Art and Commerce of Walt Disney*, revised edition (London: Michael Joseph, 1986), pp.284–92.

55 The relevant issues of *Fur Age Weekly* are those of 15 July, 5 August and 17 August 1991. The story was covered in the *New York Post* on 30 July and 22 August, and PETA's position is outlined in Michael H. Hodges, 'The fur trade traps Uncle Walt in a hairy debate', *Detroit News*, 24 August 1991, pp.1C and 3C. Briefer reports also appeared on 19 August in *U.S. News & World Report* and *Time* magazine.

Index

One purpose of this book has been to blur the sharp distinctions which are often drawn between living animals and animal representations, and this purpose is reflected in the organization of the index. Entries dealing with animals group them according to what a popular or folk taxonomy would loosely term their 'species', regardless of the particular animal's representational status or individual fame or current scientific classification. Consequently, Mickey Mouse and Spiegelman's book *Maus* appear as subheadings listed under *mice*, laboratory beagles and the British bulldog are listed under *dogs*, Rupert Bear under *bears*, and so on.

237